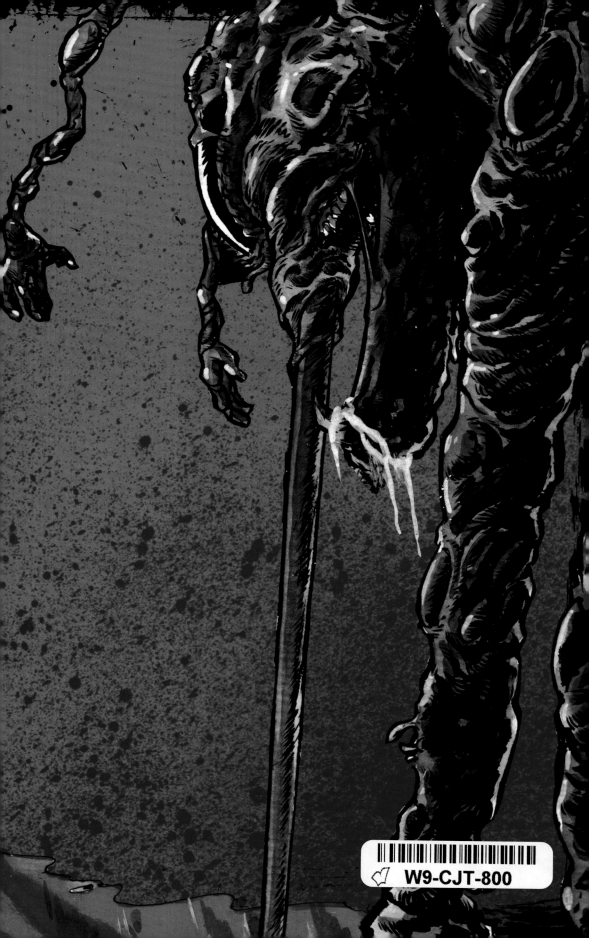

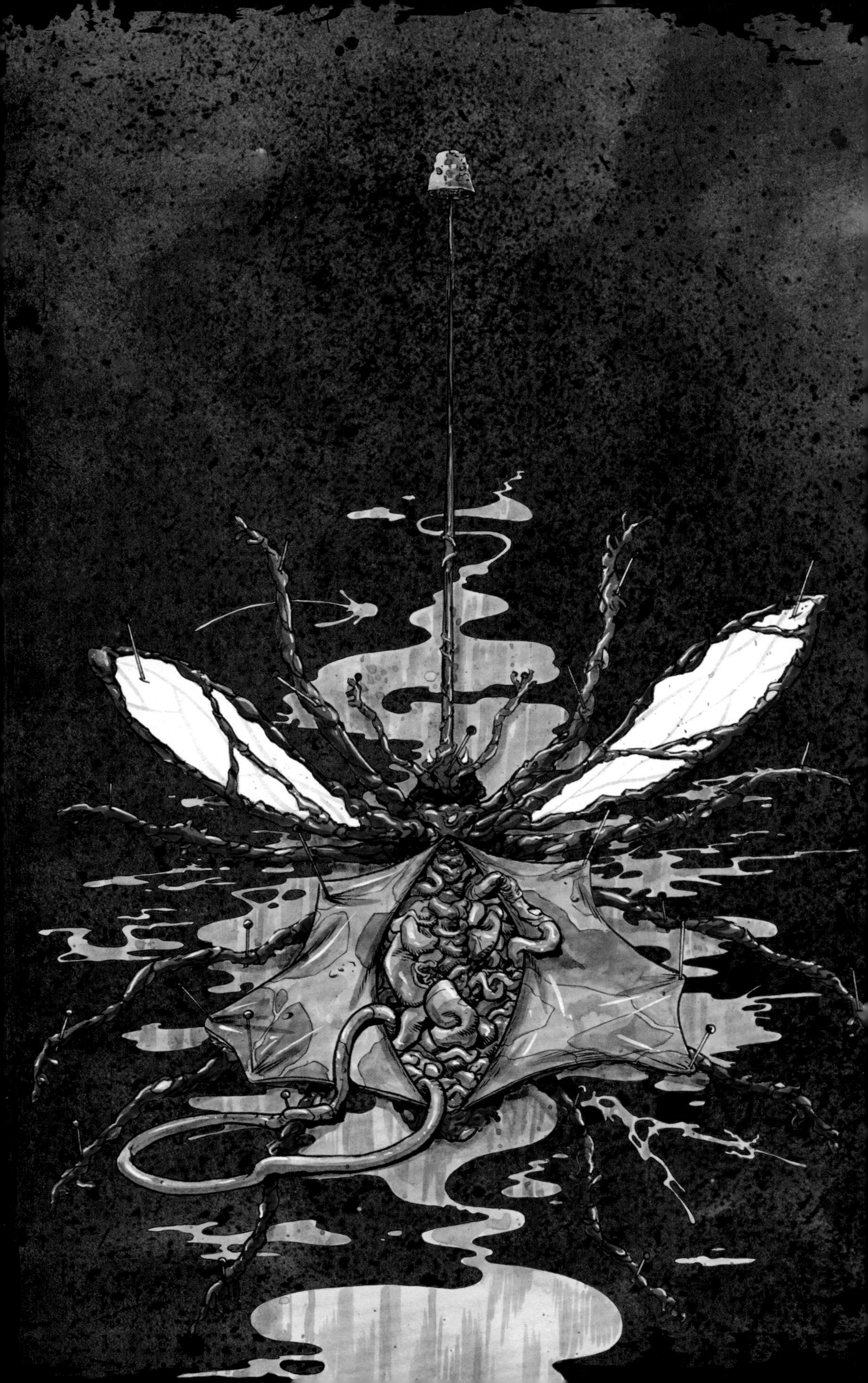

SKEETERS ™

Kelly Williams ✳ Artist

Bob Frantz & Kevin Cuffe ✳ Co-Writers

Chas! Pangburn ✳ Letterer/Editor

Camilo Sánchez ✳ Logo and Book Designer

MAD CAVE ®

LAURA CHACÓN • FOUNDER

MARK LONDON • CEO AND CHIEF CREATIVE OFFICER

MARK IRWIN • SENIOR VICE PRESIDENT

MIKE MARTS • EVP AND EDITOR-IN-CHIEF

CHRIS FERNANDEZ • PUBLISHER

CHAS! PANGBURN • SENIOR EDITOR

JAMES B. EMMETT • SENIOR EDITOR

CHRISTINA HARRINGTON • EDITOR

MARLA EIZIK • EDITOR

GIOVANNA T. OROZCO • PRODUCTION MANAGER

MIGUEL A. ZAPATA • DESIGN DIRECTOR

DIANA BERMÚDEZ • GRAPHIC DESIGNER

DAVID REYES • GRAPHIC DESIGNER

CAMILO SÁNCHEZ • GRAPHIC DESIGNER

ADRIANA T. OROZCO • INTERACTIVE MEDIA DESIGNER

NICOLÁS ZEA ARIAS • AUDIOVISUAL PRODUCTION

CECILIA MEDINA • CHIEF FINANCIAL OFFICER

STARLIN GONZALEZ • ACCOUNTING DIRECTOR

KURT NELSON • DIRECTOR OF SALES

ANA ESCALERA • DIRECT MARKET SALES MANAGER

KEITH DAVIDSEN • DIRECTOR OF MARKETING

ALLISON POND • DIRECTOR OF MARKETING

MAYA LOPEZ • MARKETING MANAGER

JAMES FACCINTO • PUBLICIST

GEOFFREY LAPID • SALES & MARKETING SPECIALIST

FRANK SILVA • MARKETING & COMMUNICATIONS COORDINATOR

PEDRO HERRERA • SHIPPING & RECEIVING MANAGER

STEPHANIE HIDALGO OFFICE MANAGER

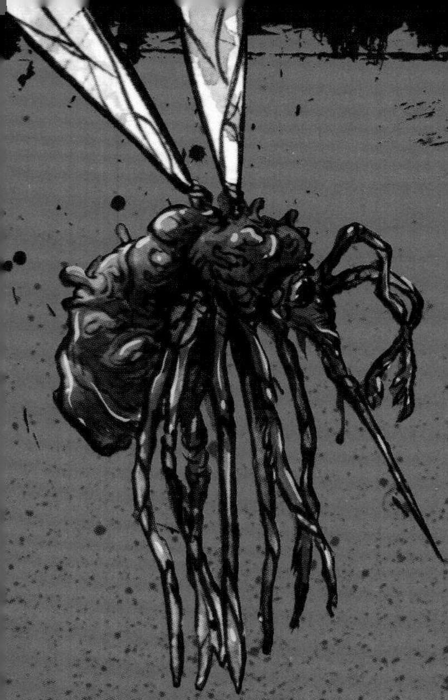

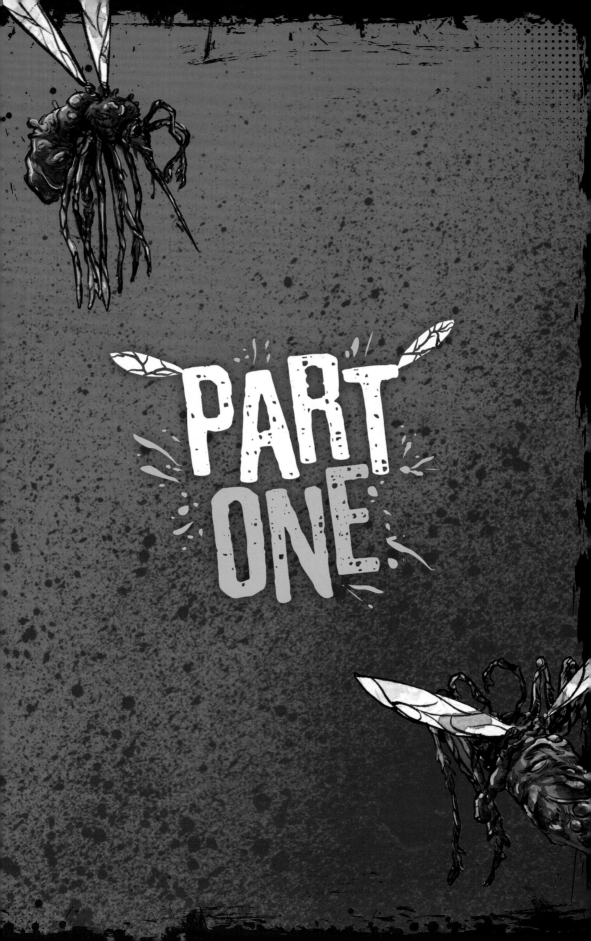

PART ONE

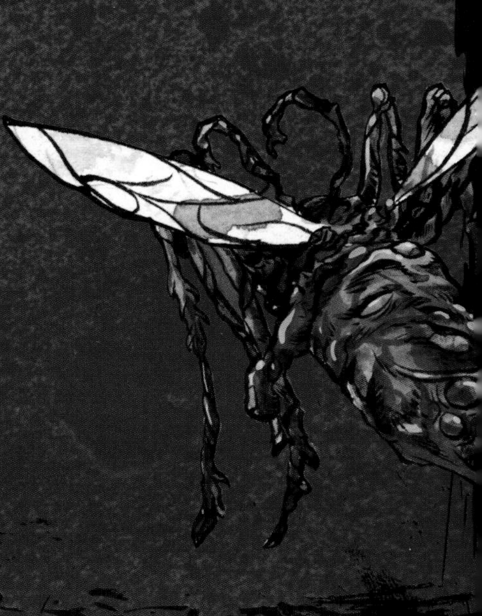

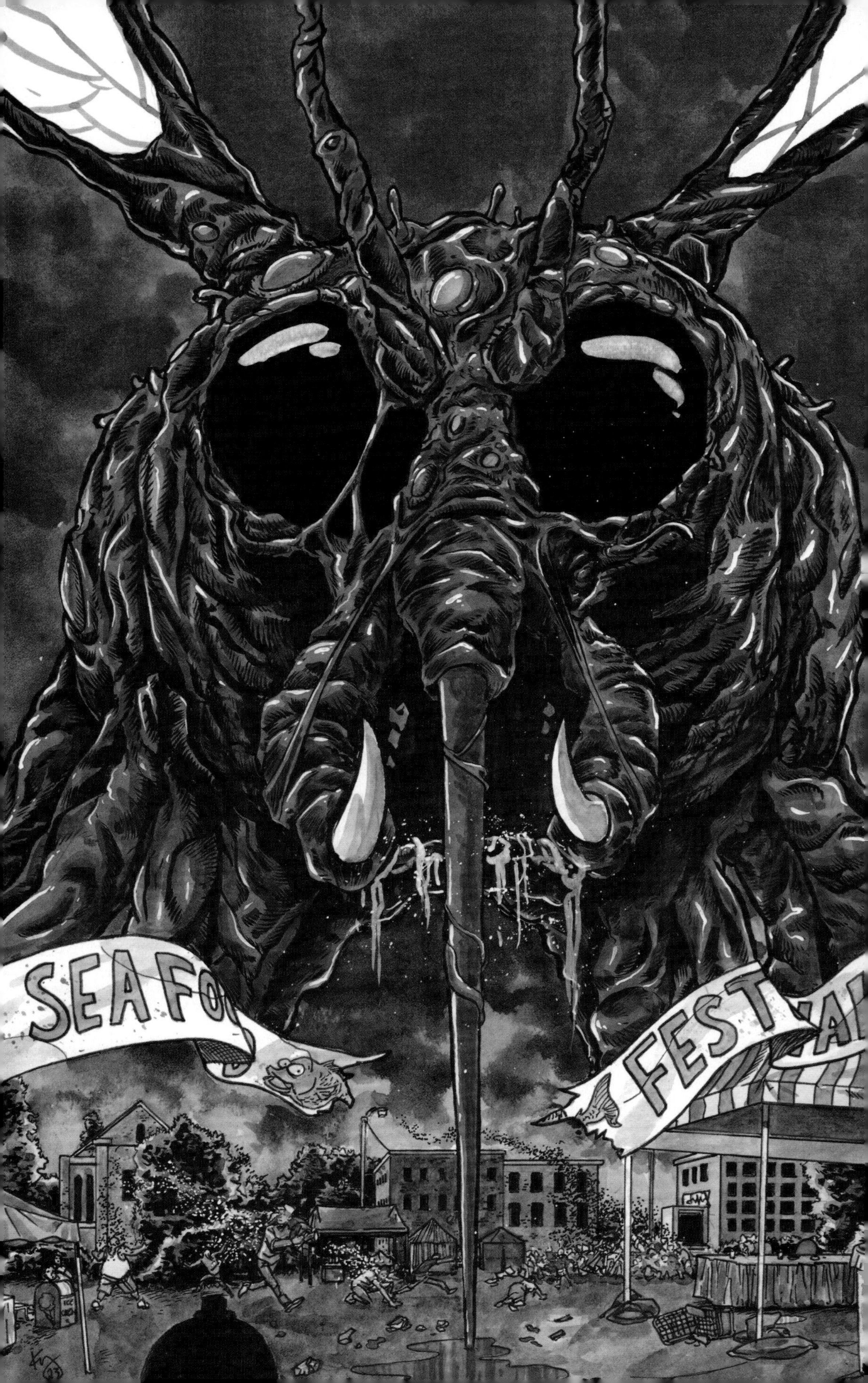
SEA FO
FEST

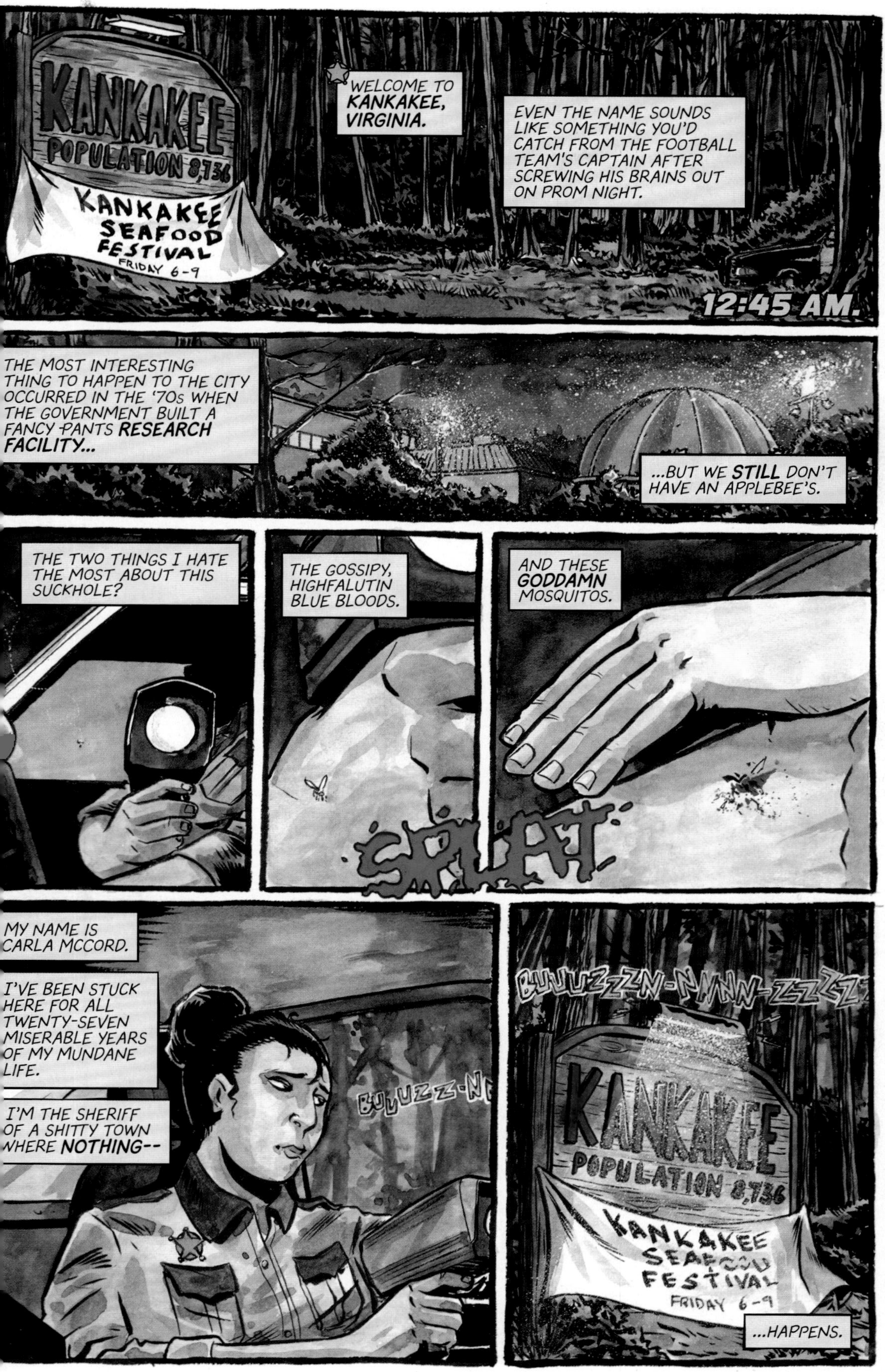
KANKAKEE
POPULATION 8,736
KANKAKEE SEAFOOD FESTIVAL
FRIDAY 6-9
WELCOME TO KANKAKEE, VIRGINIA.
EVEN THE NAME SOUNDS LIKE SOMETHING YOU'D CATCH FROM THE FOOTBALL TEAM'S CAPTAIN AFTER SCREWING HIS BRAINS OUT ON PROM NIGHT.
12:45 AM.
THE MOST INTERESTING THING TO HAPPEN TO THE CITY OCCURRED IN THE '70s WHEN THE GOVERNMENT BUILT A FANCY-PANTS RESEARCH FACILITY...
...BUT WE STILL DON'T HAVE AN APPLEBEE'S.
THE TWO THINGS I HATE THE MOST ABOUT THIS SUCKHOLE?
THE GOSSIPY, HIGHFALUTIN BLUE BLOODS.
AND THESE GODDAMN MOSQUITOS.
SPLAT
MY NAME IS CARLA MCCORD.
I'VE BEEN STUCK HERE FOR ALL TWENTY-SEVEN MISERABLE YEARS OF MY MUNDANE LIFE.
I'M THE SHERIFF OF A SHITTY TOWN WHERE NOTHING--
BUUUZZ-NE
BUUUZZZN-NNNN-ZZZZZ
KANKAKEE
POPULATION 8,736
KANKAKEE SEAFOOD FESTIVAL
FRIDAY 6-9
...HAPPENS.

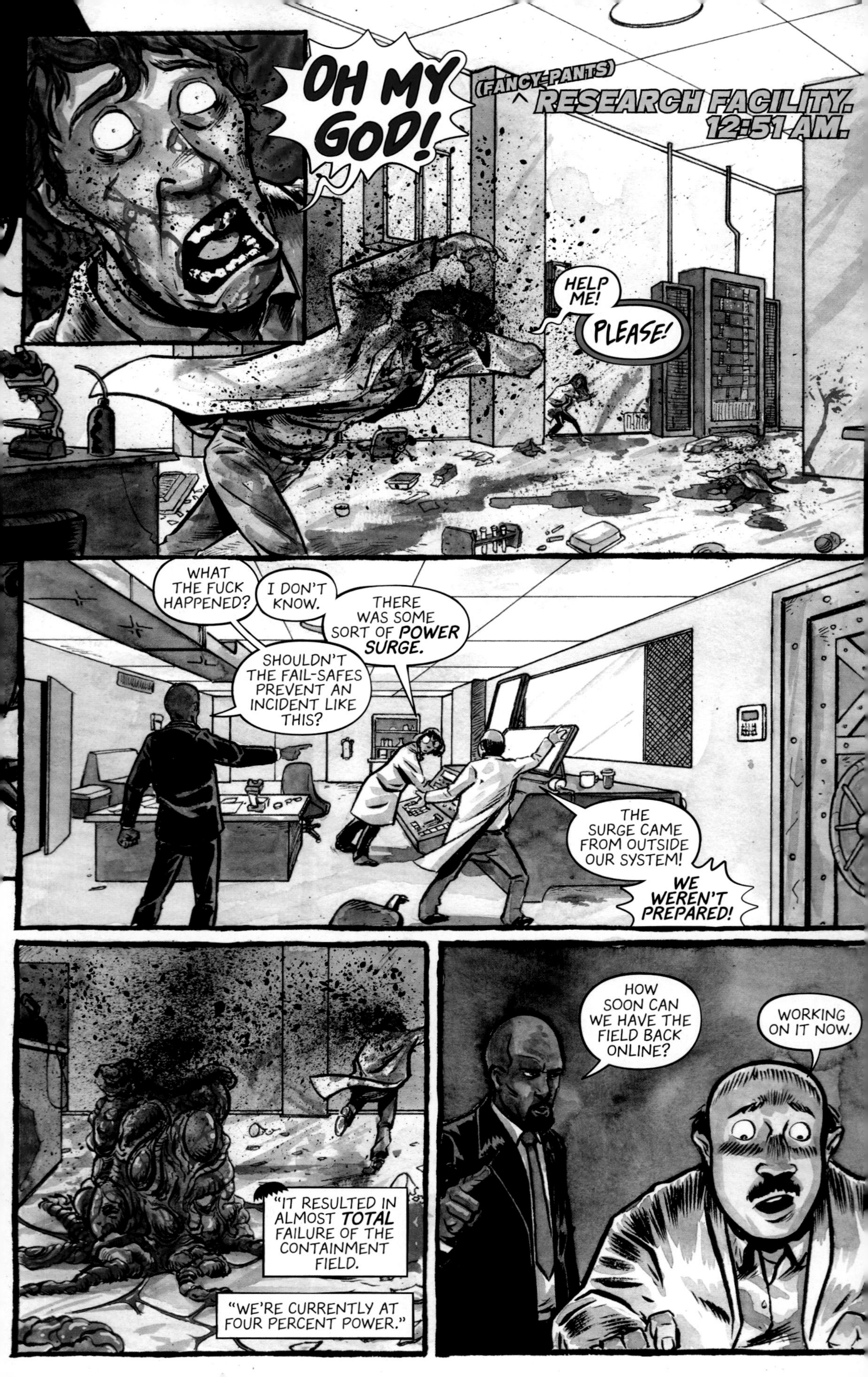
OH MY GOD!
(FANCY-PANTS) ^ RESEARCH FACILITY. 12:51 AM.
HELP ME!
PLEASE!
WHAT THE FUCK HAPPENED?
I DON'T KNOW.
THERE WAS SOME SORT OF POWER SURGE.
SHOULDN'T THE FAIL-SAFES PREVENT AN INCIDENT LIKE THIS?
THE SURGE CAME FROM OUTSIDE OUR SYSTEM!
WE WEREN'T PREPARED!
"IT RESULTED IN ALMOST TOTAL FAILURE OF THE CONTAINMENT FIELD.
"WE'RE CURRENTLY AT FOUR PERCENT POWER."
HOW SOON CAN WE HAVE THE FIELD BACK ONLINE?
WORKING ON IT NOW.

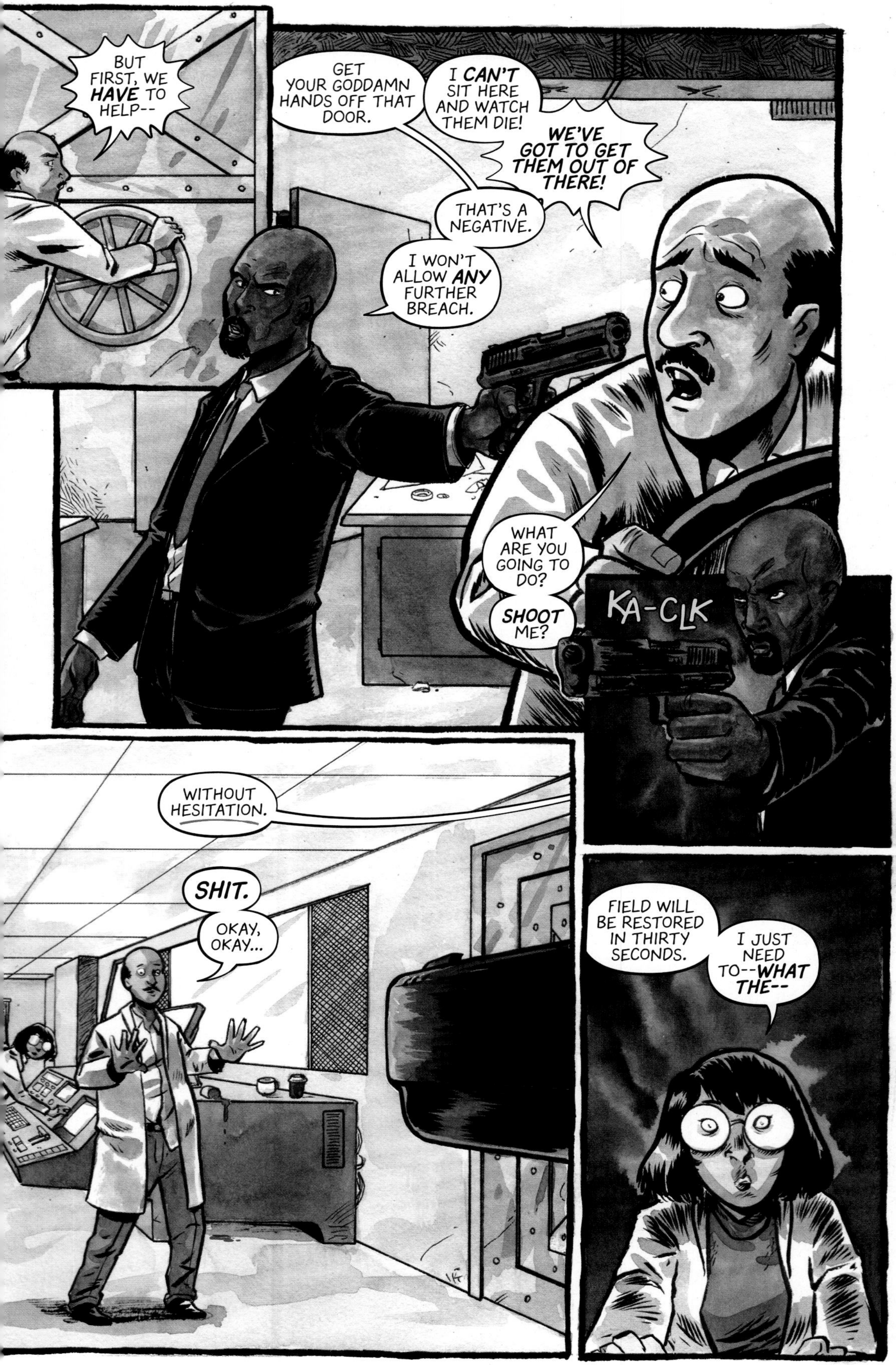
BUT FIRST, WE HAVE TO HELP--
GET YOUR GODDAMN HANDS OFF THAT DOOR.
I CAN'T SIT HERE AND WATCH THEM DIE!
WE'VE GOT TO GET THEM OUT OF THERE!
THAT'S A NEGATIVE.
I WON'T ALLOW ANY FURTHER BREACH.
WHAT ARE YOU GOING TO DO?
SHOOT ME?
KA-CLK
WITHOUT HESITATION.
SHIT.
OKAY, OKAY...
FIELD WILL BE RESTORED IN THIRTY SECONDS.
I JUST NEED TO--WHAT THE--

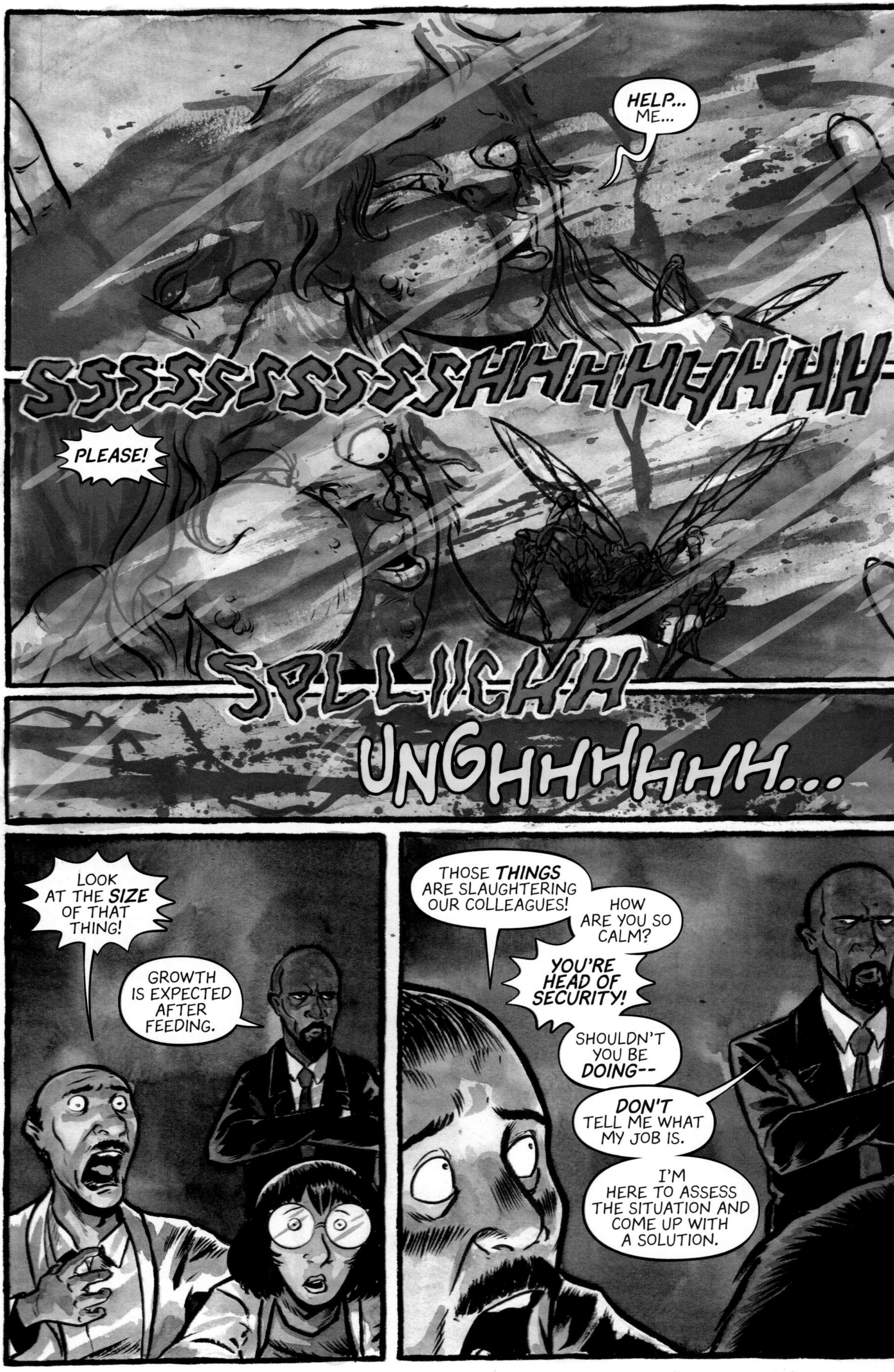
HELP... ME...
SSSSSSSSSSSSHHHHHHHHH
PLEASE!
SPLLIICHH
UNGHHHHHH...
LOOK AT THE SIZE OF THAT THING!
GROWTH IS EXPECTED AFTER FEEDING.
THOSE THINGS ARE SLAUGHTERING OUR COLLEAGUES!
HOW ARE YOU SO CALM?
YOU'RE HEAD OF SECURITY!
SHOULDN'T YOU BE DOING--
DON'T TELL ME WHAT MY JOB IS.
I'M HERE TO ASSESS THE SITUATION AND COME UP WITH A SOLUTION.

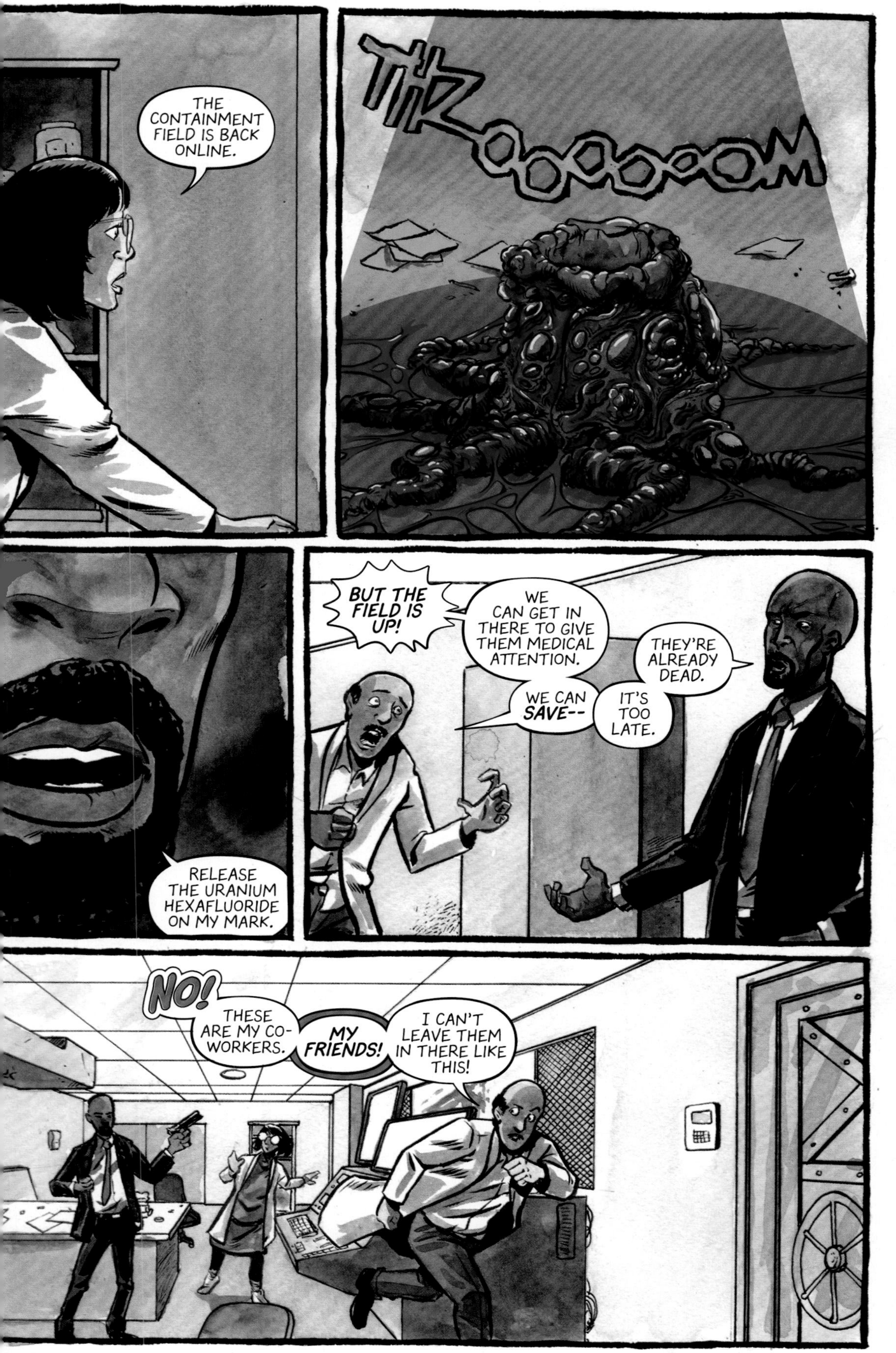
THE CONTAINMENT FIELD IS BACK ONLINE.
THZOOOOOOM
RELEASE THE URANIUM HEXAFLUORIDE ON MY MARK.
BUT THE FIELD IS UP!
WE CAN GET IN THERE TO GIVE THEM MEDICAL ATTENTION.
THEY'RE ALREADY DEAD.
WE CAN SAVE--
IT'S TOO LATE.
NO!
THESE ARE MY CO-WORKERS.
MY FRIENDS!
I CAN'T LEAVE THEM IN THERE LIKE THIS!

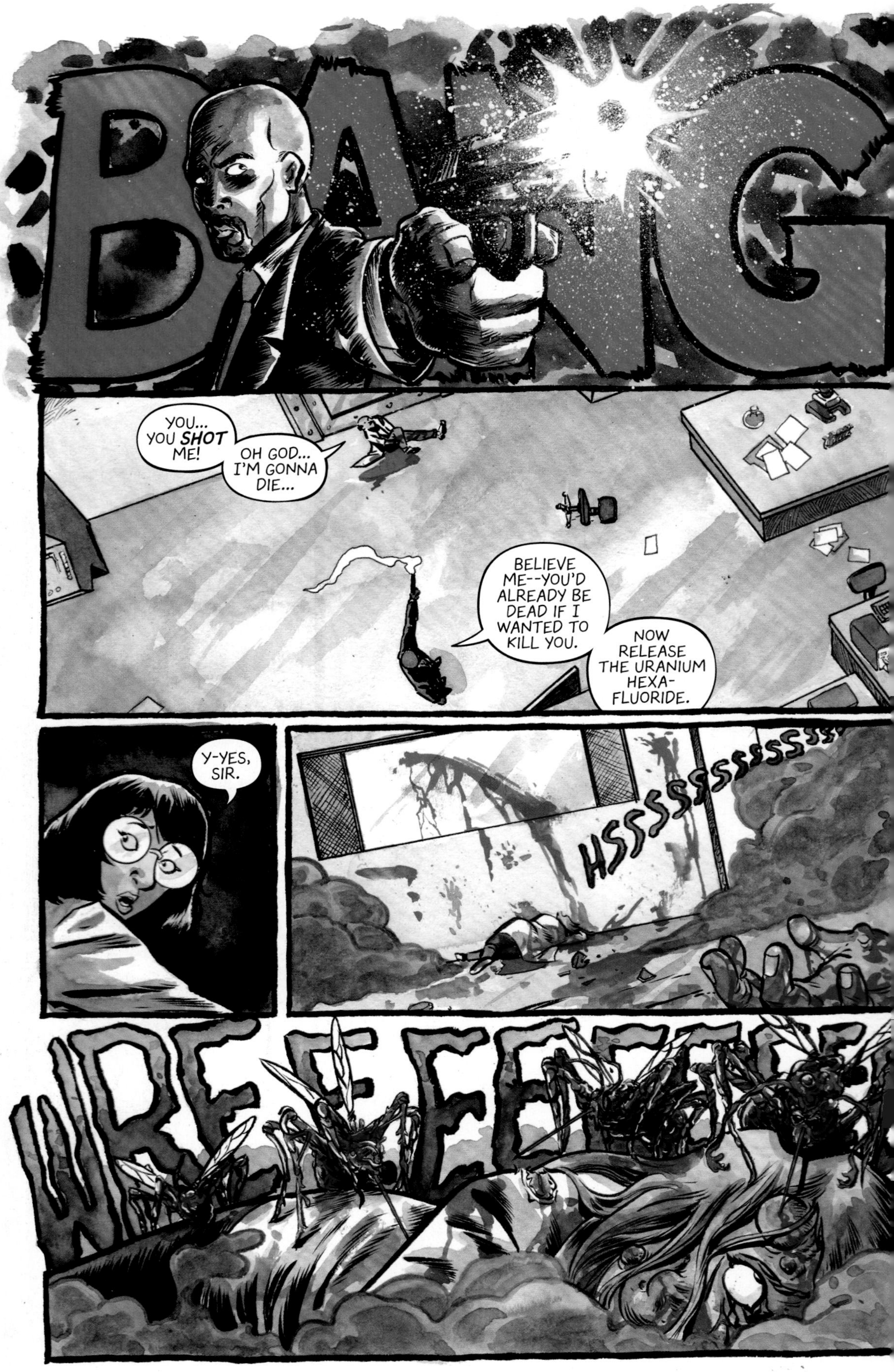
BANG
YOU... YOU SHOT ME!
OH GOD... I'M GONNA DIE...
BELIEVE ME--YOU'D ALREADY BE DEAD IF I WANTED TO KILL YOU.
NOW RELEASE THE URANIUM HEXA-FLUORIDE.
Y-YES, SIR.
HSSSSSSSSSSSSS

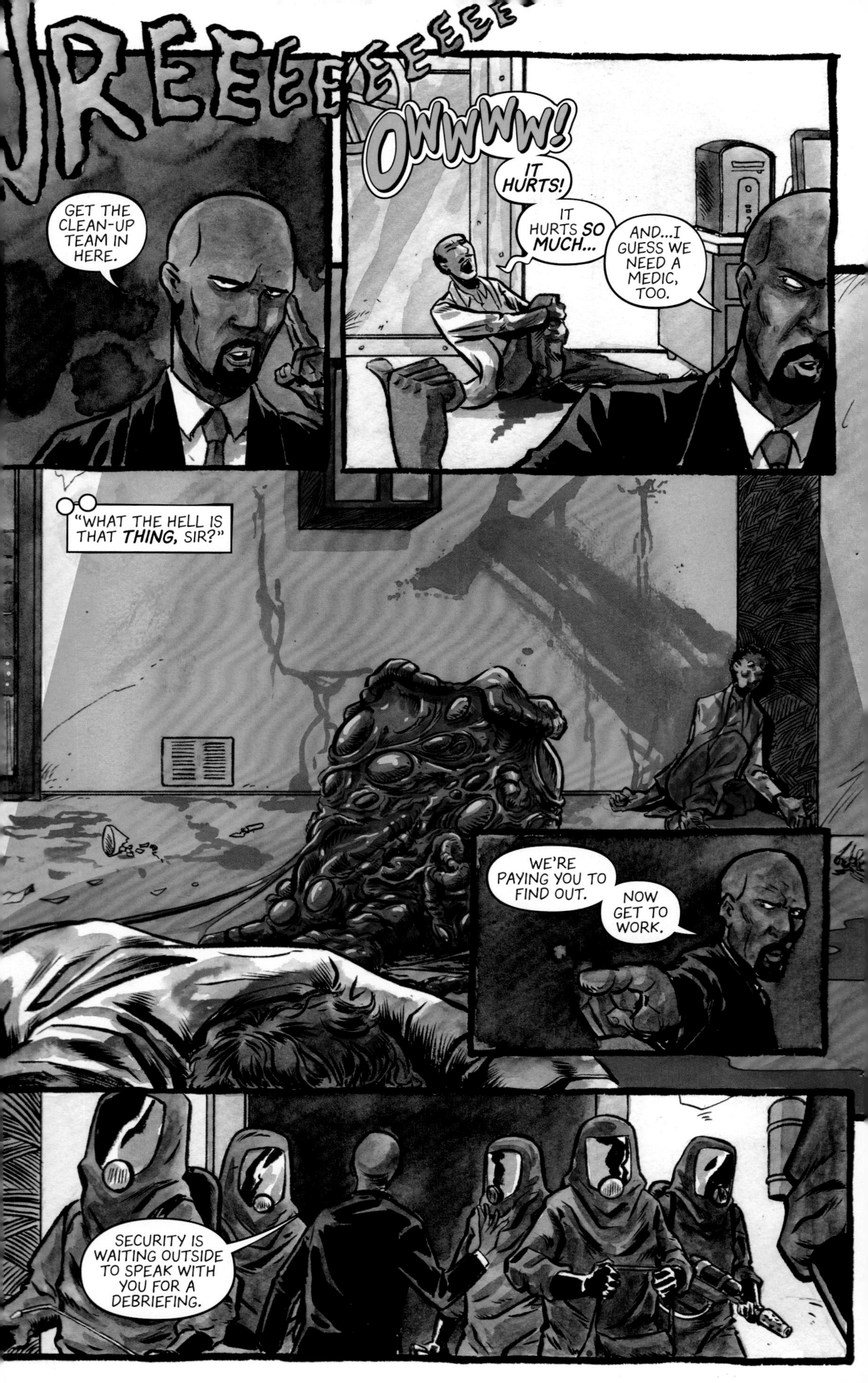
JREEEEEEEEEE
GET THE CLEAN-UP TEAM IN HERE.
OWWWW!
IT HURTS!
IT HURTS SO MUCH...
AND...I GUESS WE NEED A MEDIC, TOO.
"WHAT THE HELL IS THAT THING, SIR?"
WE'RE PAYING YOU TO FIND OUT.
NOW GET TO WORK.
SECURITY IS WAITING OUTSIDE TO SPEAK WITH YOU FOR A DEBRIEFING.

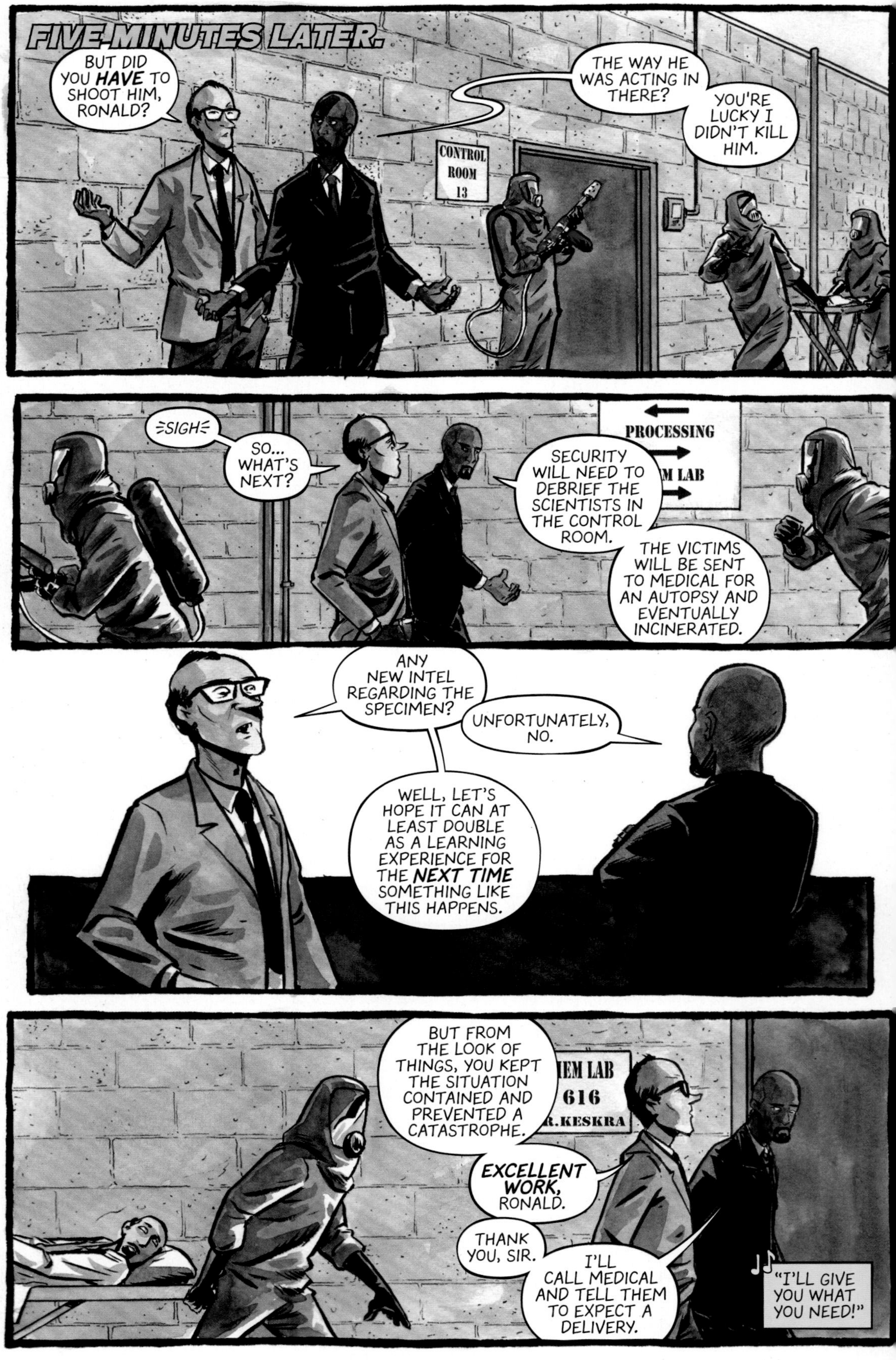
FIVE MINUTES LATER.
BUT DID YOU HAVE TO SHOOT HIM, RONALD?
THE WAY HE WAS ACTING IN THERE?
YOU'RE LUCKY I DIDN'T KILL HIM.
CONTROL ROOM 13
≈SIGH≈
SO... WHAT'S NEXT?
SECURITY WILL NEED TO DEBRIEF THE SCIENTISTS IN THE CONTROL ROOM.
THE VICTIMS WILL BE SENT TO MEDICAL FOR AN AUTOPSY AND EVENTUALLY INCINERATED.
PROCESSING
M LAB
ANY NEW INTEL REGARDING THE SPECIMEN?
UNFORTUNATELY, NO.
WELL, LET'S HOPE IT CAN AT LEAST DOUBLE AS A LEARNING EXPERIENCE FOR THE NEXT TIME SOMETHING LIKE THIS HAPPENS.
BUT FROM THE LOOK OF THINGS, YOU KEPT THE SITUATION CONTAINED AND PREVENTED A CATASTROPHE.
EXCELLENT WORK, RONALD.
THANK YOU, SIR.
I'LL CALL MEDICAL AND TELL THEM TO EXPECT A DELIVERY.
IEM LAB
616
R.KESKRA
"I'LL GIVE YOU WHAT YOU NEED!"

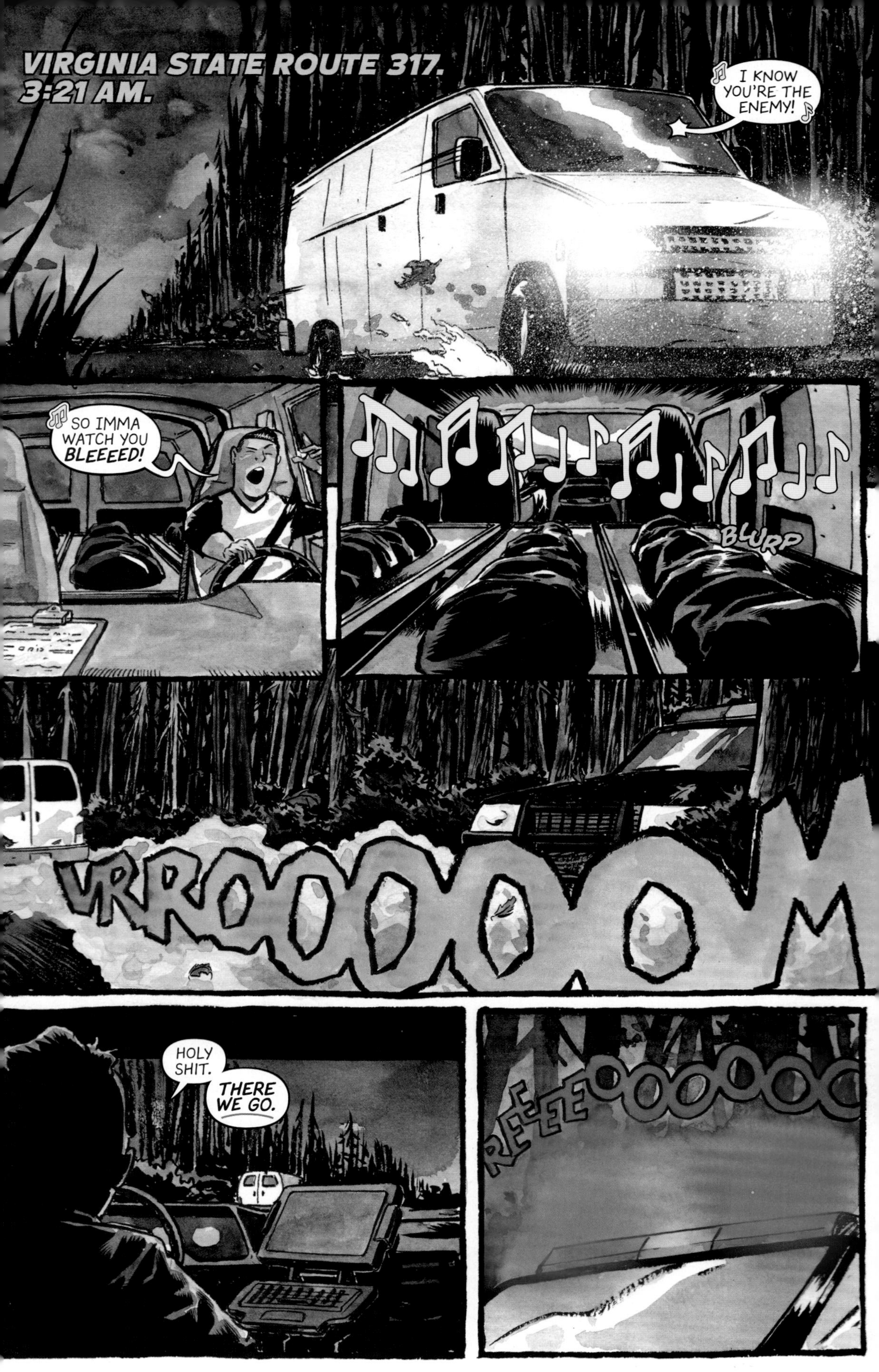
VIRGINIA STATE ROUTE 317.
3:21 AM.
I KNOW YOU'RE THE ENEMY!
SO IMMA WATCH YOU BLEEEED!
BLURP
VRROOOOOOM
HOLY SHIT.
THERE WE GO.
REEEOOOOOOO

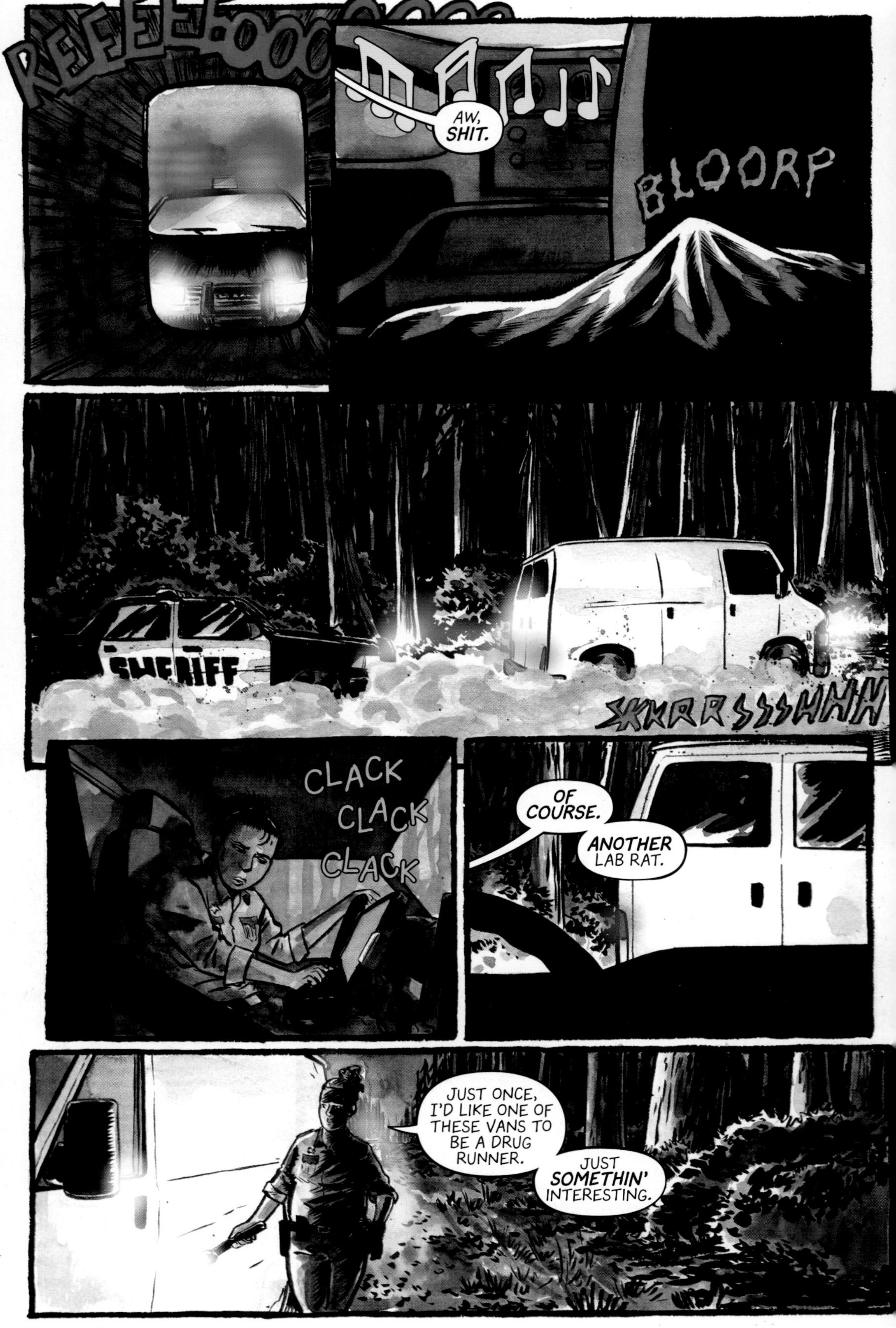
REEEEE-OOOOOOOO
AW, SHIT.
BLOORP
SHERIFF
SKKRRSSSHHH
CLACK
CLACK
CLACK
OF COURSE.
ANOTHER LAB RAT.
JUST ONCE, I'D LIKE ONE OF THESE VANS TO BE A DRUG RUNNER.
JUST SOMETHIN' INTERESTING.

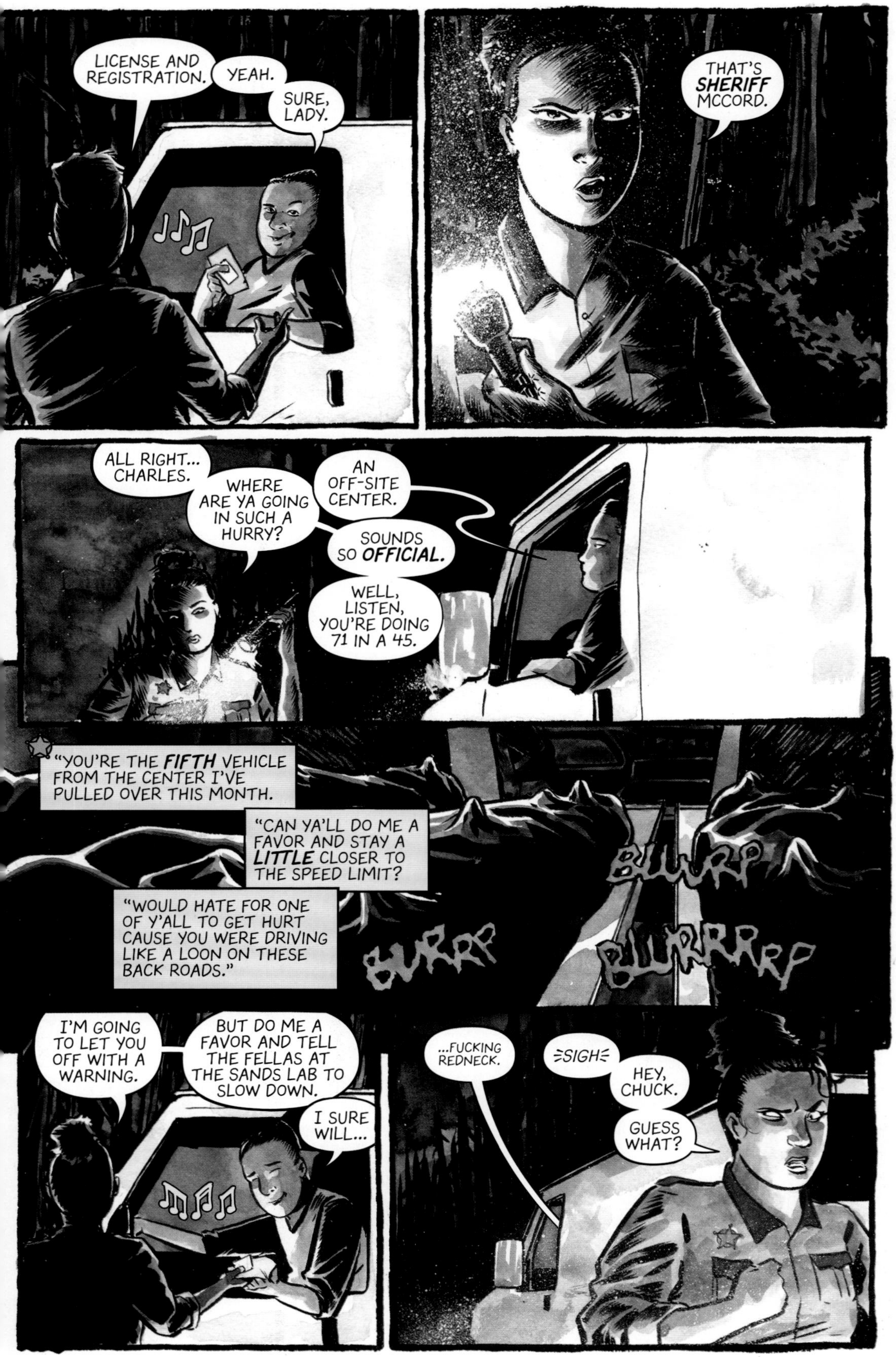
LICENSE AND REGISTRATION.
YEAH.
SURE, LADY.
THAT'S SHERIFF MCCORD.
ALL RIGHT... CHARLES.
WHERE ARE YA GOING IN SUCH A HURRY?
AN OFF-SITE CENTER.
SOUNDS SO OFFICIAL.
WELL, LISTEN, YOU'RE DOING 71 IN A 45.
"YOU'RE THE FIFTH VEHICLE FROM THE CENTER I'VE PULLED OVER THIS MONTH.
"CAN YA'LL DO ME A FAVOR AND STAY A LITTLE CLOSER TO THE SPEED LIMIT?
"WOULD HATE FOR ONE OF Y'ALL TO GET HURT CAUSE YOU WERE DRIVING LIKE A LOON ON THESE BACK ROADS."
BLUURP
BURRP
BLURRRRP
I'M GOING TO LET YOU OFF WITH A WARNING.
BUT DO ME A FAVOR AND TELL THE FELLAS AT THE SANDS LAB TO SLOW DOWN.
I SURE WILL...
...FUCKING REDNECK.
SIGH
HEY, CHUCK.
GUESS WHAT?

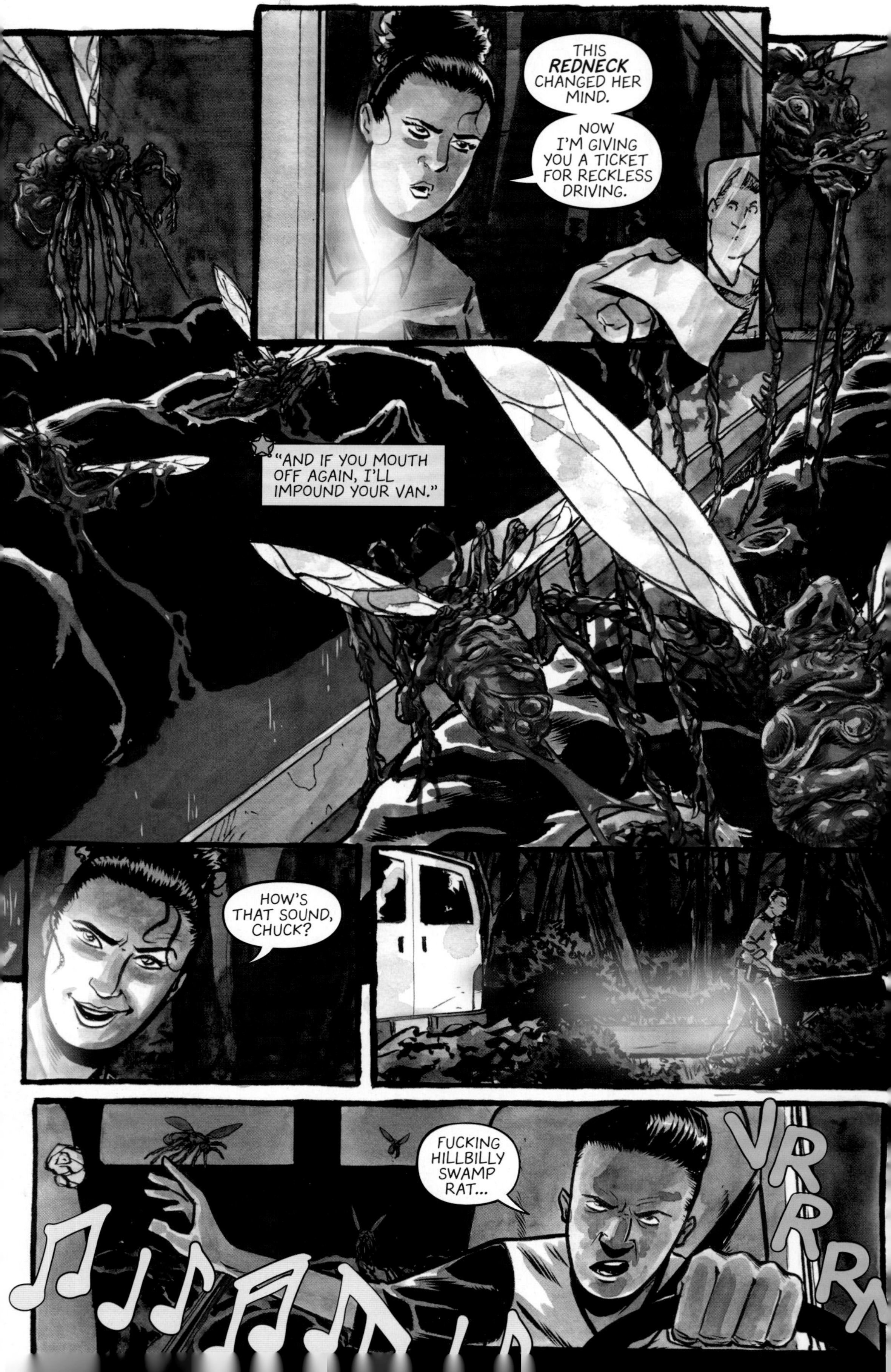
THIS REDNECK CHANGED HER MIND.
NOW I'M GIVING YOU A TICKET FOR RECKLESS DRIVING.
"AND IF YOU MOUTH OFF AGAIN, I'LL IMPOUND YOUR VAN."
HOW'S THAT SOUND, CHUCK?
FUCKING HILLBILLY SWAMP RAT...
VRRRR

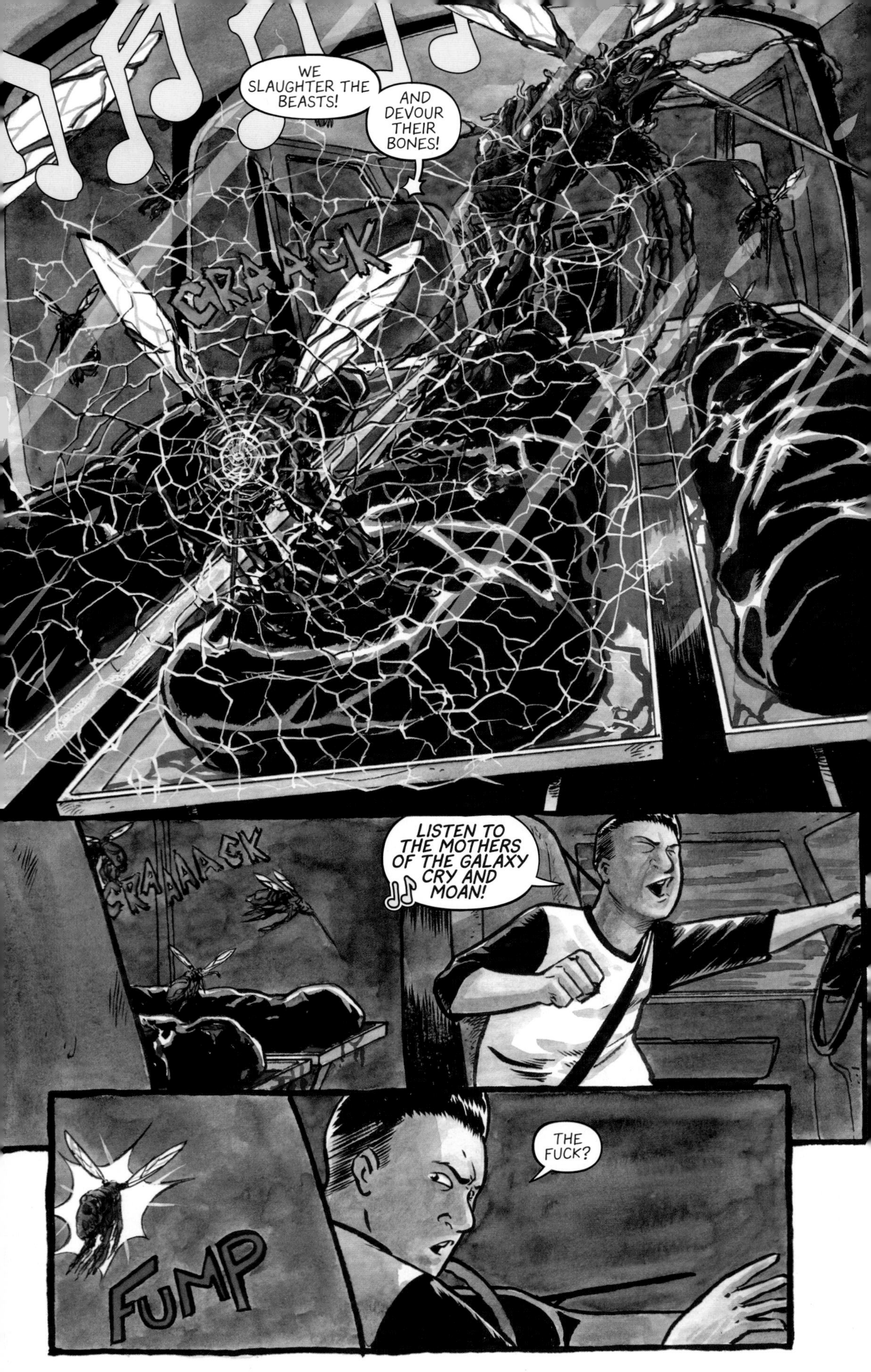
WE SLAUGHTER THE BEASTS!
AND DEVOUR THEIR BONES!
CRAACK
CRAAAACK
LISTEN TO THE MOTHERS OF THE GALAXY CRY AND MOAN!
THE FUCK?
FUMP

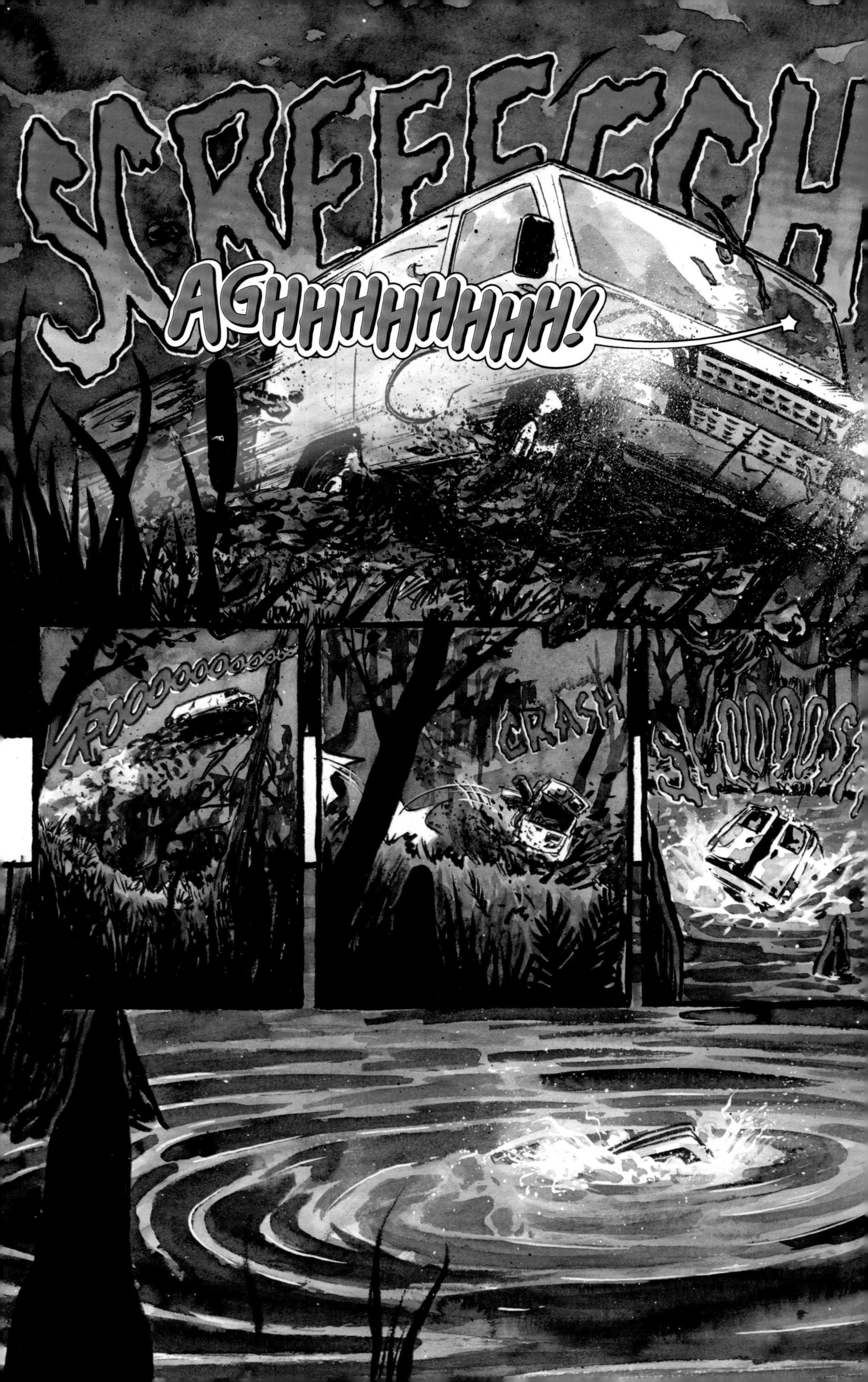
SCREEECH
AGHHHHHHHH!
VROOOOOOOSSSS...
CRASH
SLOOOOSH

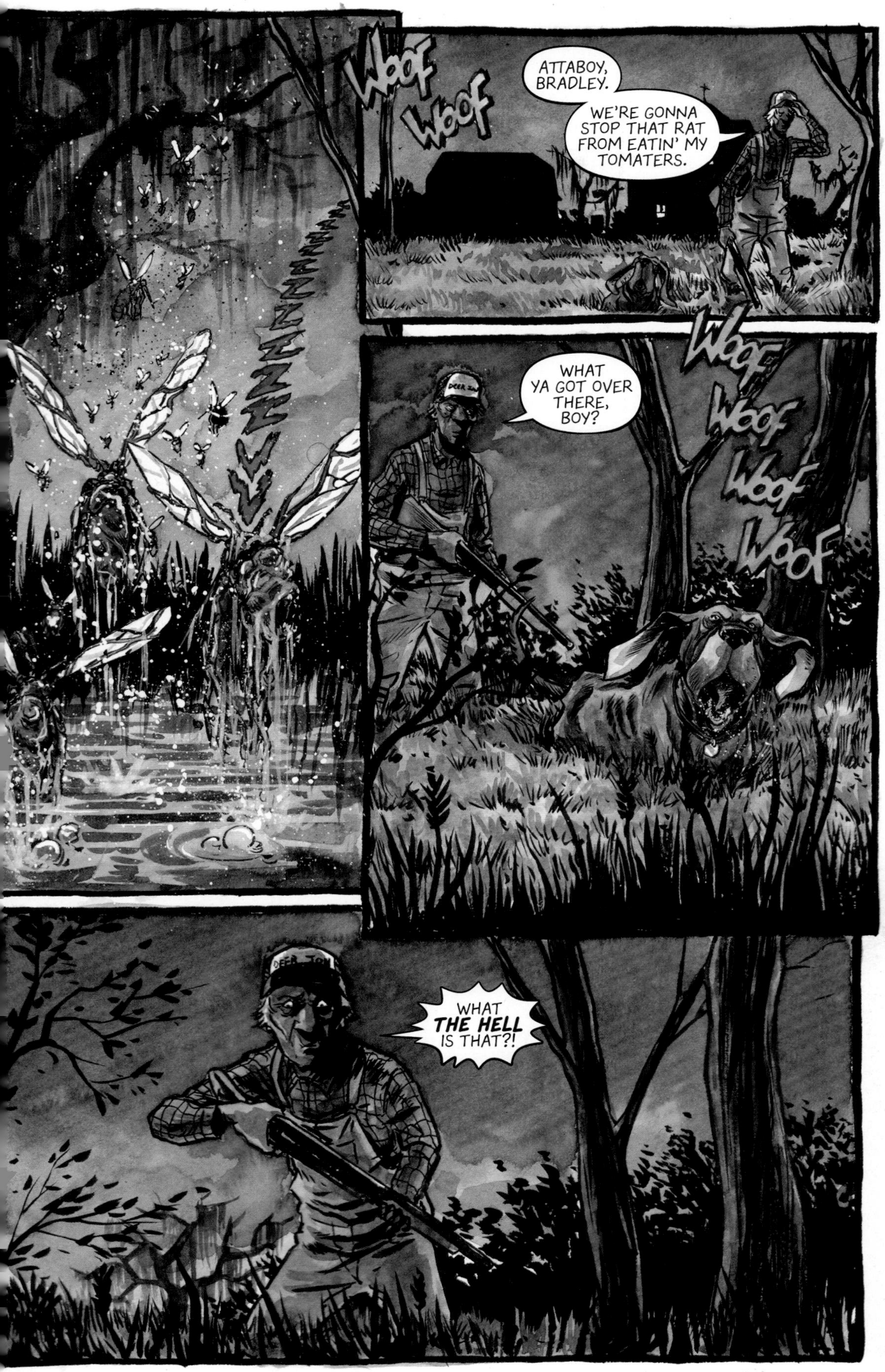
ZZZZZZZZZZZ
WOOF
WOOF
ATTABOY, BRADLEY.
WE'RE GONNA STOP THAT RAT FROM EATIN' MY TOMATERS.
WOOF
WOOF
WOOF
WOOF
WHAT YA GOT OVER THERE, BOY?
WHAT **THE HELL** IS THAT?!

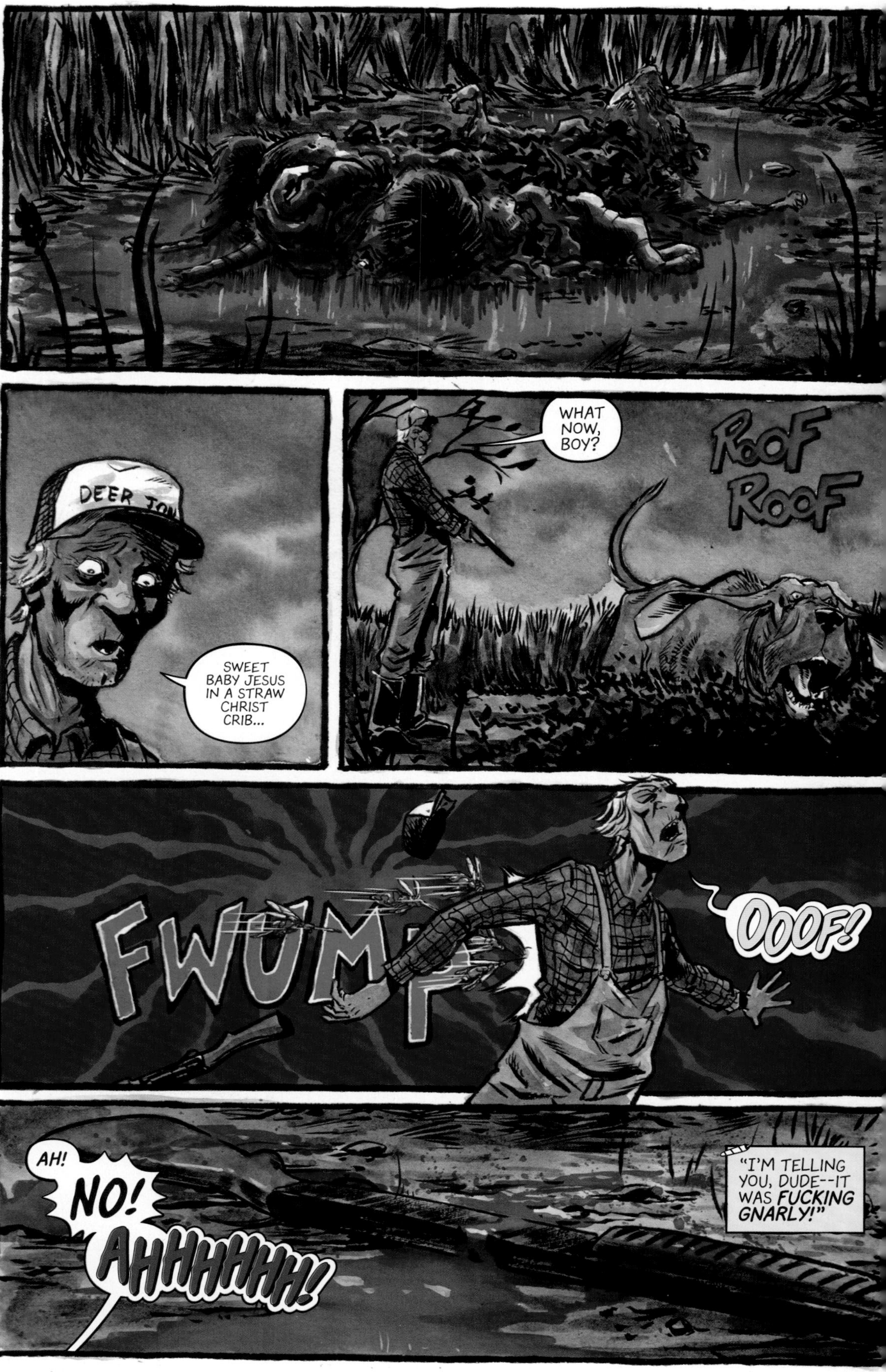
DEER JO
SWEET BABY JESUS IN A STRAW CHRIST CRIB...
WHAT NOW, BOY?
ROOF ROOF
FWUMP
OOOF!
AH!
NO!
AHHHHHH!
"I'M TELLING YOU, DUDE--IT WAS FUCKING GNARLY!"

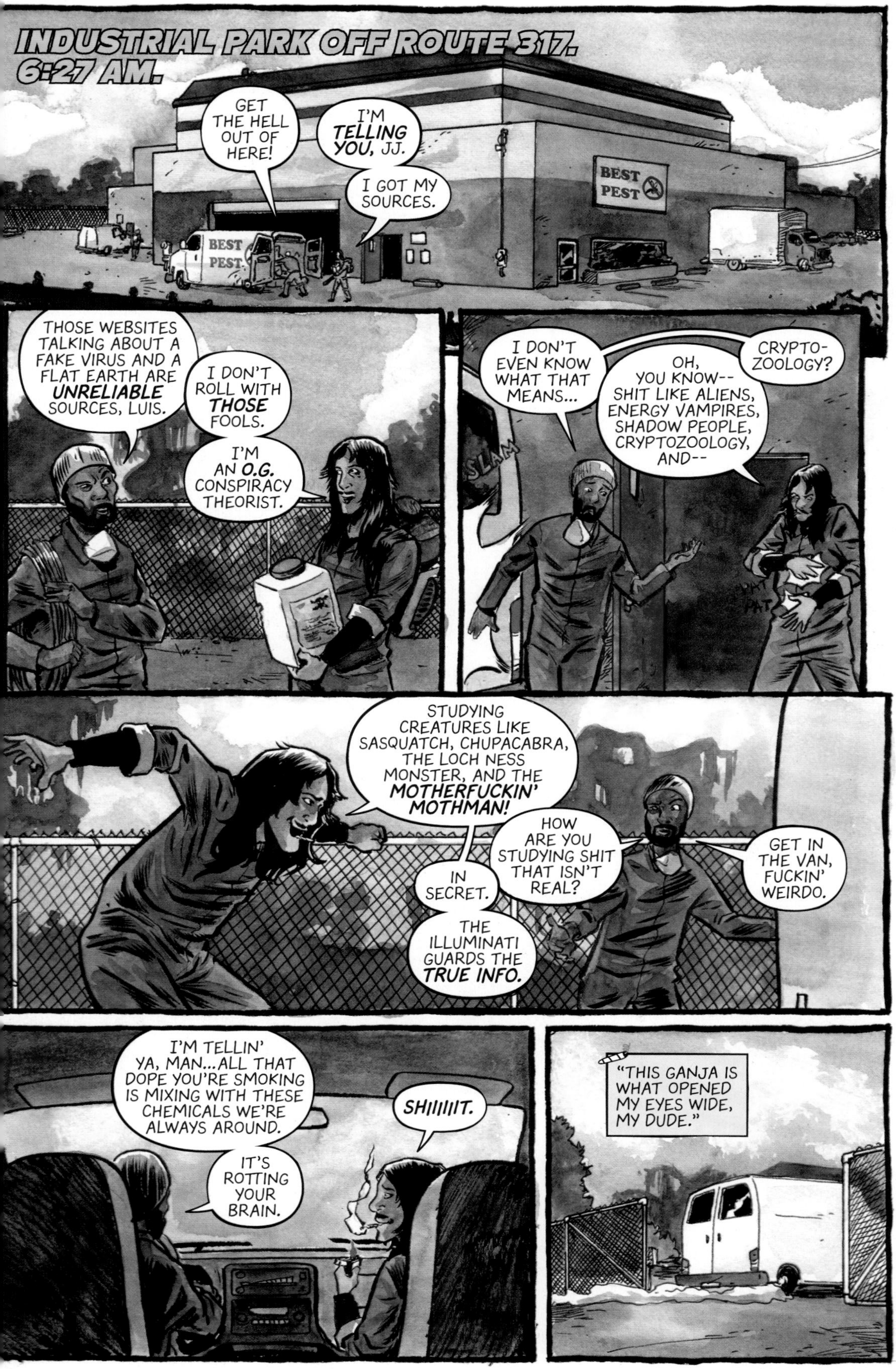
INDUSTRIAL PARK OFF ROUTE 317. 6:27 AM.
GET THE HELL OUT OF HERE!
I'M TELLING YOU, JJ.
I GOT MY SOURCES.
BEST PEST
BEST PEST
THOSE WEBSITES TALKING ABOUT A FAKE VIRUS AND A FLAT EARTH ARE UNRELIABLE SOURCES, LUIS.
I DON'T ROLL WITH THOSE FOOLS.
I'M AN O.G. CONSPIRACY THEORIST.
I DON'T EVEN KNOW WHAT THAT MEANS...
OH, YOU KNOW-- SHIT LIKE ALIENS, ENERGY VAMPIRES, SHADOW PEOPLE, CRYPTOZOOLOGY, AND--
CRYPTO-ZOOLOGY?
SLAM
PAT
STUDYING CREATURES LIKE SASQUATCH, CHUPACABRA, THE LOCH NESS MONSTER, AND THE MOTHERFUCKIN' MOTHMAN!
HOW ARE YOU STUDYING SHIT THAT ISN'T REAL?
GET IN THE VAN, FUCKIN' WEIRDO.
IN SECRET.
THE ILLUMINATI GUARDS THE TRUE INFO.
I'M TELLIN' YA, MAN...ALL THAT DOPE YOU'RE SMOKING IS MIXING WITH THESE CHEMICALS WE'RE ALWAYS AROUND.
IT'S ROTTING YOUR BRAIN.
SHIIIIIT.
"THIS GANJA IS WHAT OPENED MY EYES WIDE, MY DUDE."

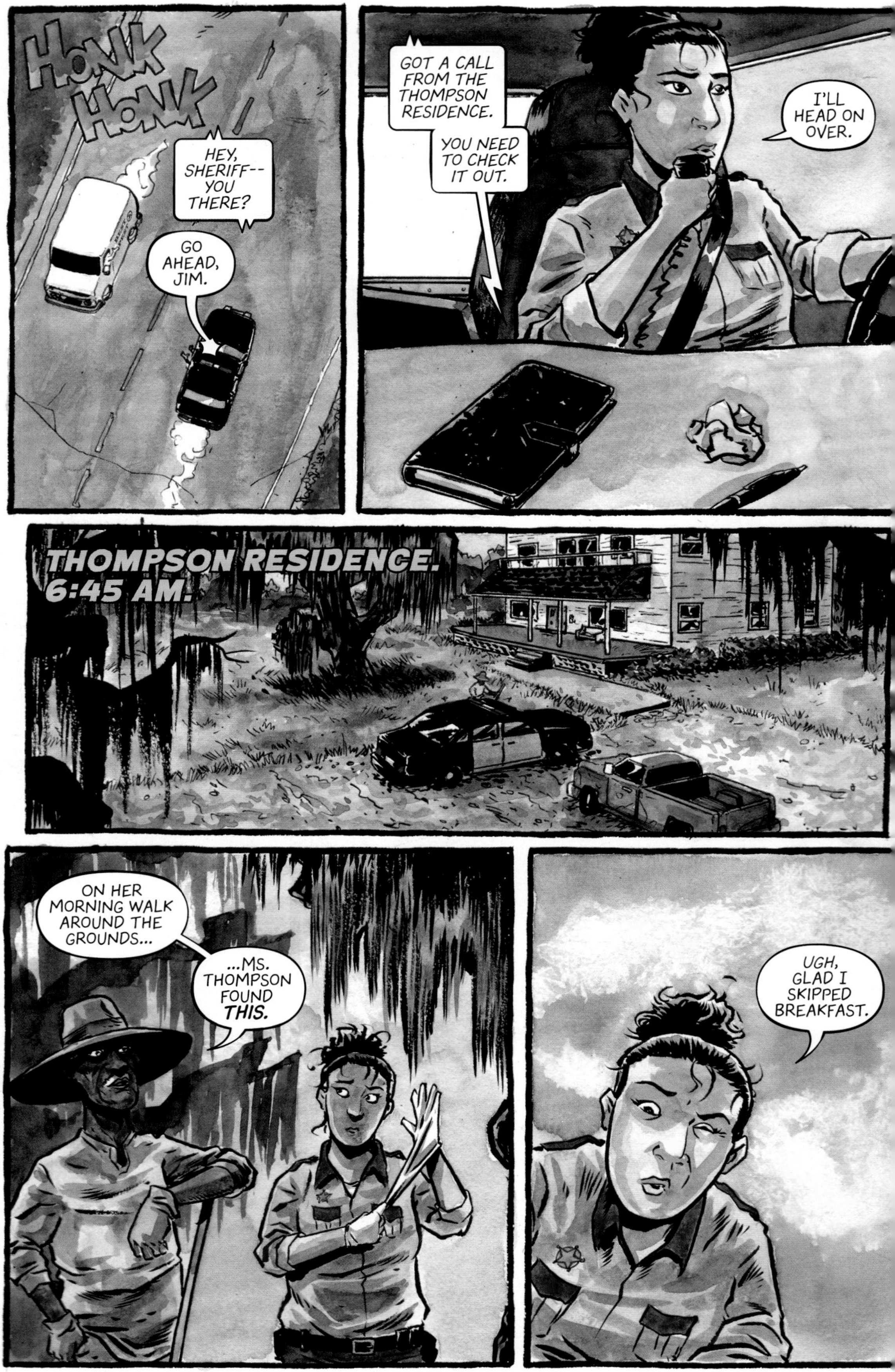
HONK HONK
HEY, SHERIFF-- YOU THERE?
GO AHEAD, JIM.
GOT A CALL FROM THE THOMPSON RESIDENCE.
YOU NEED TO CHECK IT OUT.
I'LL HEAD ON OVER.
THOMPSON RESIDENCE. 6:45 AM.
ON HER MORNING WALK AROUND THE GROUNDS...
...MS. THOMPSON FOUND THIS.
UGH, GLAD I SKIPPED BREAKFAST.

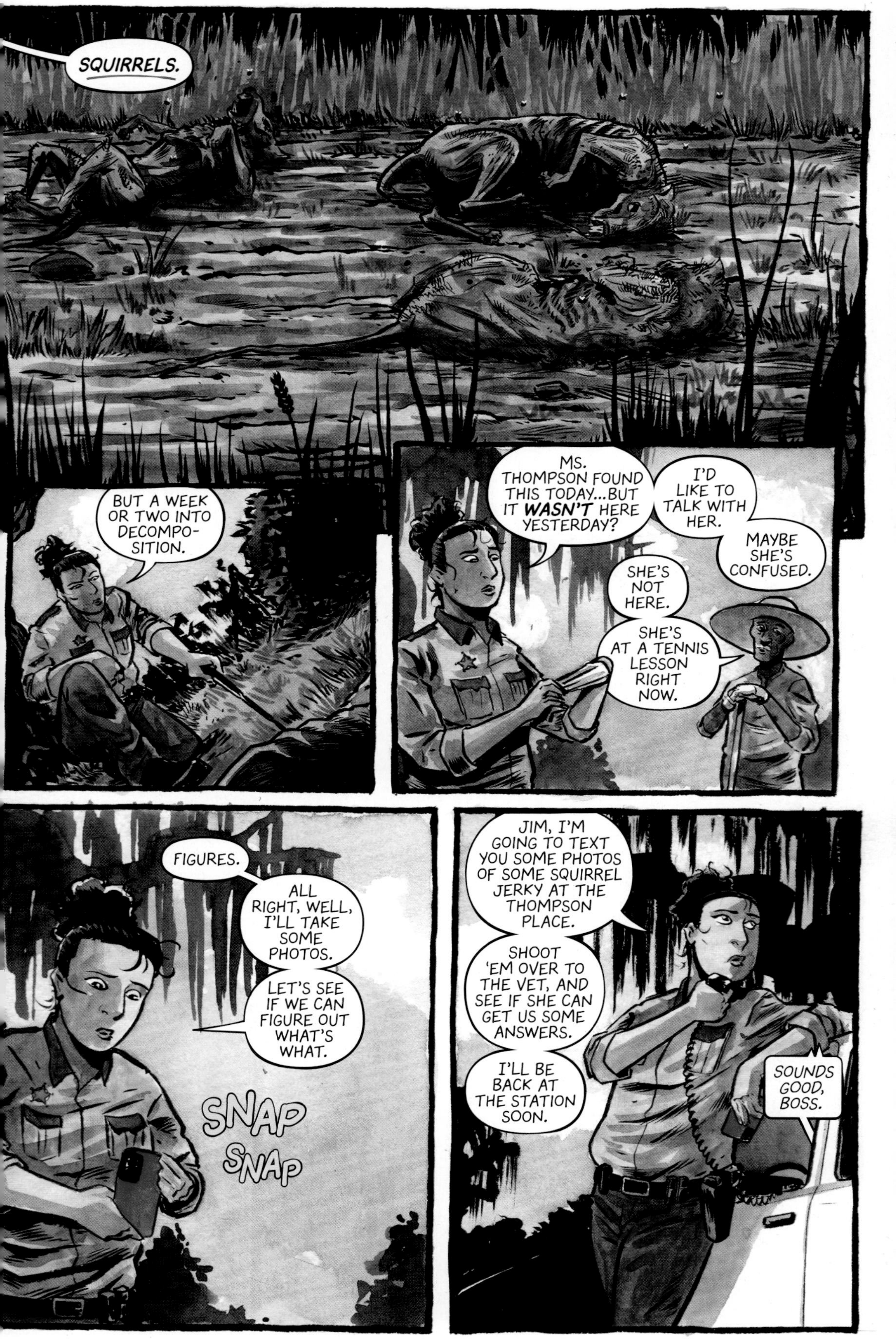
SQUIRRELS.
BUT A WEEK OR TWO INTO DECOMPO-SITION.
MS. THOMPSON FOUND THIS TODAY...BUT IT **WASN'T** HERE YESTERDAY?
I'D LIKE TO TALK WITH HER.
MAYBE SHE'S CONFUSED.
SHE'S NOT HERE.
SHE'S AT A TENNIS LESSON RIGHT NOW.
FIGURES.
ALL RIGHT, WELL, I'LL TAKE SOME PHOTOS.
LET'S SEE IF WE CAN FIGURE OUT WHAT'S WHAT.
SNAP
SNAP
JIM, I'M GOING TO TEXT YOU SOME PHOTOS OF SOME SQUIRREL JERKY AT THE THOMPSON PLACE.
SHOOT 'EM OVER TO THE VET, AND SEE IF SHE CAN GET US SOME ANSWERS.
I'LL BE BACK AT THE STATION SOON.
SOUNDS GOOD, BOSS.

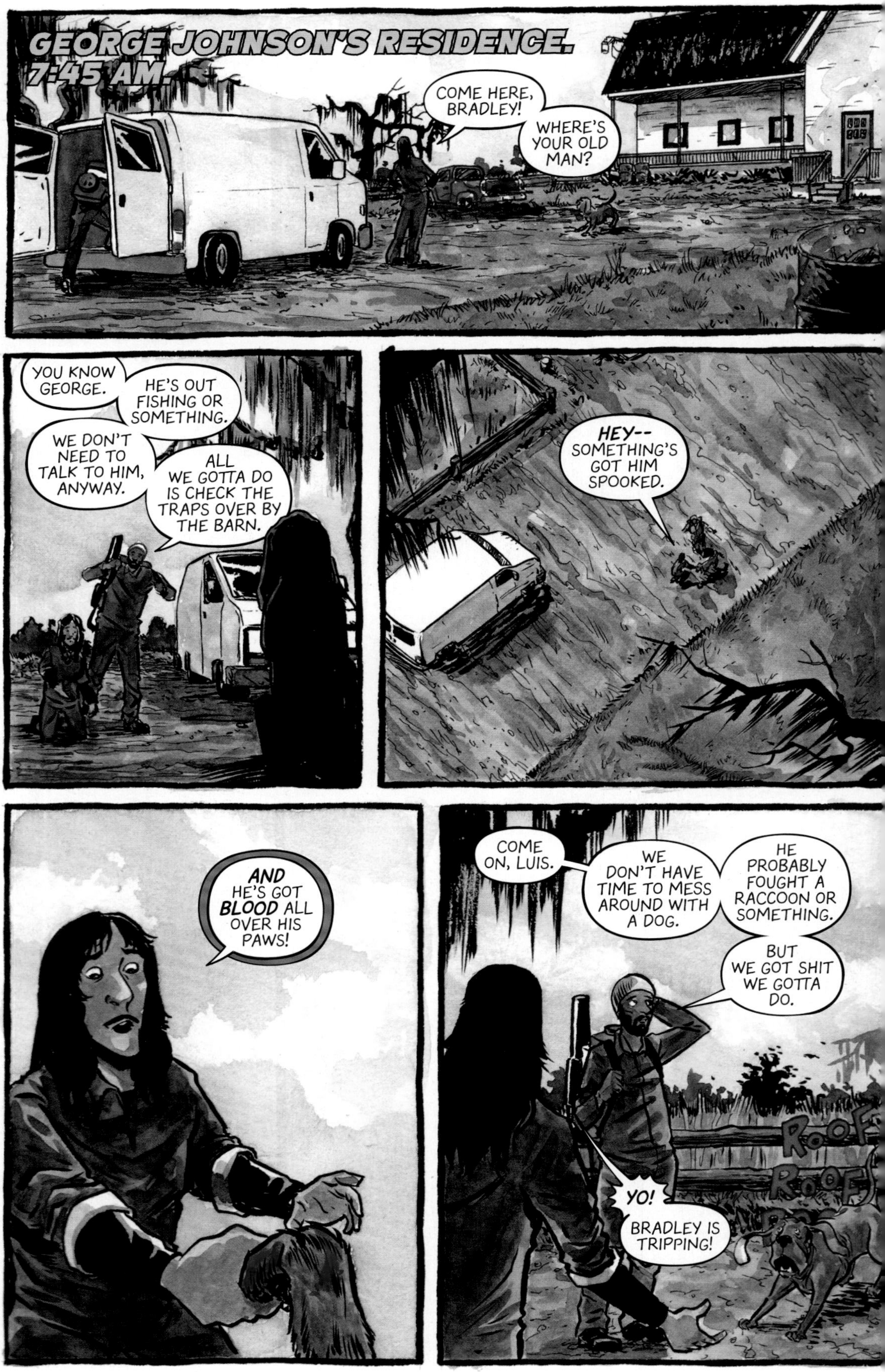
GEORGE JOHNSON'S RESIDENCE.
7:45 AM.
COME HERE, BRADLEY!
WHERE'S YOUR OLD MAN?
YOU KNOW GEORGE.
HE'S OUT FISHING OR SOMETHING.
WE DON'T NEED TO TALK TO HIM, ANYWAY.
ALL WE GOTTA DO IS CHECK THE TRAPS OVER BY THE BARN.
HEY-- SOMETHING'S GOT HIM SPOOKED.
AND HE'S GOT BLOOD ALL OVER HIS PAWS!
COME ON, LUIS.
WE DON'T HAVE TIME TO MESS AROUND WITH A DOG.
HE PROBABLY FOUGHT A RACCOON OR SOMETHING.
BUT WE GOT SHIT WE GOTTA DO.
YO!
BRADLEY IS TRIPPING!
ROOF
ROOF

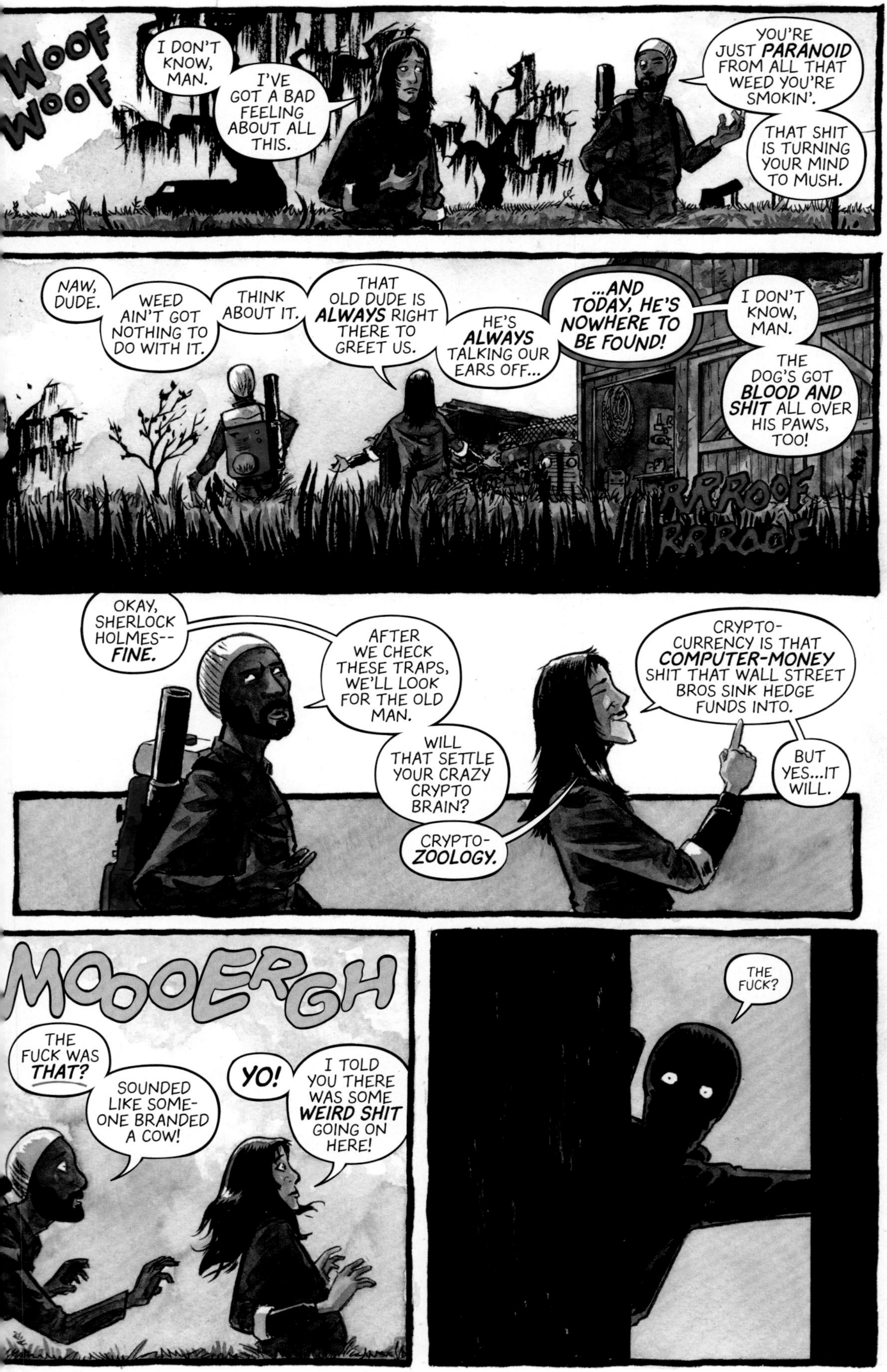
WOOF WOOF
I DON'T KNOW, MAN.
I'VE GOT A BAD FEELING ABOUT ALL THIS.
YOU'RE JUST PARANOID FROM ALL THAT WEED YOU'RE SMOKIN'.
THAT SHIT IS TURNING YOUR MIND TO MUSH.
NAW, DUDE.
WEED AIN'T GOT NOTHING TO DO WITH IT.
THINK ABOUT IT.
THAT OLD DUDE IS ALWAYS RIGHT THERE TO GREET US.
HE'S ALWAYS TALKING OUR EARS OFF...
...AND TODAY, HE'S NOWHERE TO BE FOUND!
I DON'T KNOW, MAN.
THE DOG'S GOT BLOOD AND SHIT ALL OVER HIS PAWS, TOO!
RRROOF RRROOF
OKAY, SHERLOCK HOLMES-- FINE.
AFTER WE CHECK THESE TRAPS, WE'LL LOOK FOR THE OLD MAN.
WILL THAT SETTLE YOUR CRAZY CRYPTO BRAIN?
CRYPTO-ZOOLOGY.
CRYPTO-CURRENCY IS THAT COMPUTER-MONEY SHIT THAT WALL STREET BROS SINK HEDGE FUNDS INTO.
BUT YES...IT WILL.
MOOOERGH
THE FUCK WAS THAT?
SOUNDED LIKE SOME-ONE BRANDED A COW!
YO!
I TOLD YOU THERE WAS SOME WEIRD SHIT GOING ON HERE!
THE FUCK?

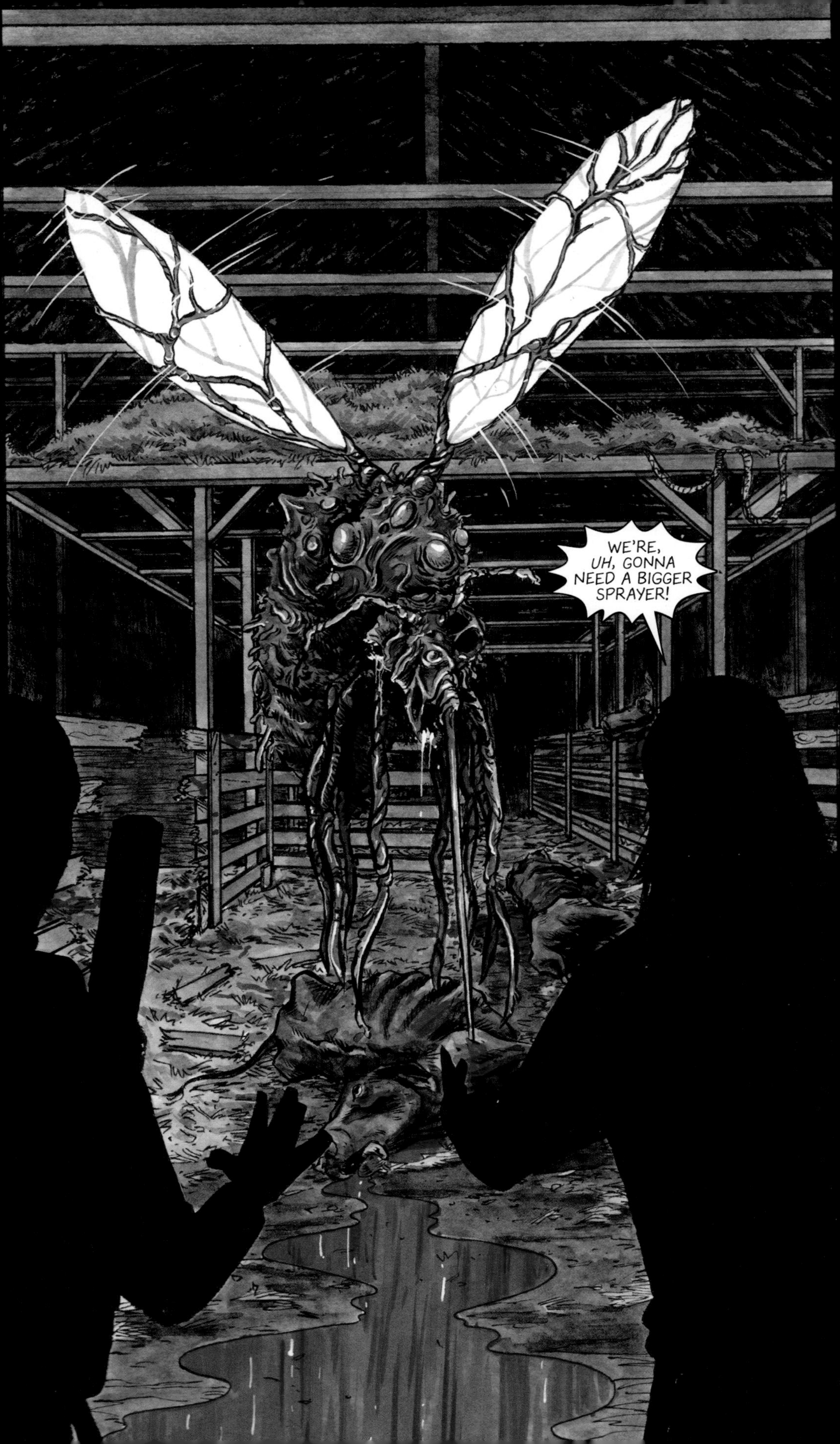
WE'RE, *UH*, GONNA NEED A BIGGER SPRAYER!

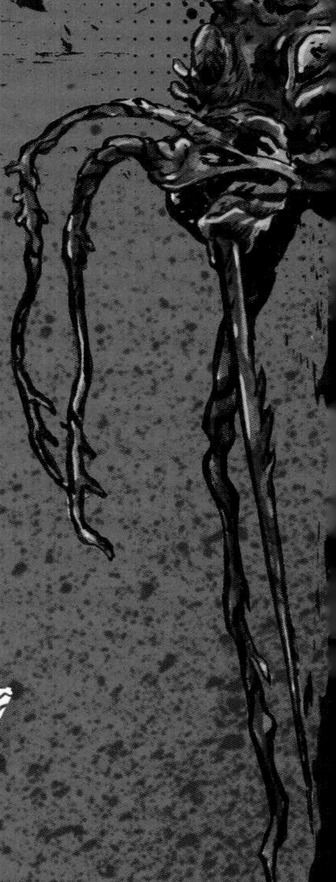

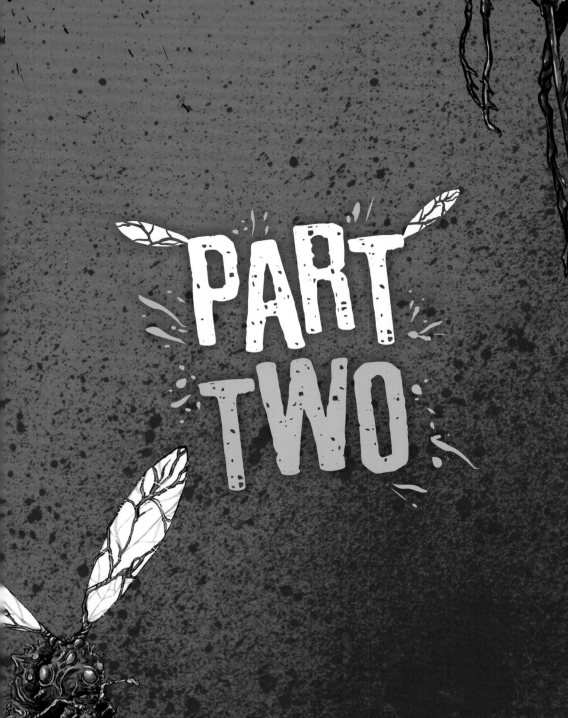

PART TWO

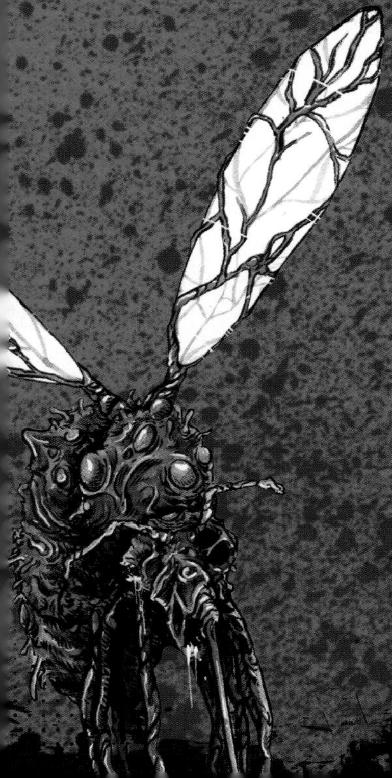

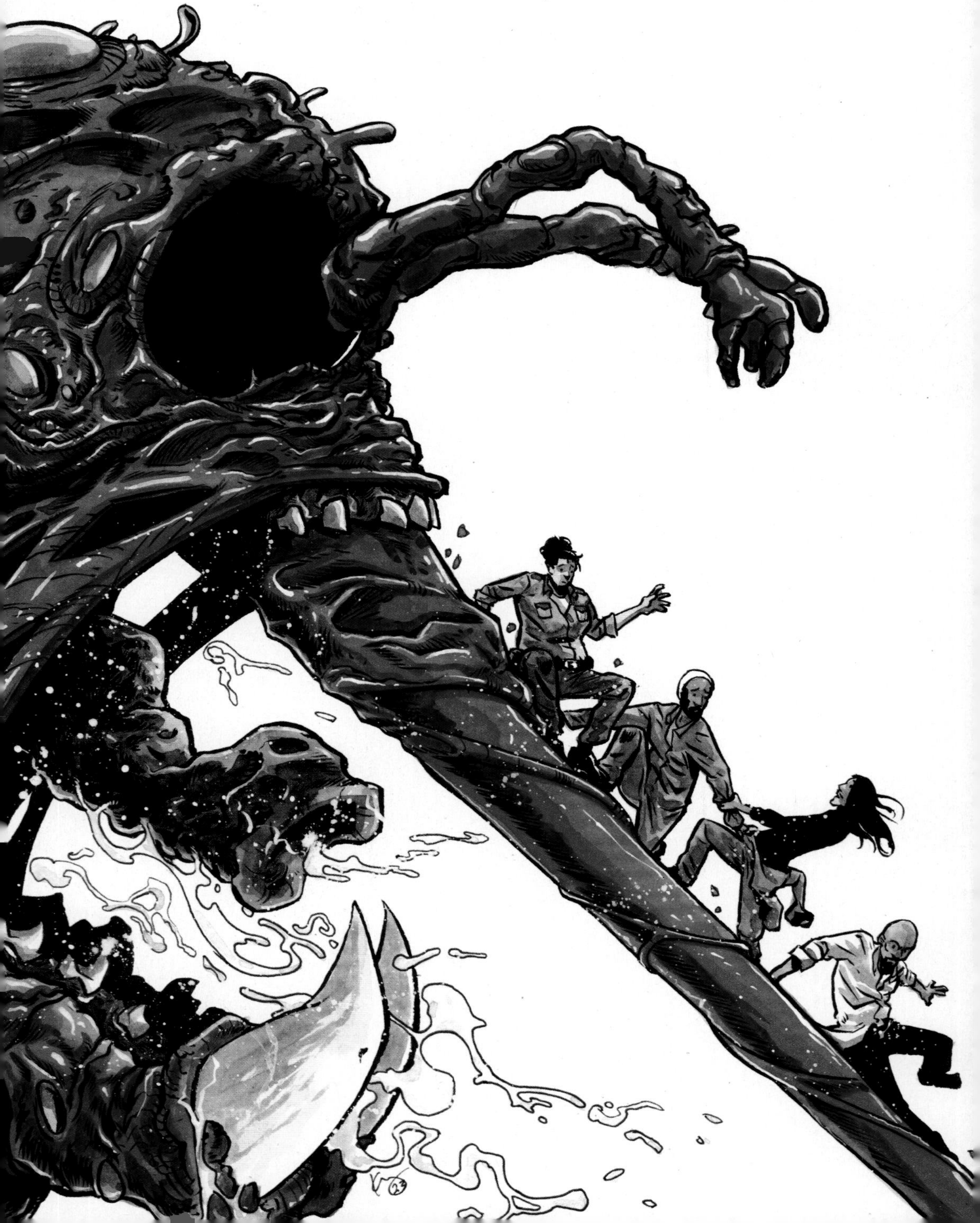

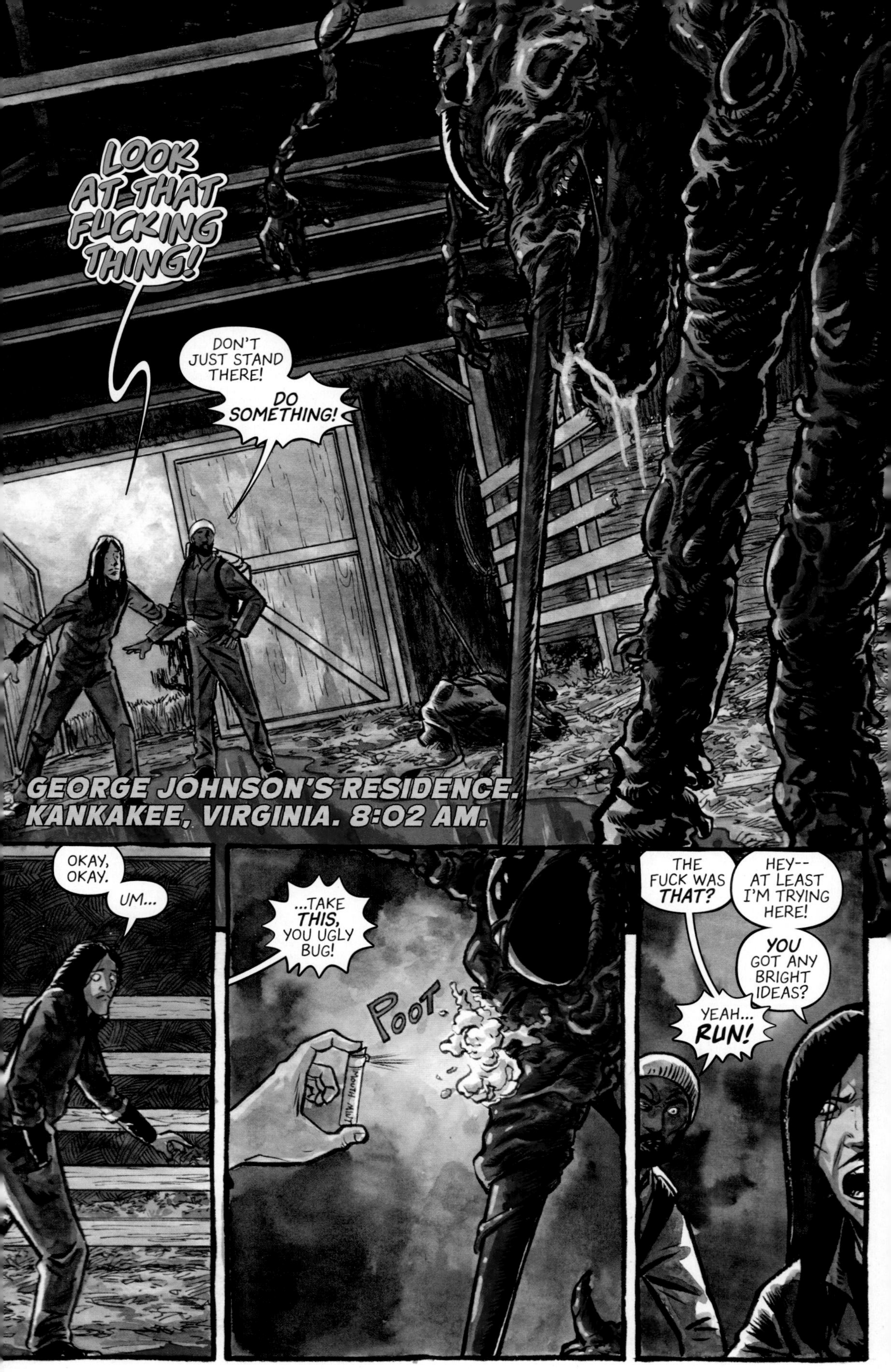
LOOK AT THAT FUCKING THING!
DON'T JUST STAND THERE!
DO SOMETHING!
GEORGE JOHNSON'S RESIDENCE. KANKAKEE, VIRGINIA. 8:02 AM.
OKAY, OKAY.
UM...
...TAKE THIS, YOU UGLY BUG!
POOT.
MOUTH MIST
THE FUCK WAS THAT?
HEY-- AT LEAST I'M TRYING HERE!
YOU GOT ANY BRIGHT IDEAS?
YEAH... RUN!

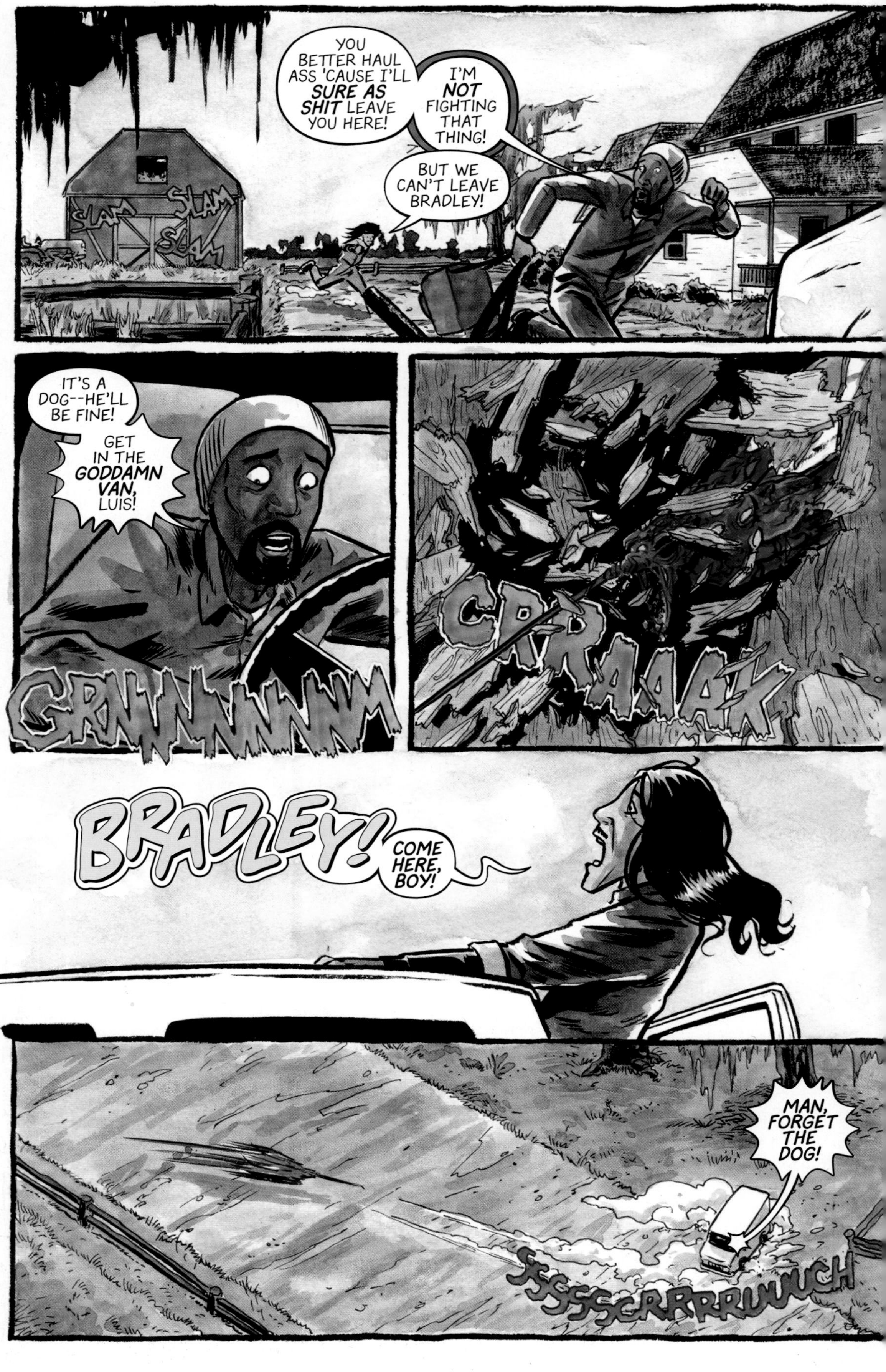
SLAM
SLAM
SLAM
YOU BETTER HAUL ASS 'CAUSE I'LL SURE AS SHIT LEAVE YOU HERE!
I'M NOT FIGHTING THAT THING!
BUT WE CAN'T LEAVE BRADLEY!
IT'S A DOG--HE'LL BE FINE!
GET IN THE GODDAMN VAN, LUIS!
GRNNNNNNM
CRRAAAK
BRADLEY!
COME HERE, BOY!
MAN, FORGET THE DOG!
SSSSSCRRRRUUUCH

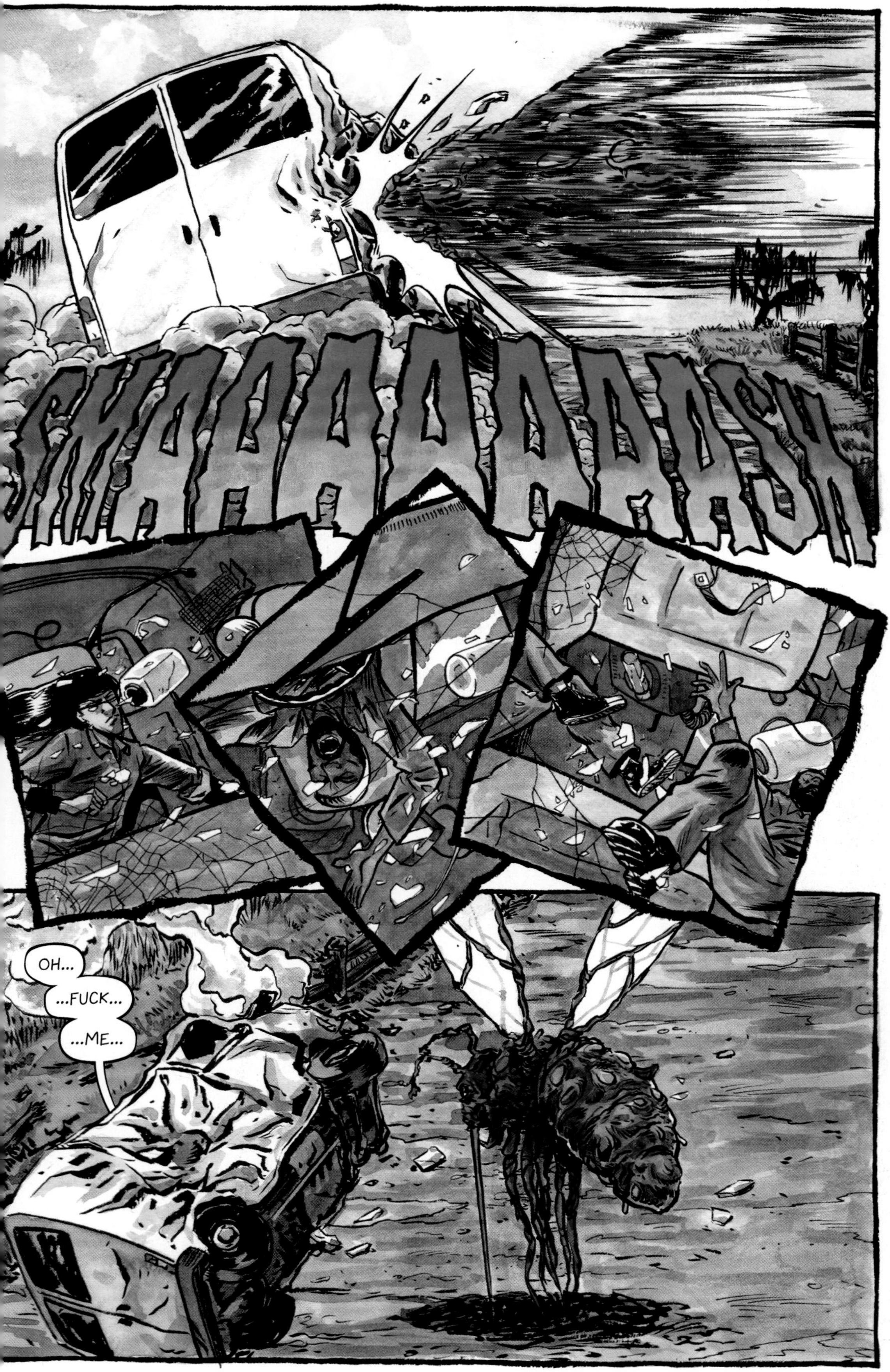
SKRAAAAAASH
OH...
...FUCK...
...ME...

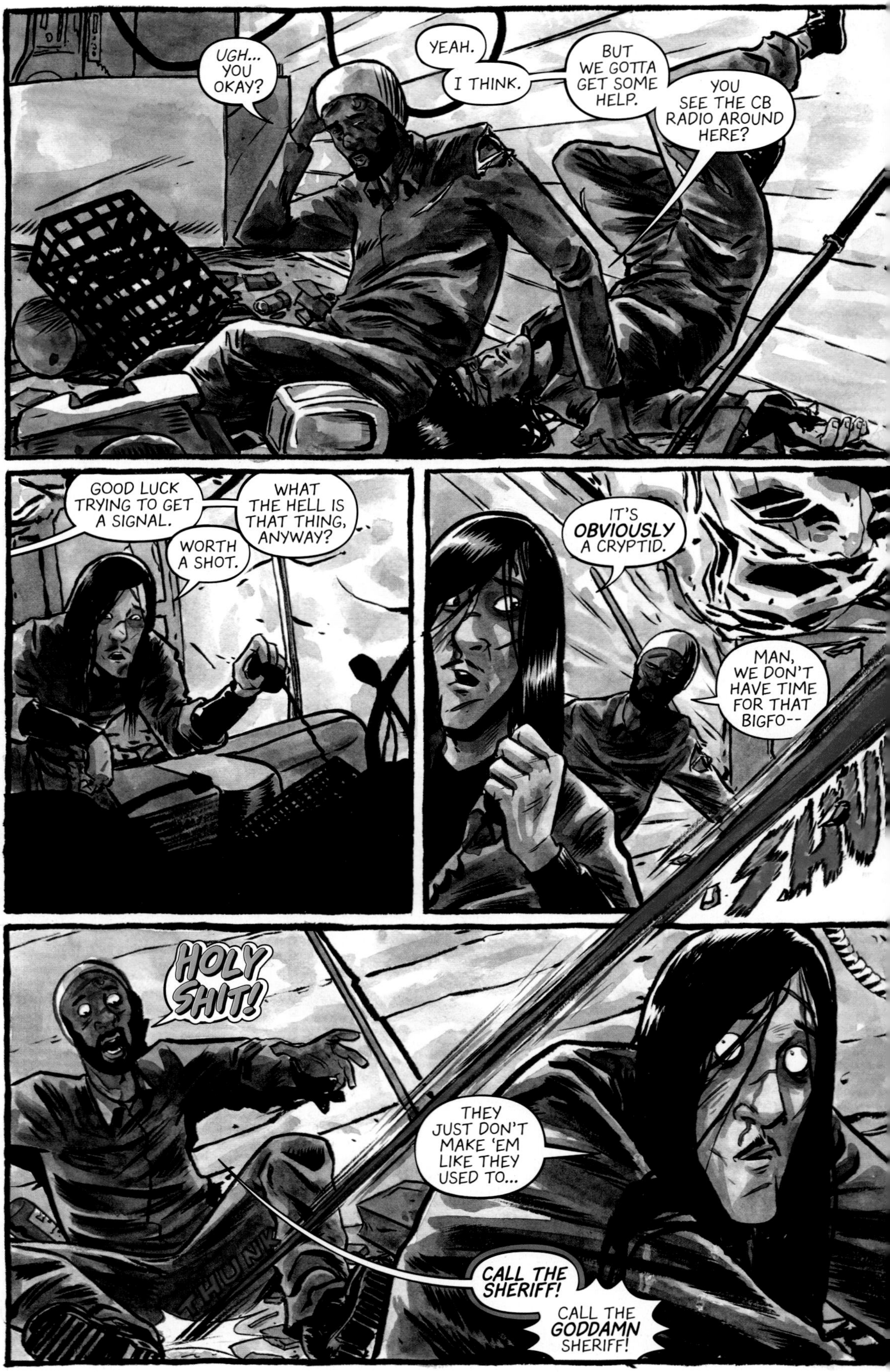
UGH... YOU OKAY?
YEAH.
I THINK.
BUT WE GOTTA GET SOME HELP.
YOU SEE THE CB RADIO AROUND HERE?
GOOD LUCK TRYING TO GET A SIGNAL.
WORTH A SHOT.
WHAT THE HELL IS THAT THING, ANYWAY?
IT'S OBVIOUSLY A CRYPTID.
MAN, WE DON'T HAVE TIME FOR THAT BIGFO--
HOLY SHIT!
THEY JUST DON'T MAKE 'EM LIKE THEY USED TO...
THUNK
CALL THE SHERIFF!
CALL THE GODDAMN SHERIFF!

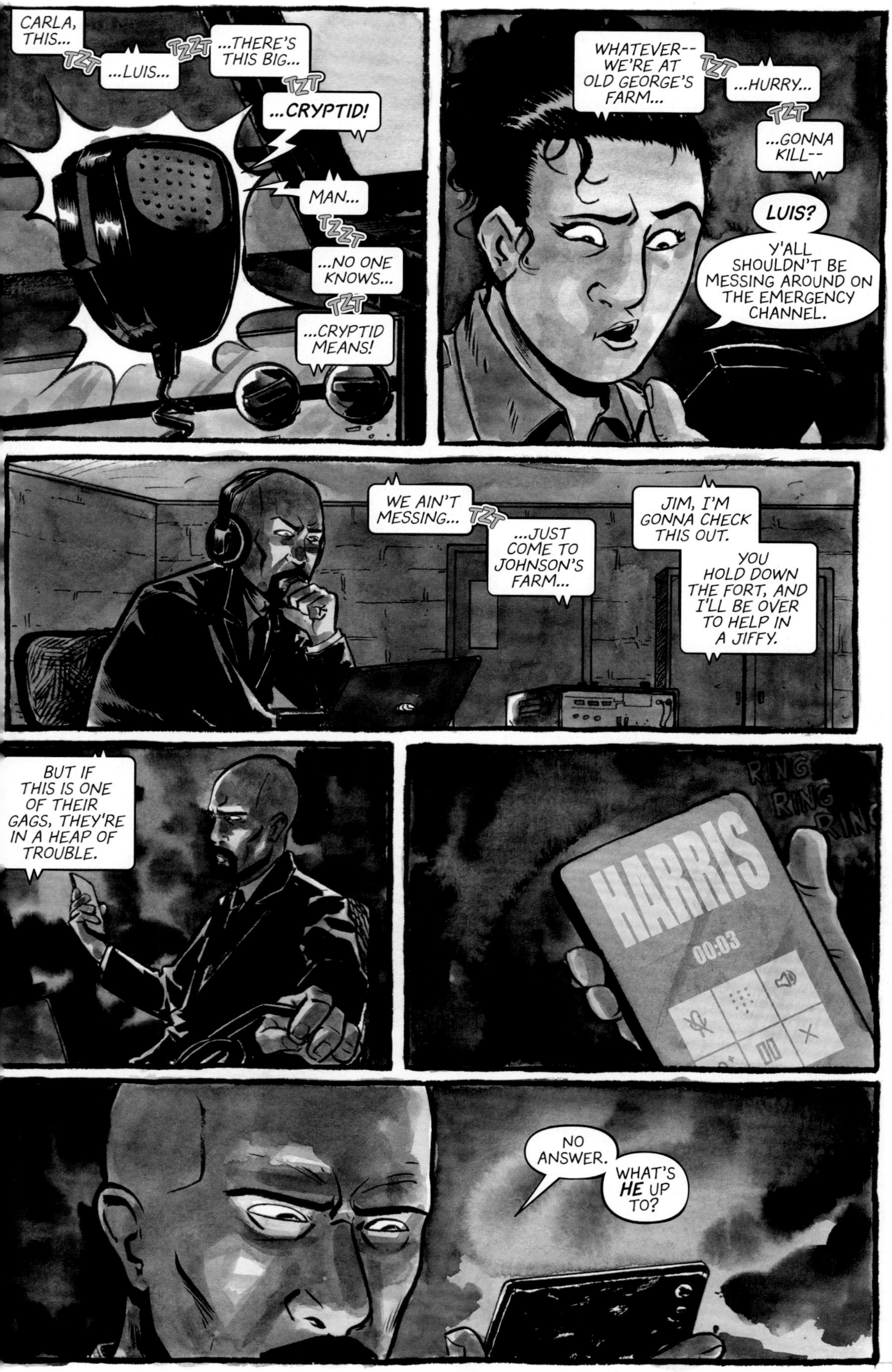
CARLA, THIS...
TZT
...LUIS...
TZZT
...THERE'S THIS BIG...
TZT
...CRYPTID!
MAN...
TZZT
...NO ONE KNOWS...
TZT
...CRYPTID MEANS!
WHATEVER-- WE'RE AT OLD GEORGE'S FARM...
TZT
...HURRY...
TZT
...GONNA KILL--
LUIS?
Y'ALL SHOULDN'T BE MESSING AROUND ON THE EMERGENCY CHANNEL.
WE AIN'T MESSING...
TZT
...JUST COME TO JOHNSON'S FARM...
JIM, I'M GONNA CHECK THIS OUT.
YOU HOLD DOWN THE FORT, AND I'LL BE OVER TO HELP IN A JIFFY.
BUT IF THIS IS ONE OF THEIR GAGS, THEY'RE IN A HEAP OF TROUBLE.
RING RING RING
HARRIS
00:03
NO ANSWER.
WHAT'S HE UP TO?

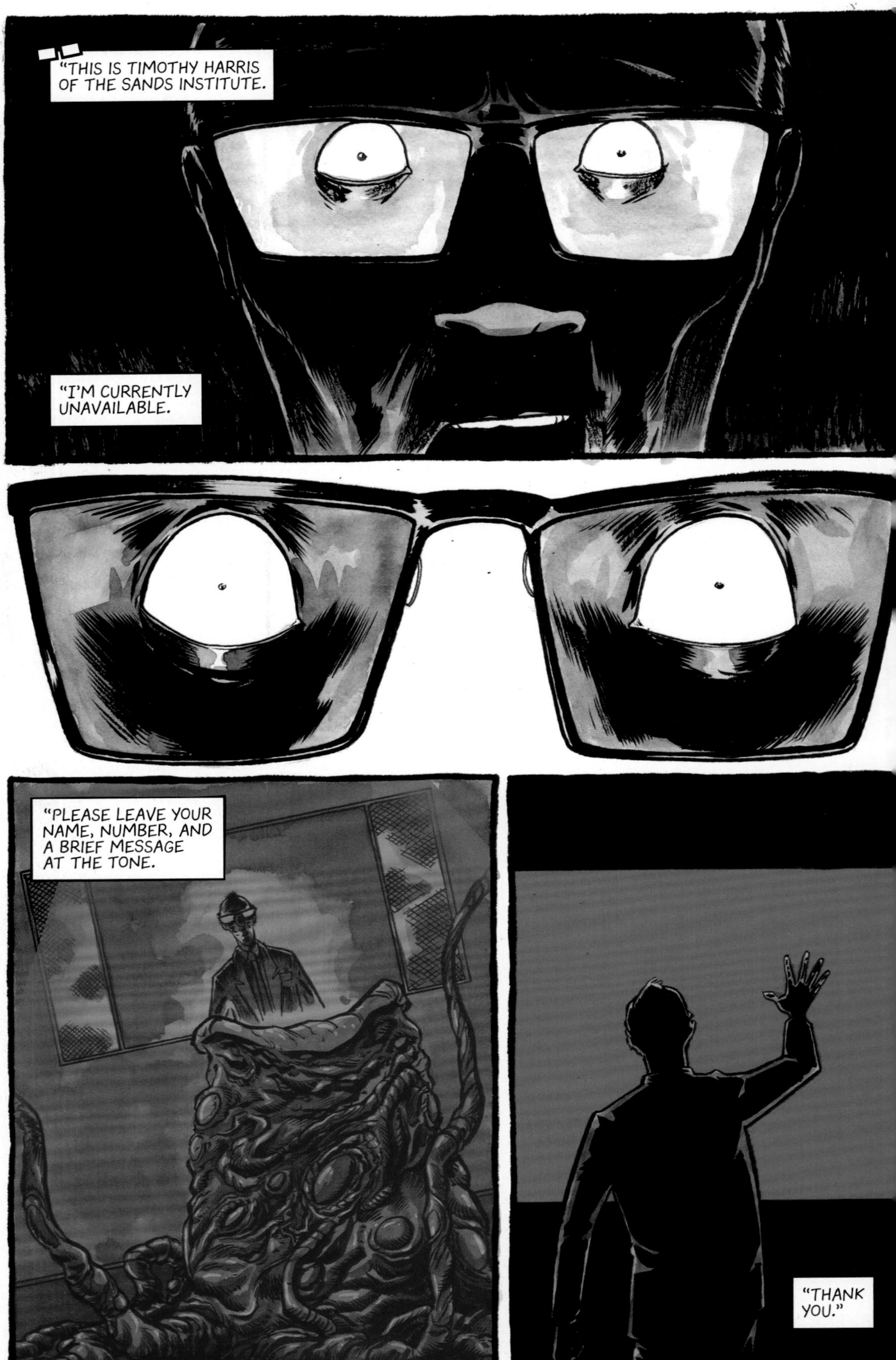
"THIS IS TIMOTHY HARRIS OF THE SANDS INSTITUTE.
"I'M CURRENTLY UNAVAILABLE.
"PLEASE LEAVE YOUR NAME, NUMBER, AND A BRIEF MESSAGE AT THE TONE.
"THANK YOU."

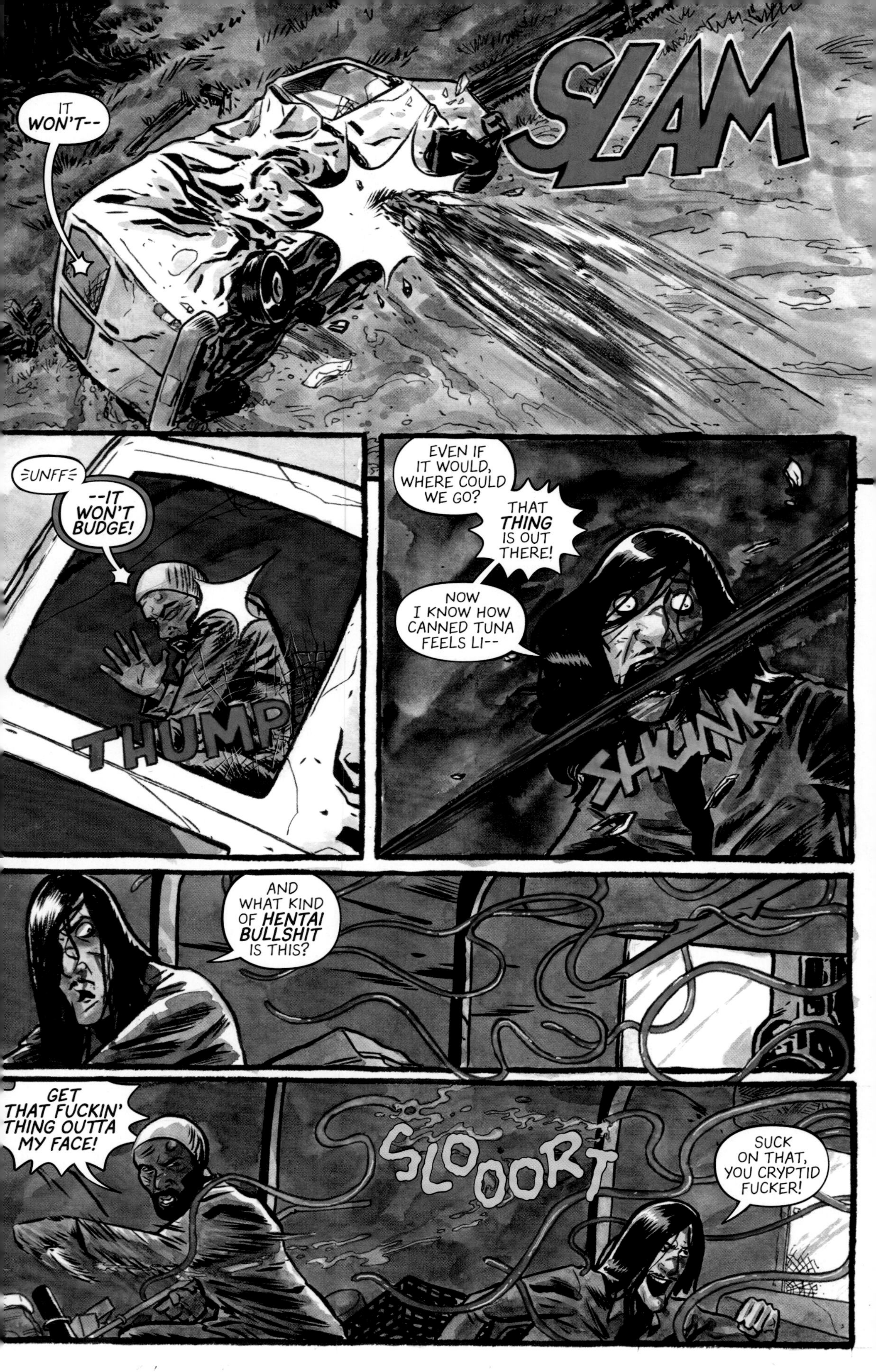
IT WON'T--
SLAM
UNFF
--IT WON'T BUDGE!
THUMP
EVEN IF IT WOULD, WHERE COULD WE GO?
THAT THING IS OUT THERE!
NOW I KNOW HOW CANNED TUNA FEELS LI--
SHUNK
AND WHAT KIND OF HENTAI BULLSHIT IS THIS?
GET THAT FUCKIN' THING OUTTA MY FACE!
SLOOORT
SUCK ON THAT, YOU CRYPTID FUCKER!

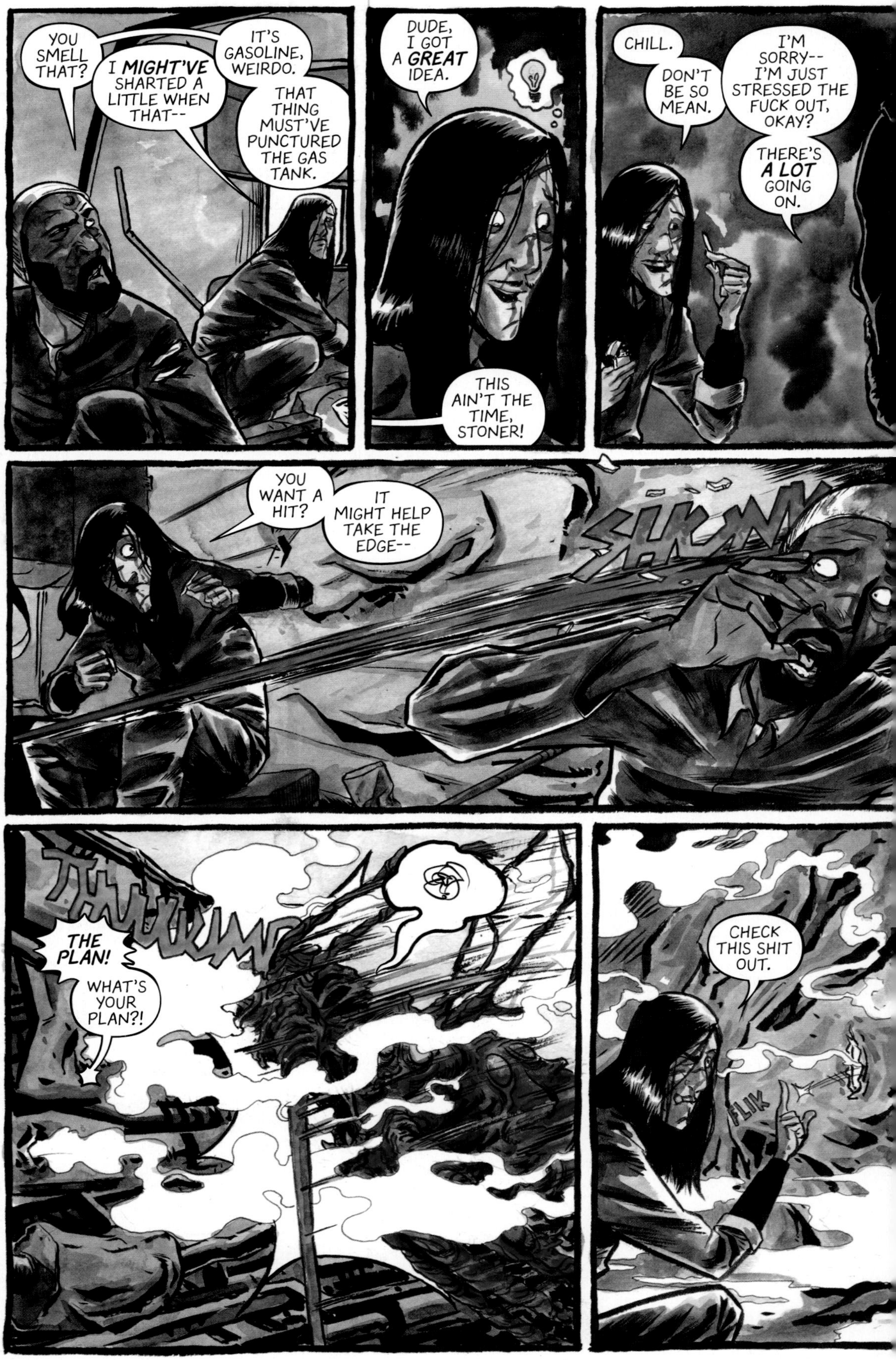
YOU SMELL THAT?
I **MIGHT'VE** SHARTED A LITTLE WHEN THAT--
IT'S GASOLINE, WEIRDO.
THAT THING MUST'VE PUNCTURED THE GAS TANK.
DUDE, I GOT A **GREAT** IDEA.
THIS AIN'T THE TIME, STONER!
CHILL.
DON'T BE SO MEAN.
I'M SORRY-- I'M JUST STRESSED THE FUCK OUT, OKAY?
THERE'S **A LOT** GOING ON.
YOU WANT A HIT?
IT MIGHT HELP TAKE THE EDGE--
SHUNK
THUUUMP
THE PLAN!
WHAT'S YOUR PLAN?!
CHECK THIS SHIT OUT.
FLIK

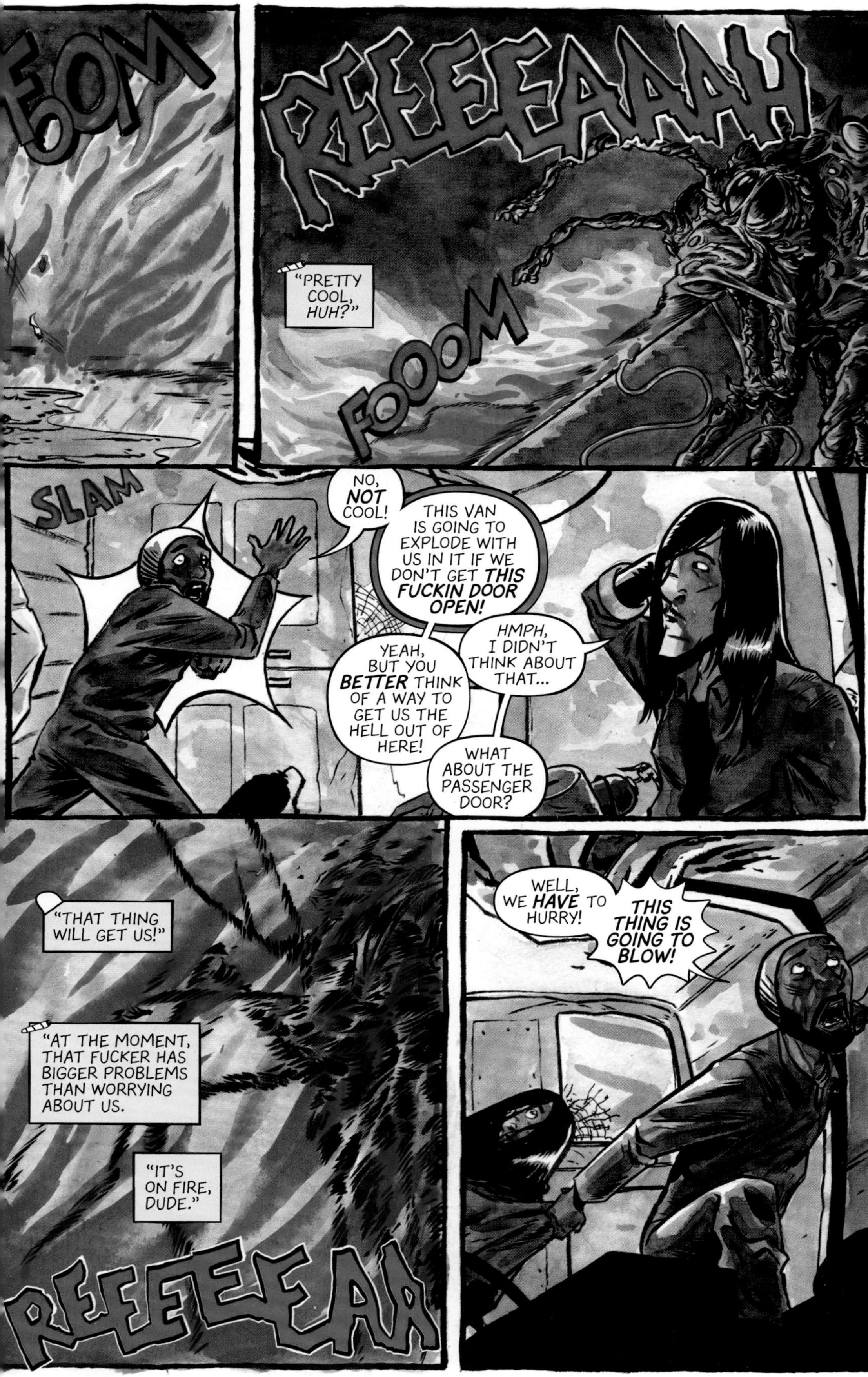
FOOM
REEEEAAAH
"PRETTY COOL, HUH?"
FOOOM
SLAM
NO, NOT COOL!
THIS VAN IS GOING TO EXPLODE WITH US IN IT IF WE DON'T GET THIS FUCKIN DOOR OPEN!
YEAH, BUT YOU BETTER THINK OF A WAY TO GET US THE HELL OUT OF HERE!
HMPH, I DIDN'T THINK ABOUT THAT...
WHAT ABOUT THE PASSENGER DOOR?
"THAT THING WILL GET US!"
"AT THE MOMENT, THAT FUCKER HAS BIGGER PROBLEMS THAN WORRYING ABOUT US.
"IT'S ON FIRE, DUDE."
REEEEAA
WELL, WE HAVE TO HURRY!
THIS THING IS GOING TO BLOW!

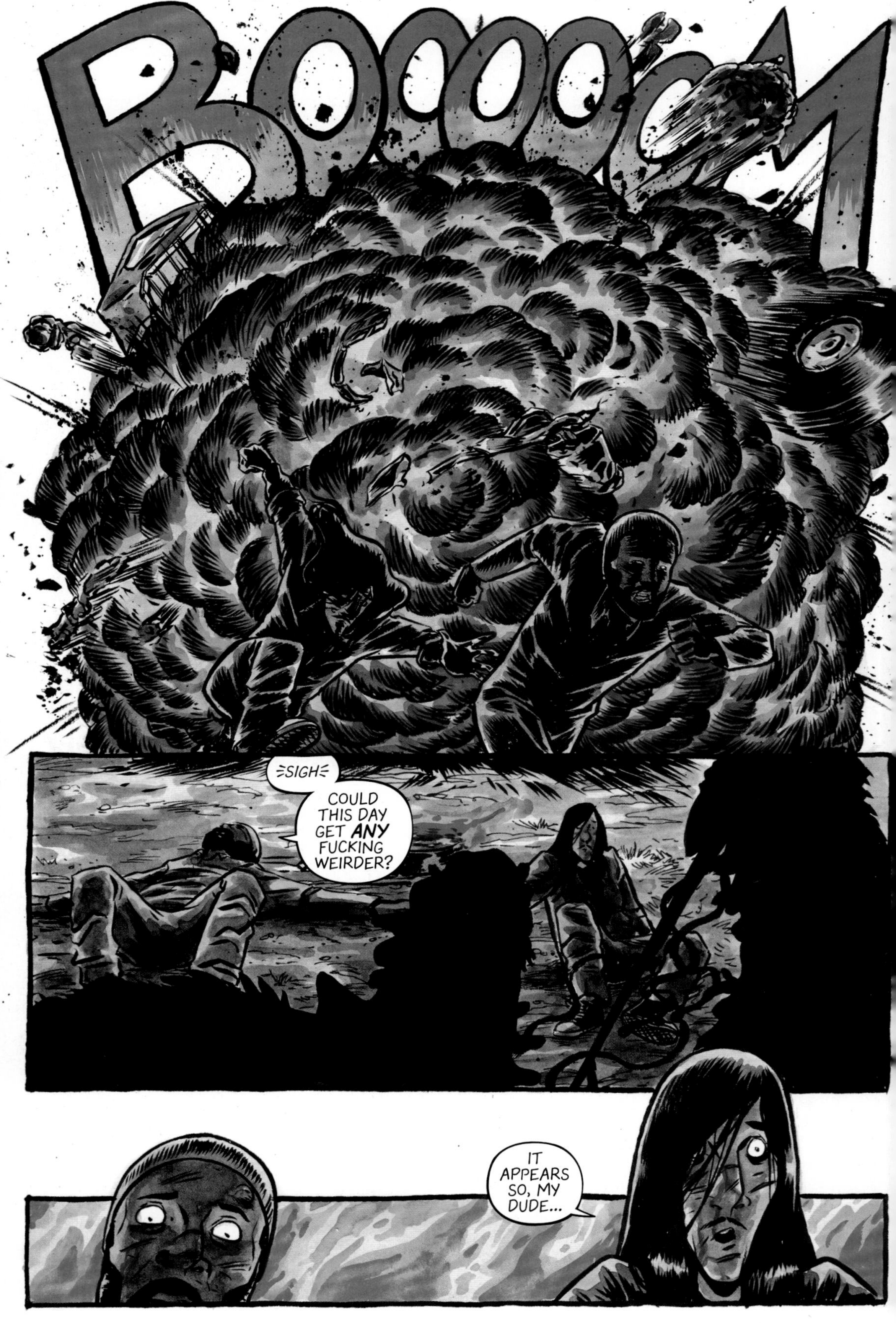
BOOOOOM
SIGH
COULD THIS DAY GET ANY FUCKING WEIRDER?
IT APPEARS SO, MY DUDE...

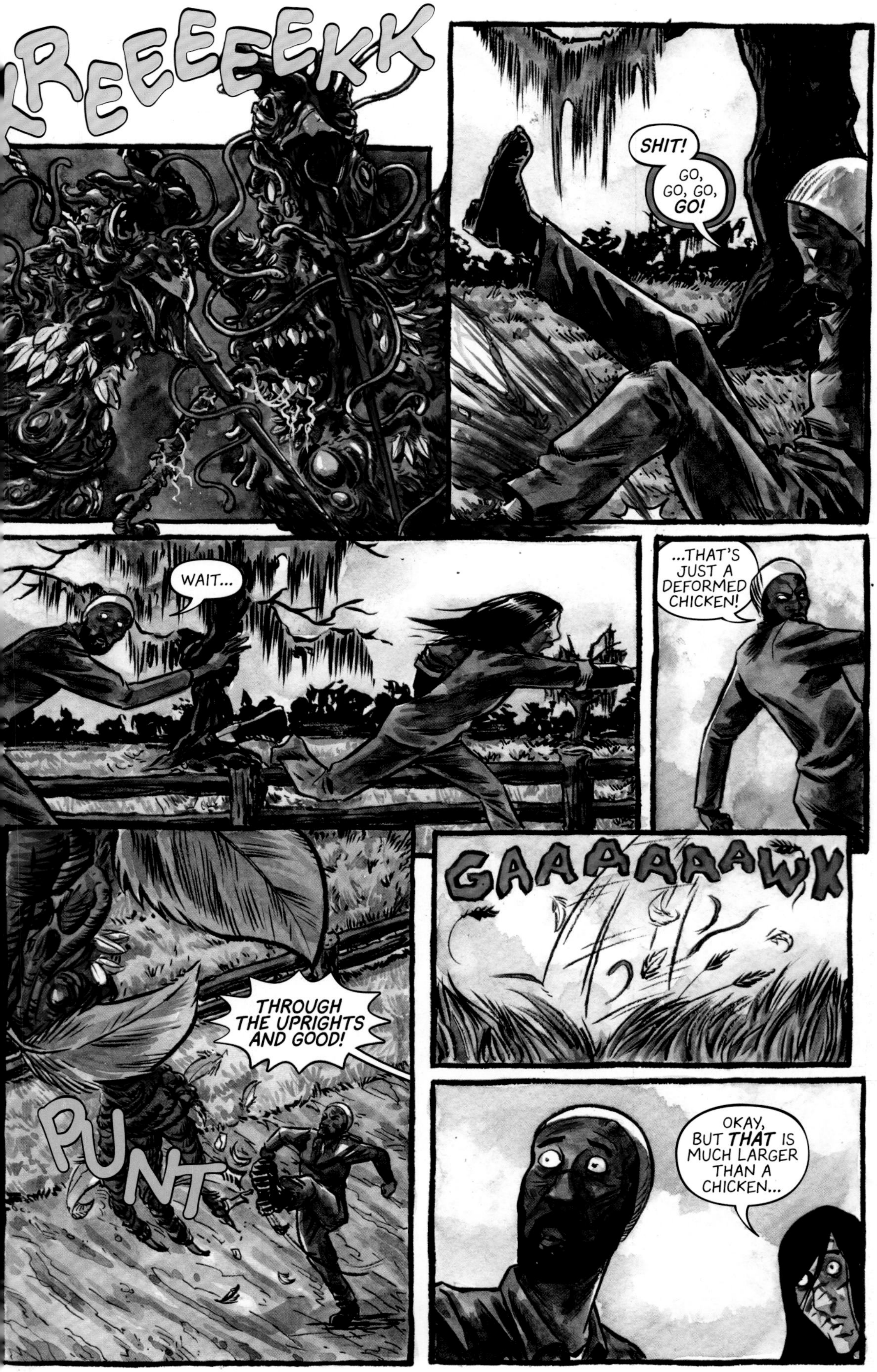

KREEEEEEKK
SHIT!
GO, GO, GO, GO!
WAIT...
...THAT'S JUST A DEFORMED CHICKEN!
THROUGH THE UPRIGHTS AND GOOD!
PUNT
GAAAAAAWK
OKAY, BUT THAT IS MUCH LARGER THAN A CHICKEN...

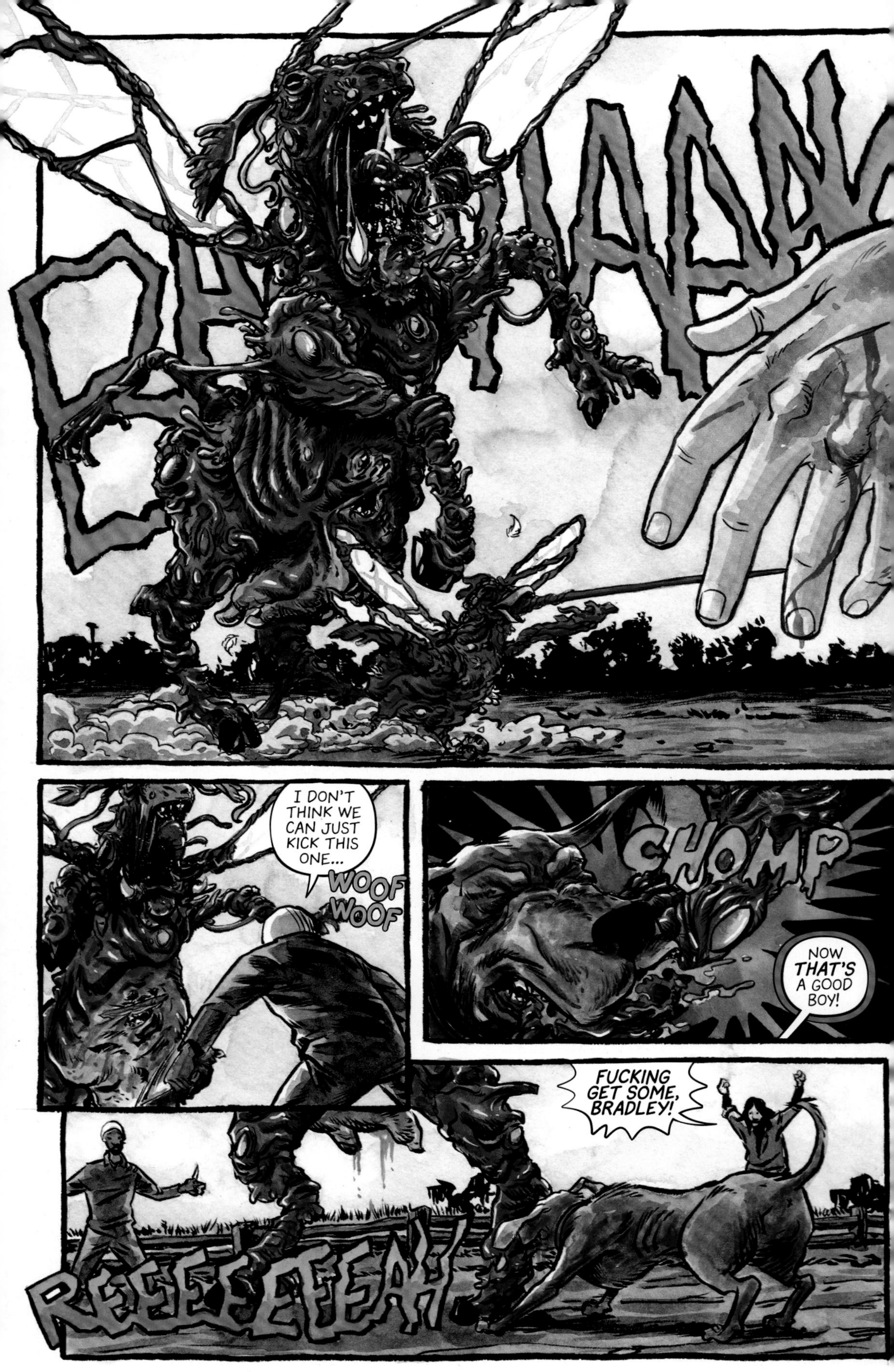
I DON'T THINK WE CAN JUST KICK THIS ONE...
WOOF WOOF
CHOMP
NOW THAT'S A GOOD BOY!
FUCKING GET SOME, BRADLEY!

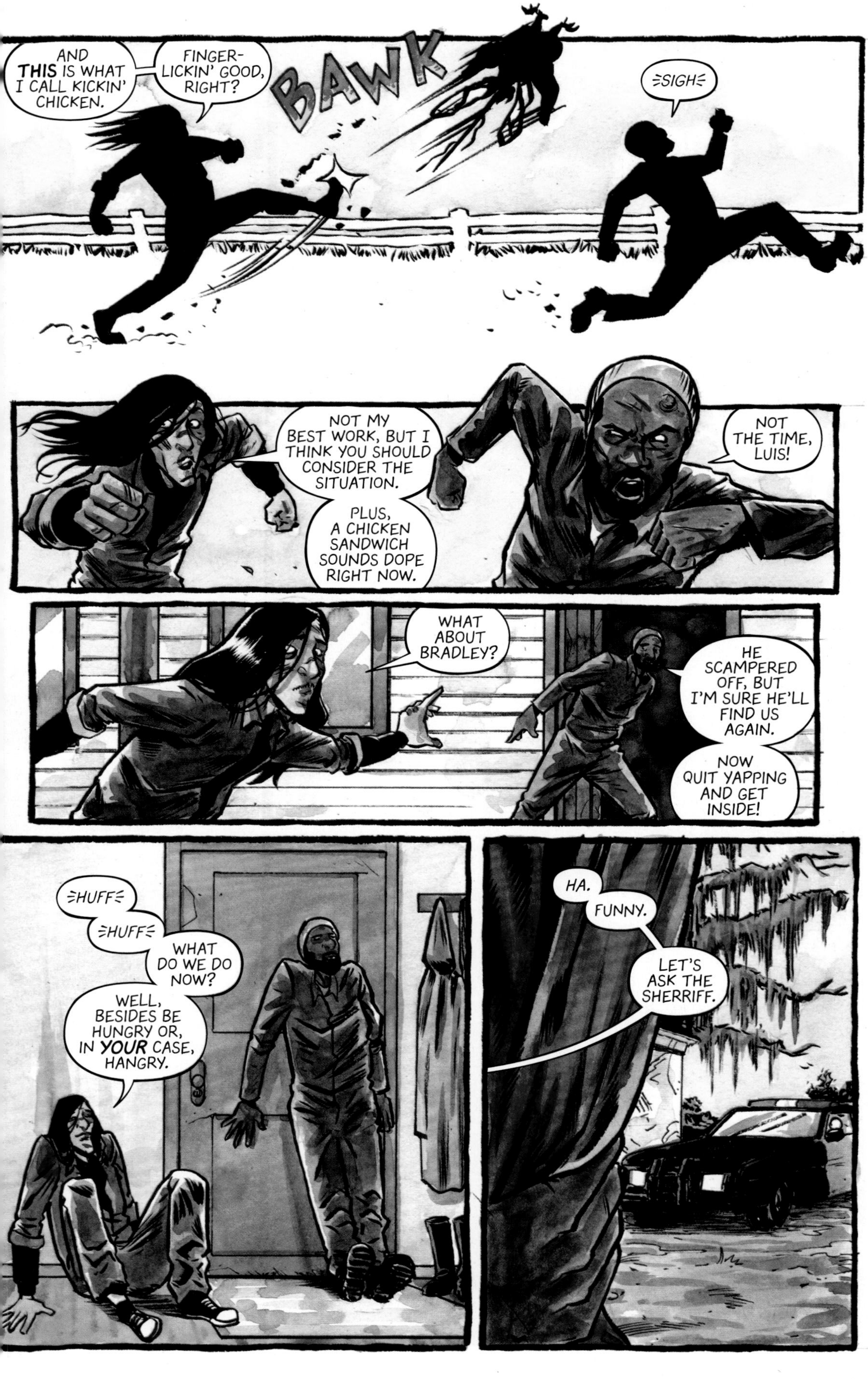
AND THIS IS WHAT I CALL KICKIN' CHICKEN.
FINGER-LICKIN' GOOD, RIGHT?
BAWK
SIGH
NOT MY BEST WORK, BUT I THINK YOU SHOULD CONSIDER THE SITUATION.
PLUS, A CHICKEN SANDWICH SOUNDS DOPE RIGHT NOW.
NOT THE TIME, LUIS!
WHAT ABOUT BRADLEY?
HE SCAMPERED OFF, BUT I'M SURE HE'LL FIND US AGAIN.
NOW QUIT YAPPING AND GET INSIDE!
HUFF
HUFF
WHAT DO WE DO NOW?
WELL, BESIDES BE HUNGRY OR, IN YOUR CASE, HANGRY.
HA.
FUNNY.
LET'S ASK THE SHERRIFF.

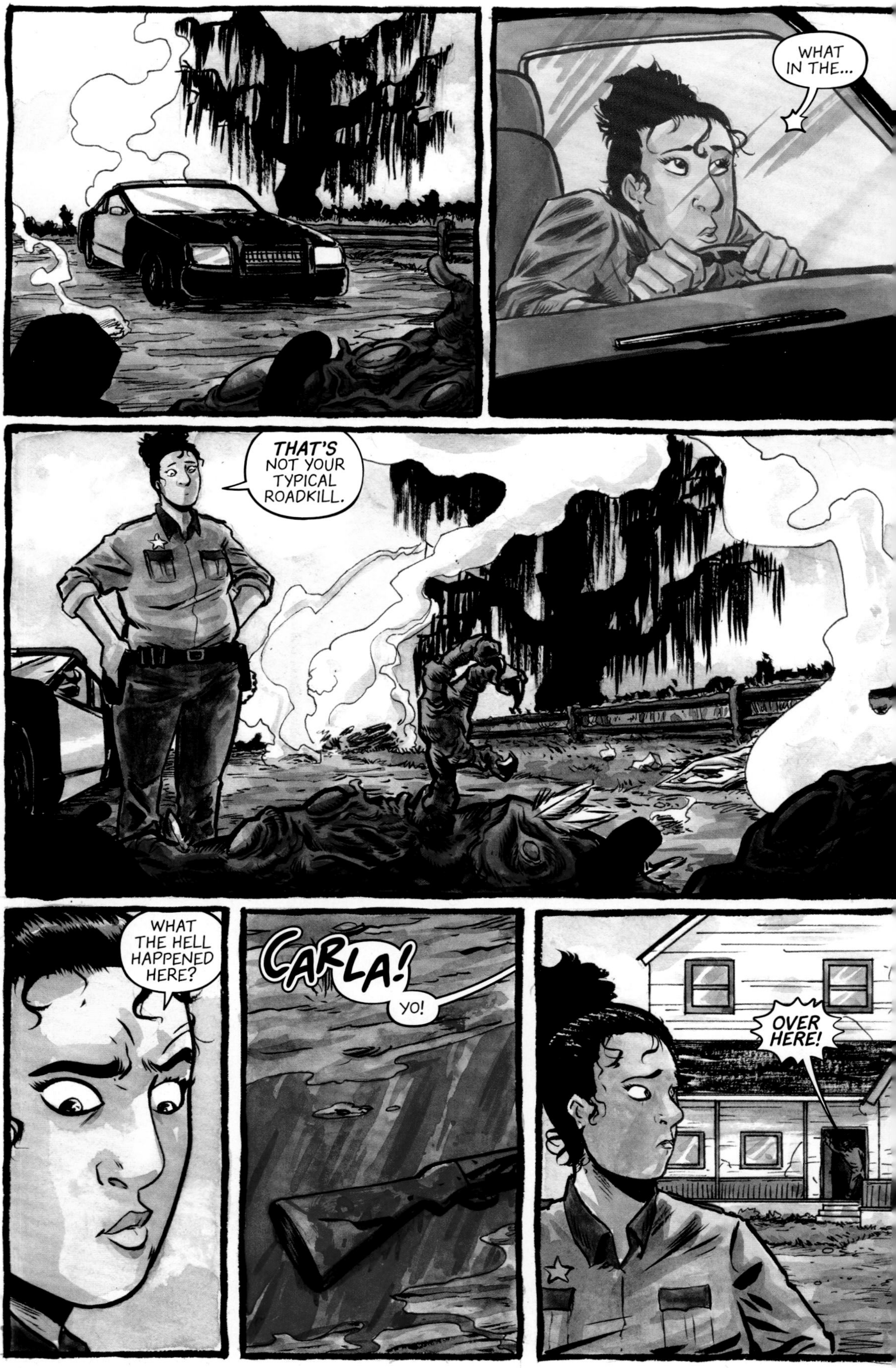
WHAT IN THE...
THAT'S NOT YOUR TYPICAL ROADKILL.
WHAT THE HELL HAPPENED HERE?
CARLA!
YO!
OVER HERE!

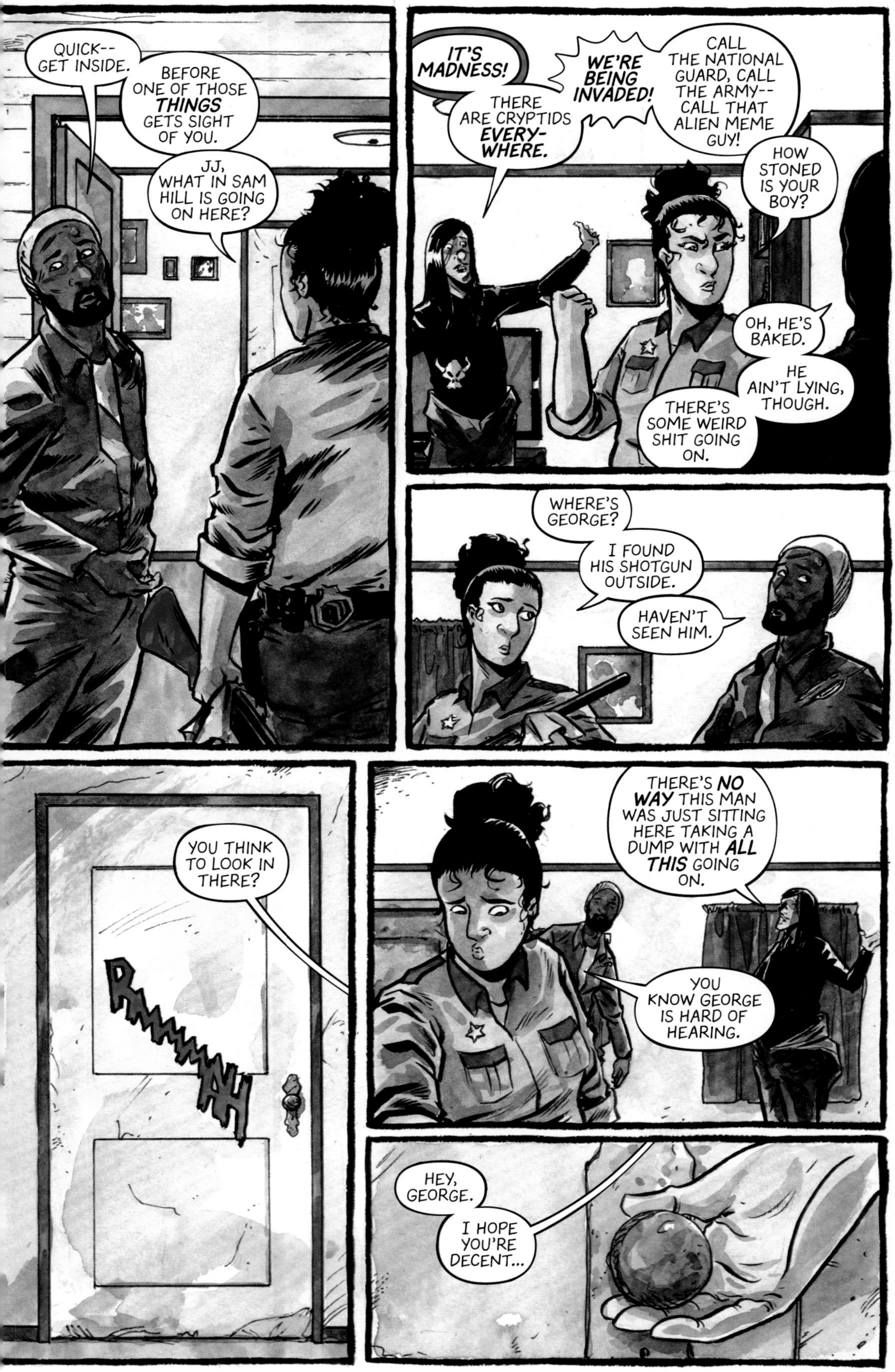
QUICK--
GET INSIDE.
BEFORE ONE OF THOSE THINGS GETS SIGHT OF YOU.
JJ, WHAT IN SAM HILL IS GOING ON HERE?
IT'S MADNESS!
THERE ARE CRYPTIDS EVERY-WHERE.
WE'RE BEING INVADED!
CALL THE NATIONAL GUARD, CALL THE ARMY-- CALL THAT ALIEN MEME GUY!
HOW STONED IS YOUR BOY?
OH, HE'S BAKED.
HE AIN'T LYING, THOUGH.
THERE'S SOME WEIRD SHIT GOING ON.
WHERE'S GEORGE?
I FOUND HIS SHOTGUN OUTSIDE.
HAVEN'T SEEN HIM.
YOU THINK TO LOOK IN THERE?
RAWWAH
THERE'S NO WAY THIS MAN WAS JUST SITTING HERE TAKING A DUMP WITH ALL THIS GOING ON.
YOU KNOW GEORGE IS HARD OF HEARING.
HEY, GEORGE.
I HOPE YOU'RE DECENT...

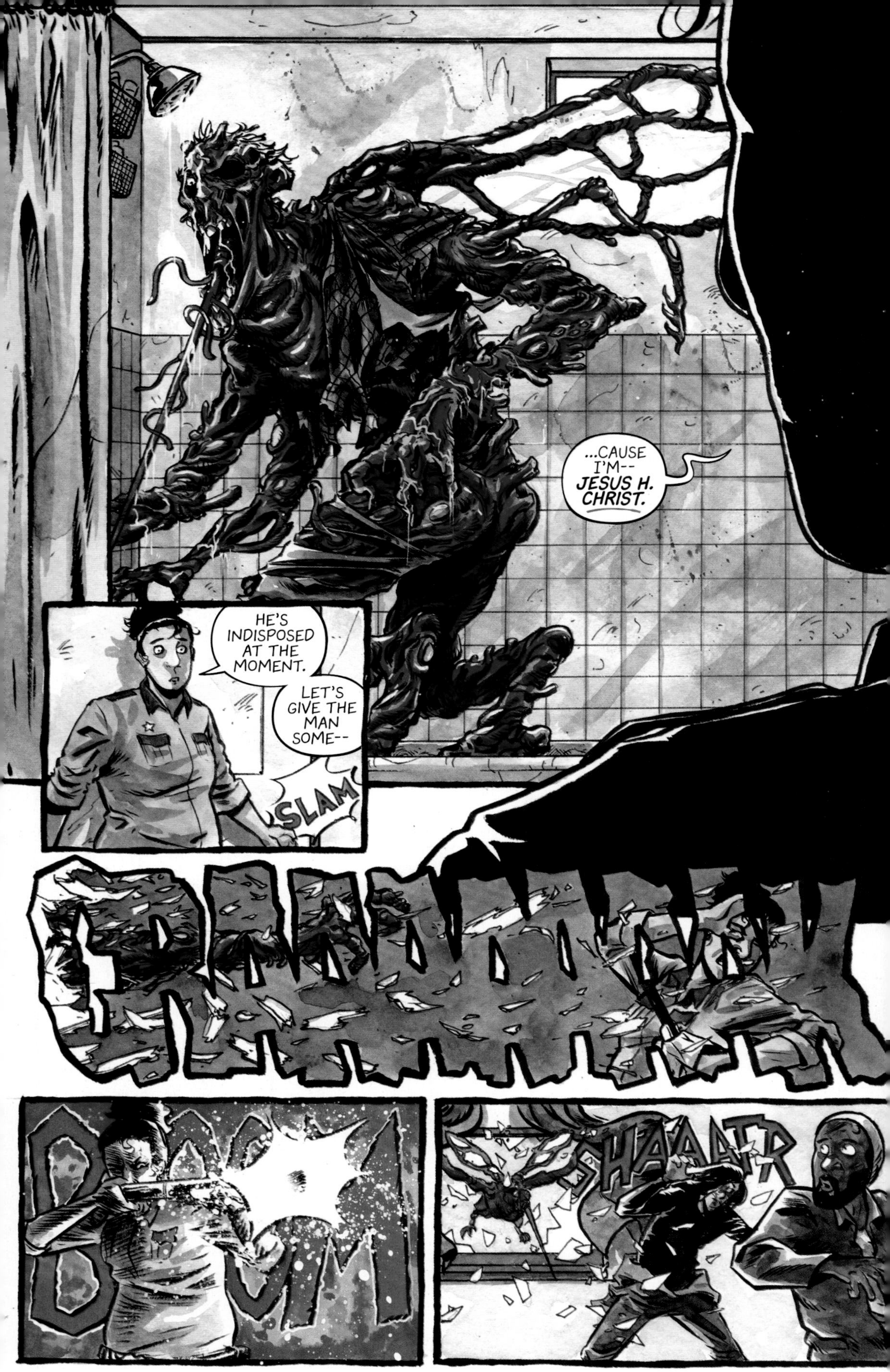
...CAUSE I'M-- JESUS H. CHRIST.
HE'S INDISPOSED AT THE MOMENT.
LET'S GIVE THE MAN SOME--
SLAM

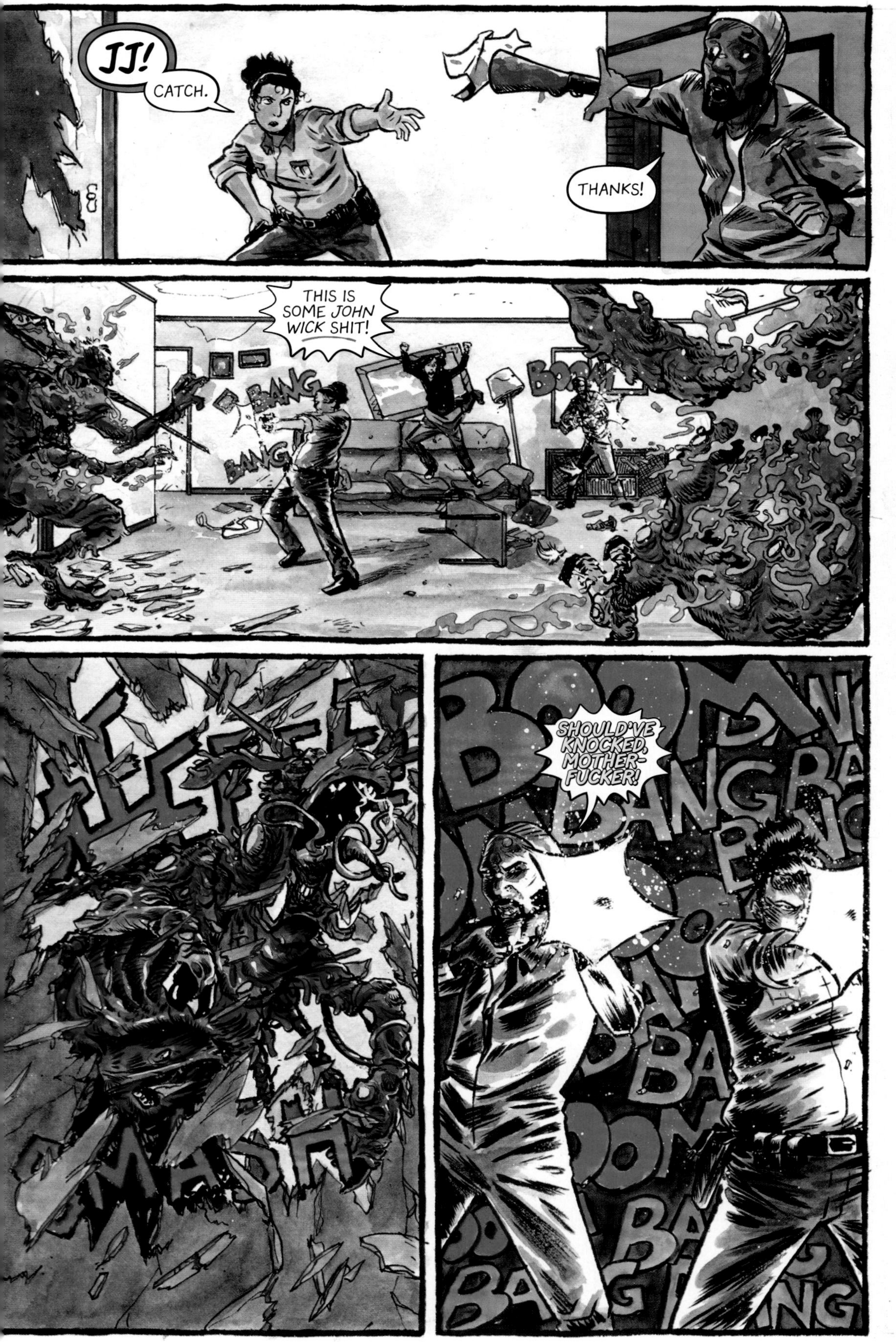
JJ!
CATCH.
THANKS!
THIS IS SOME JOHN WICK SHIT!
BANG
BANG
BOOM
SHOULD'VE KNOCKED, MOTHER-FUCKER!

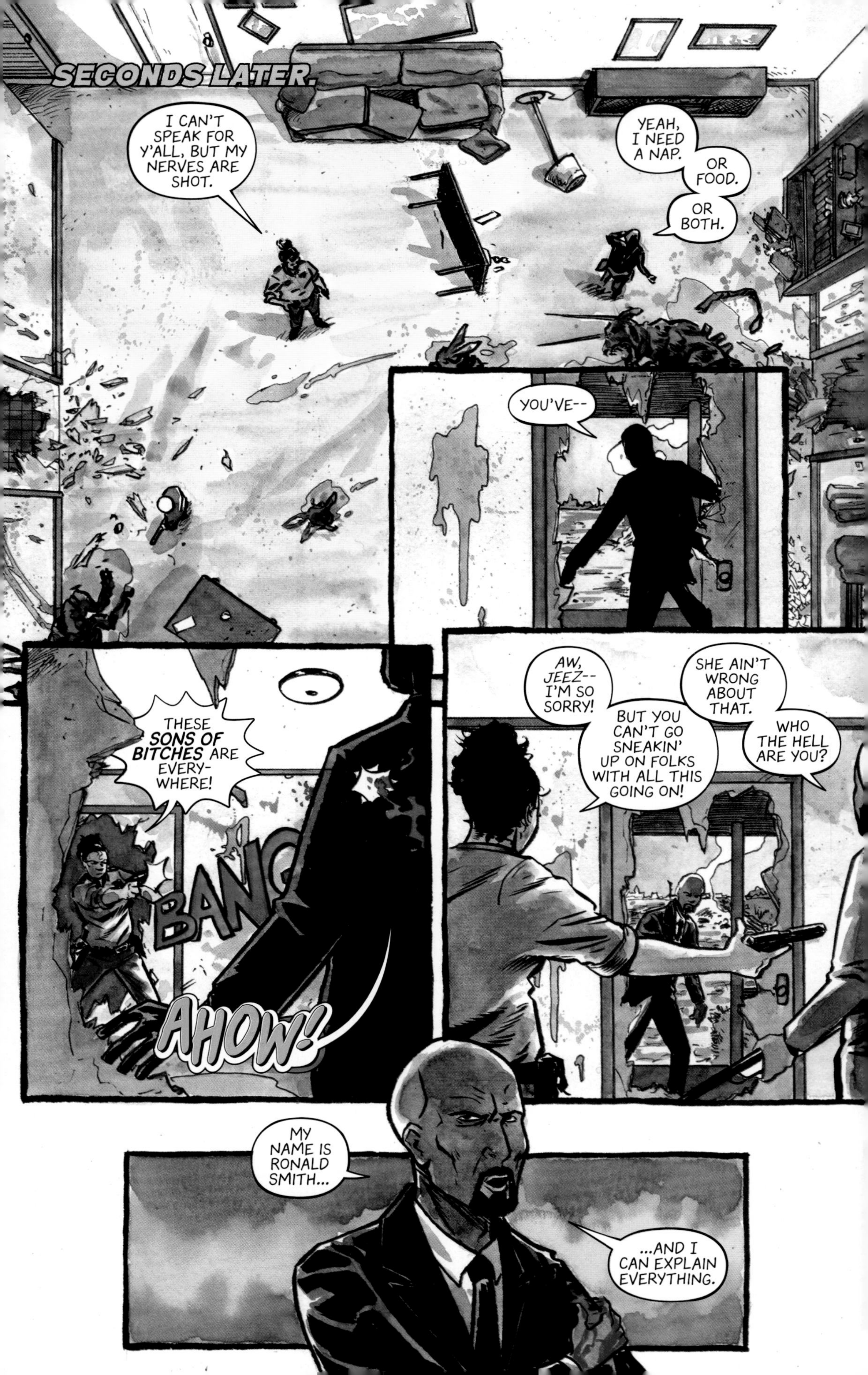
SECONDS LATER.
I CAN'T SPEAK FOR Y'ALL, BUT MY NERVES ARE SHOT.
YEAH, I NEED A NAP.
OR FOOD.
OR BOTH.
YOU'VE--
THESE **SONS OF BITCHES** ARE EVERY-WHERE!
BANG
AHOW!
AW, JEEZ-- I'M SO SORRY!
BUT YOU CAN'T GO SNEAKIN' UP ON FOLKS WITH ALL THIS GOING ON!
SHE AIN'T WRONG ABOUT THAT.
WHO THE HELL ARE YOU?
MY NAME IS RONALD SMITH...
...AND I CAN EXPLAIN EVERYTHING.

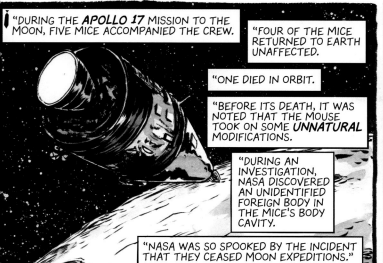

"DURING THE **APOLLO 17** MISSION TO THE MOON, FIVE MICE ACCOMPANIED THE CREW.

"FOUR OF THE MICE RETURNED TO EARTH UNAFFECTED.

"ONE DIED IN ORBIT.

"BEFORE ITS DEATH, IT WAS NOTED THAT THE MOUSE TOOK ON SOME **UNNATURAL** MODIFICATIONS.

"DURING AN INVESTIGATION, NASA DISCOVERED AN UNIDENTIFIED FOREIGN BODY IN THE MICE'S BODY CAVITY.

"NASA WAS SO SPOOKED BY THE INCIDENT THAT THEY CEASED MOON EXPEDITIONS."

OH, I READ ABOUT THAT ON A MESSAGE BOARD.

I THINK--

LET ME FINISH.

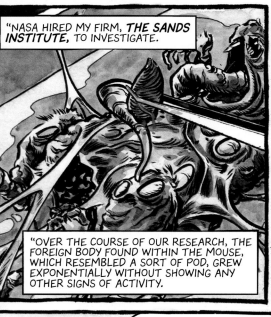

"NASA HIRED MY FIRM, **THE SANDS INSTITUTE,** TO INVESTIGATE.

"OVER THE COURSE OF OUR RESEARCH, THE FOREIGN BODY FOUND WITHIN THE MOUSE, WHICH RESEMBLED A SORT OF POD, GREW EXPONENTIALLY WITHOUT SHOWING ANY OTHER SIGNS OF ACTIVITY.

"THAT IS, UNTIL LAST NIGHT."

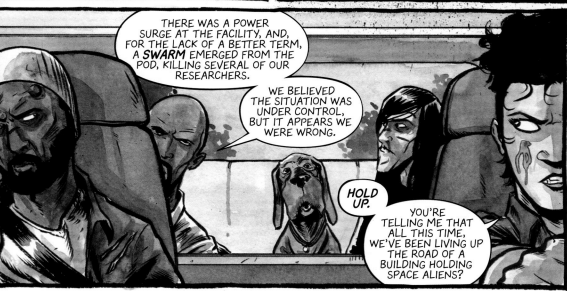

THERE WAS A POWER SURGE AT THE FACILITY, AND, FOR THE LACK OF A BETTER TERM, A **SWARM** EMERGED FROM THE POD, KILLING SEVERAL OF OUR RESEARCHERS.

WE BELIEVED THE SITUATION WAS UNDER CONTROL, BUT IT APPEARS WE WERE WRONG.

HOLD UP.

YOU'RE TELLING ME THAT ALL THIS TIME, WE'VE BEEN LIVING UP THE ROAD OF A BUILDING HOLDING SPACE ALIENS?

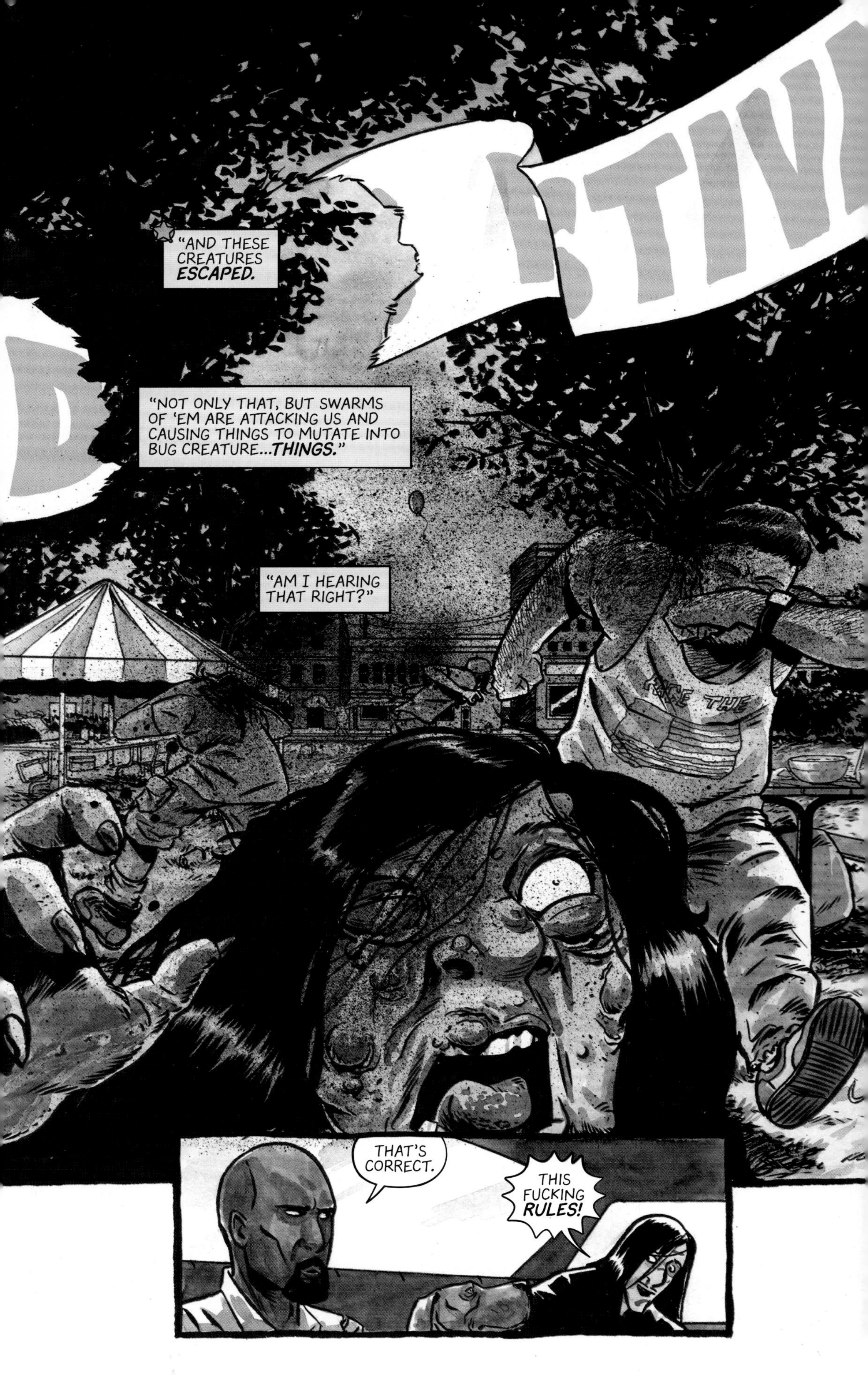
"AND THESE CREATURES ***ESCAPED.***
"NOT ONLY THAT, BUT SWARMS OF 'EM ARE ATTACKING US AND CAUSING THINGS TO MUTATE INTO BUG CREATURE...***THINGS.***"
"AM I HEARING THAT RIGHT?"
THAT'S CORRECT.
THIS FUCKING ***RULES!***

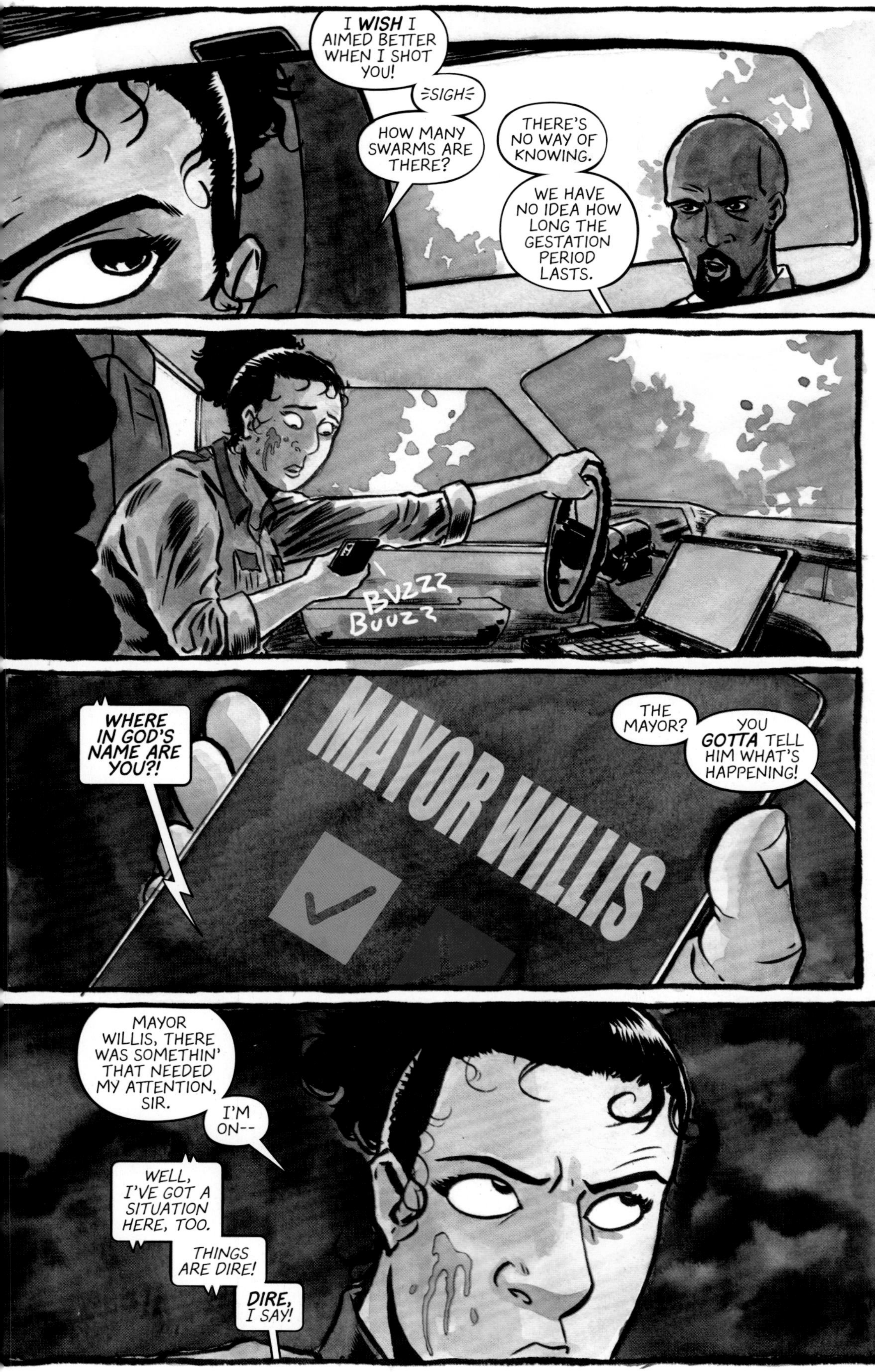
I WISH I AIMED BETTER WHEN I SHOT YOU!
≡SIGH≡
HOW MANY SWARMS ARE THERE?
THERE'S NO WAY OF KNOWING.
WE HAVE NO IDEA HOW LONG THE GESTATION PERIOD LASTS.
BUZZZ BUUZZ
MAYOR WILLIS
WHERE IN GOD'S NAME ARE YOU?!
THE MAYOR?
YOU GOTTA TELL HIM WHAT'S HAPPENING!
MAYOR WILLIS, THERE WAS SOMETHIN' THAT NEEDED MY ATTENTION, SIR.
I'M ON--
WELL, I'VE GOT A SITUATION HERE, TOO.
THINGS ARE DIRE!
DIRE, I SAY!

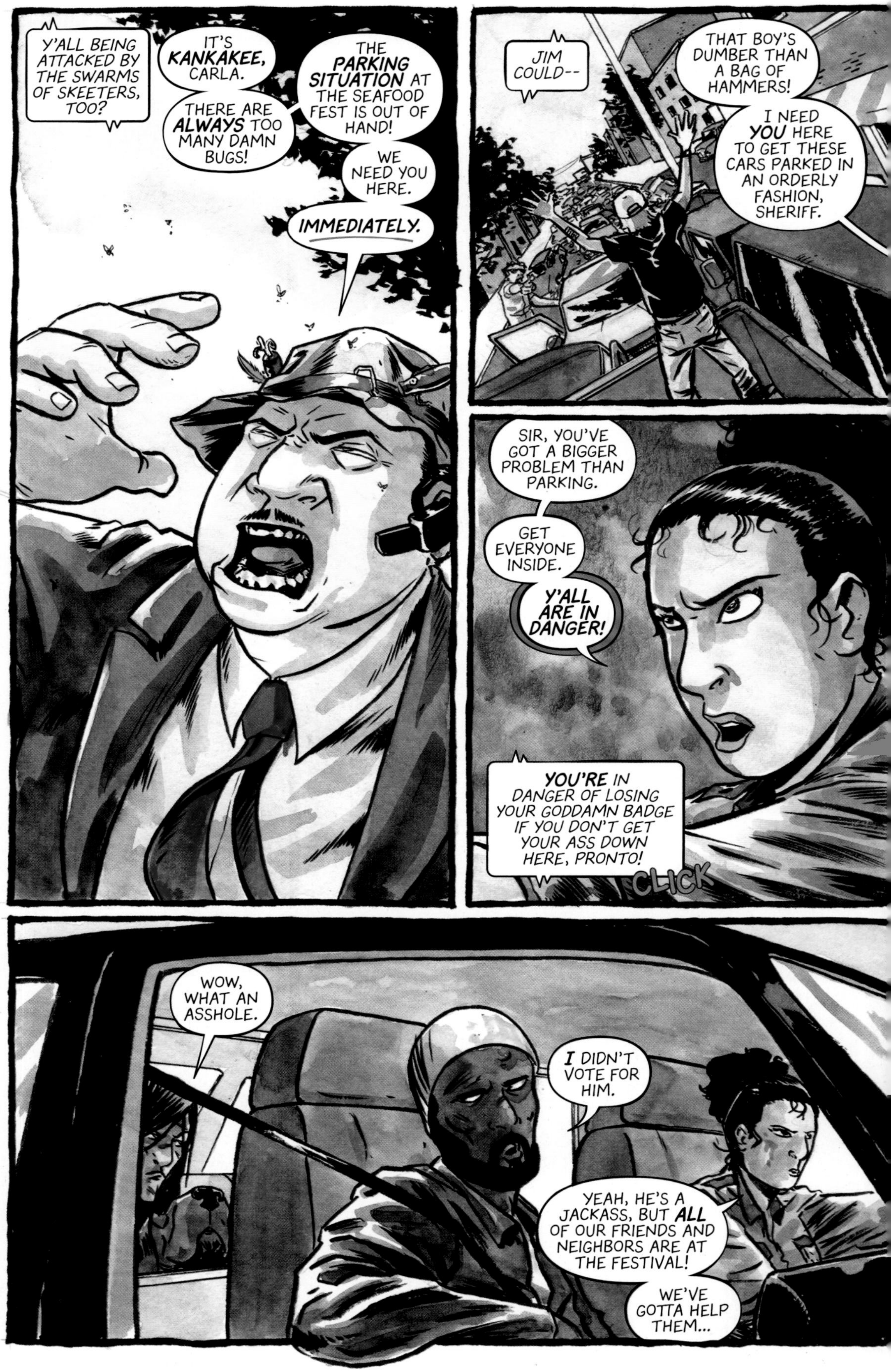
Y'ALL BEING ATTACKED BY THE SWARMS OF SKEETERS, TOO?
IT'S KANKAKEE, CARLA.
THERE ARE ALWAYS TOO MANY DAMN BUGS!
THE PARKING SITUATION AT THE SEAFOOD FEST IS OUT OF HAND!
WE NEED YOU HERE.
IMMEDIATELY.
JIM COULD--
THAT BOY'S DUMBER THAN A BAG OF HAMMERS!
I NEED YOU HERE TO GET THESE CARS PARKED IN AN ORDERLY FASHION, SHERIFF.
SIR, YOU'VE GOT A BIGGER PROBLEM THAN PARKING.
GET EVERYONE INSIDE.
Y'ALL ARE IN DANGER!
YOU'RE IN DANGER OF LOSING YOUR GODDAMN BADGE IF YOU DON'T GET YOUR ASS DOWN HERE, PRONTO!
CLICK
WOW, WHAT AN ASSHOLE.
I DIDN'T VOTE FOR HIM.
YEAH, HE'S A JACKASS, BUT ALL OF OUR FRIENDS AND NEIGHBORS ARE AT THE FESTIVAL!
WE'VE GOTTA HELP THEM...

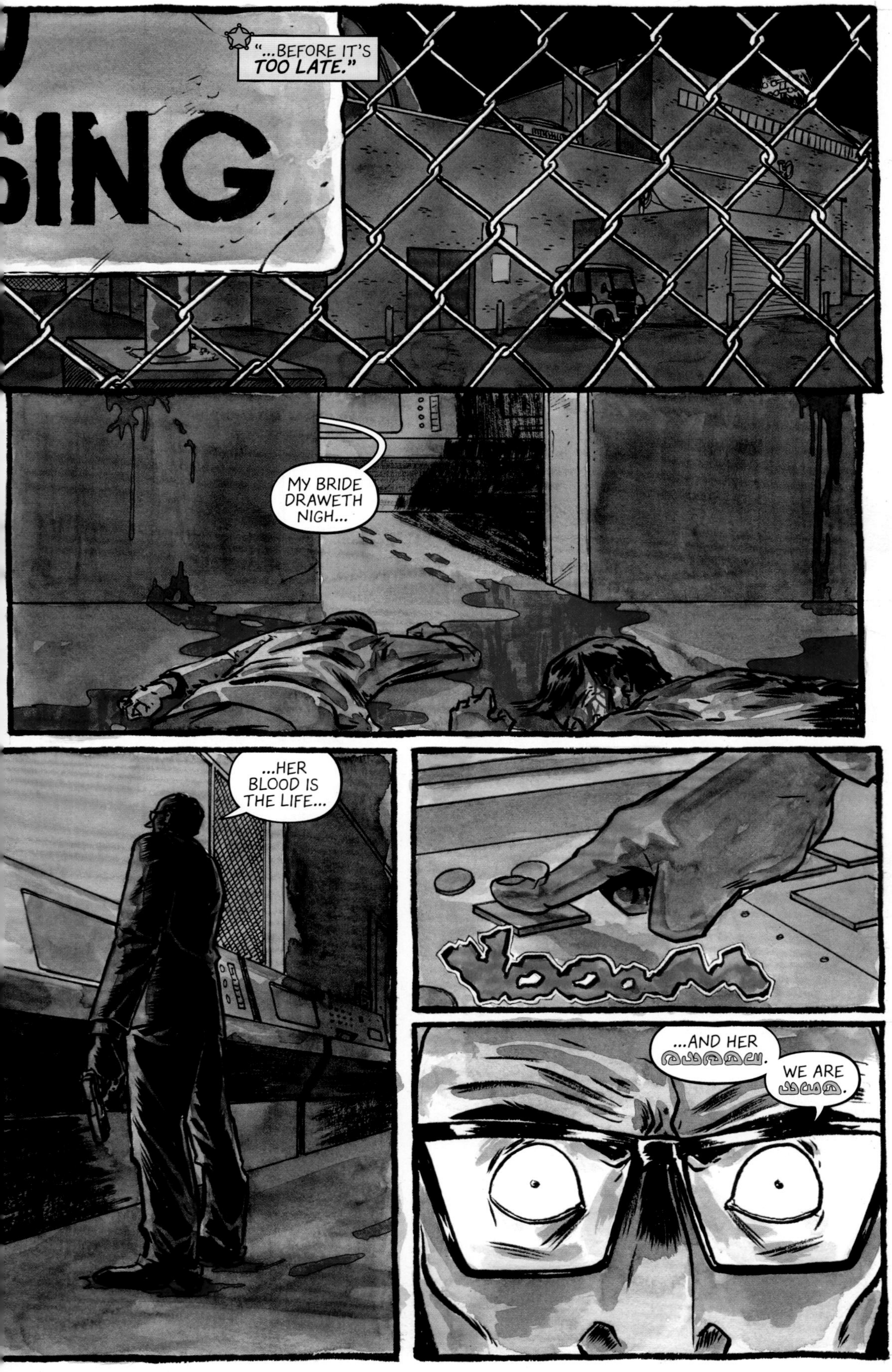
"...BEFORE IT'S TOO LATE."
SING
MY BRIDE DRAWETH NIGH...
...HER BLOOD IS THE LIFE...
...AND HER .
WE ARE .

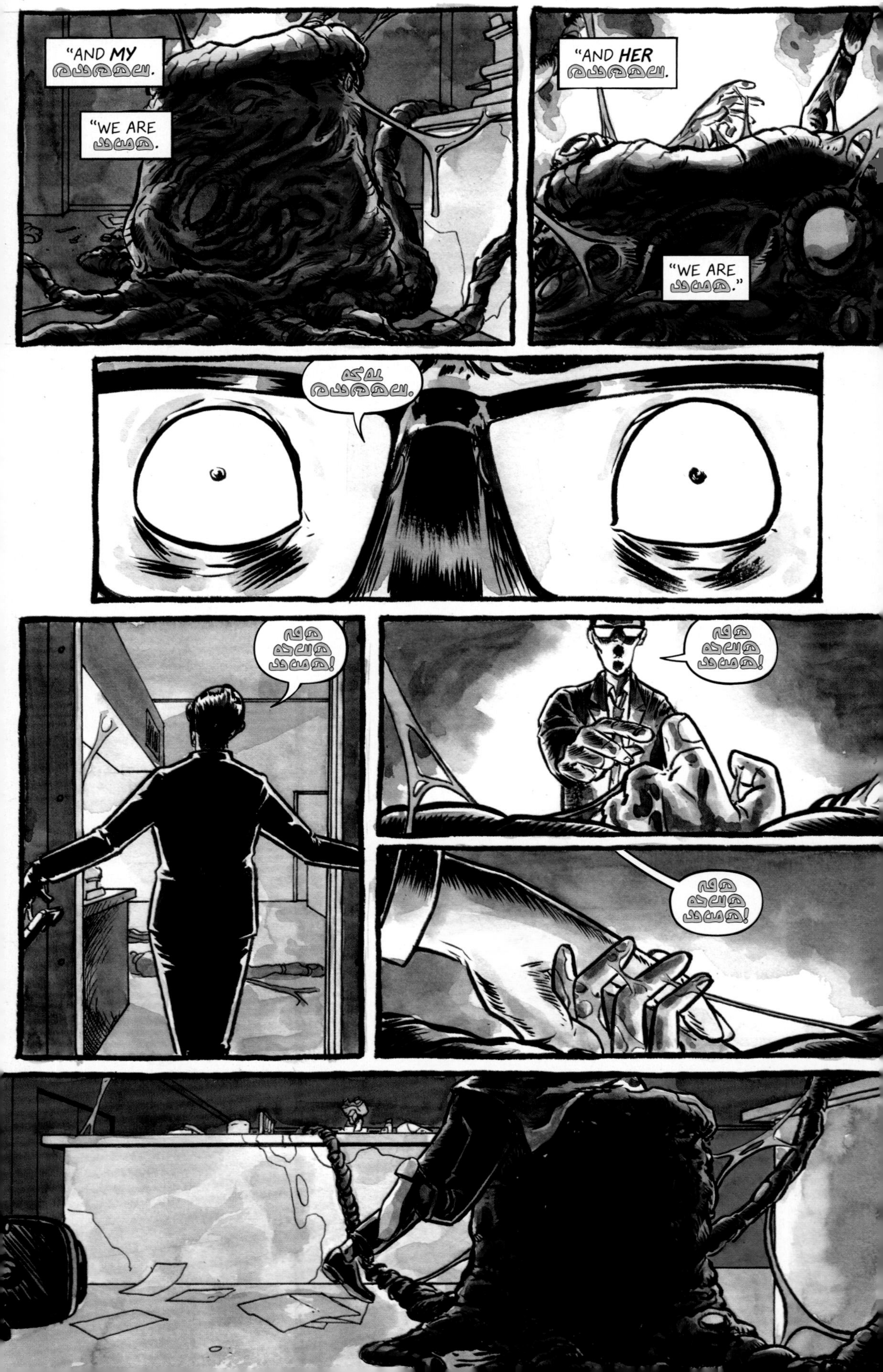

“AND **MY**
“WE ARE
“AND **HER**
“WE ARE

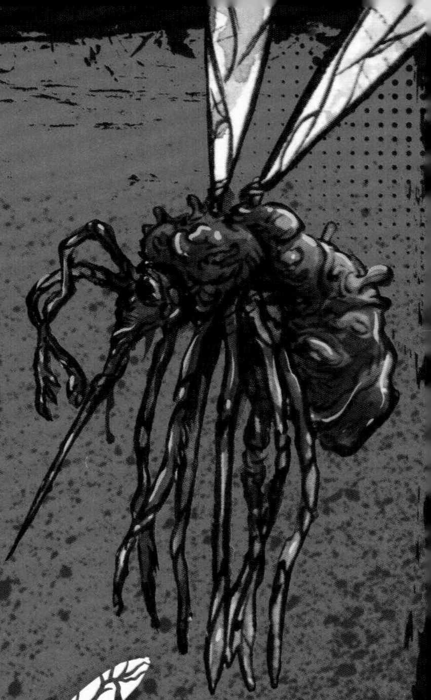

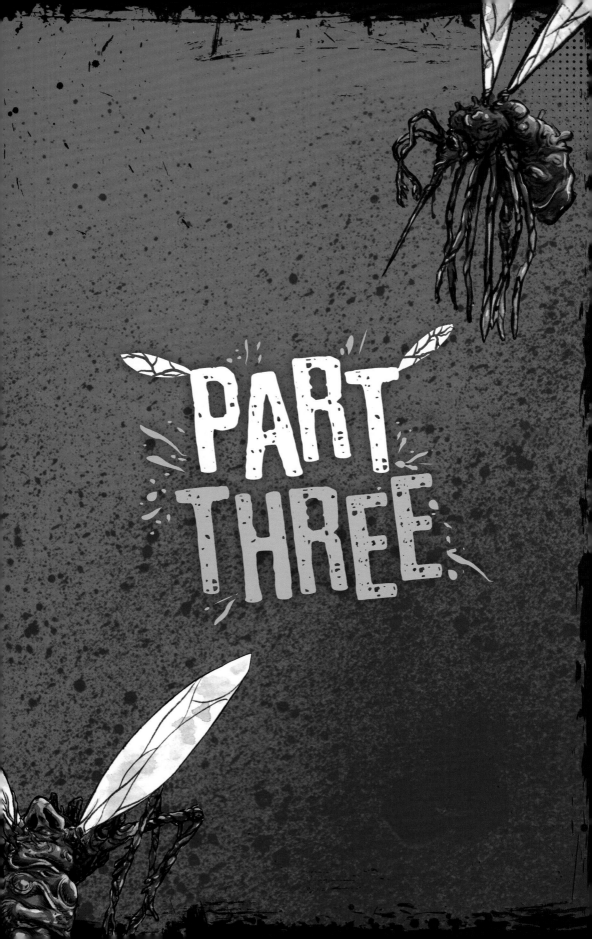

PART THREE

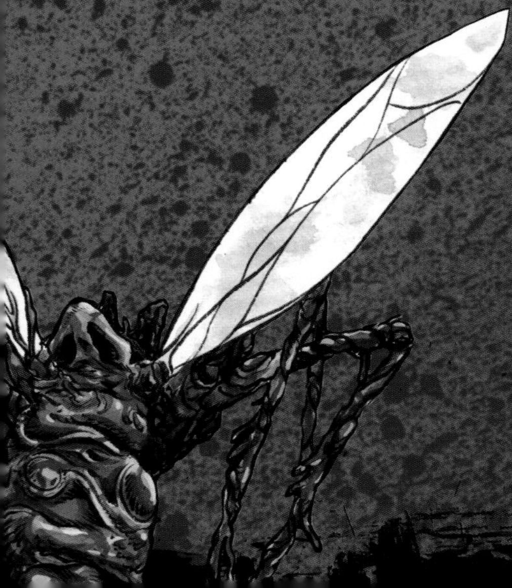

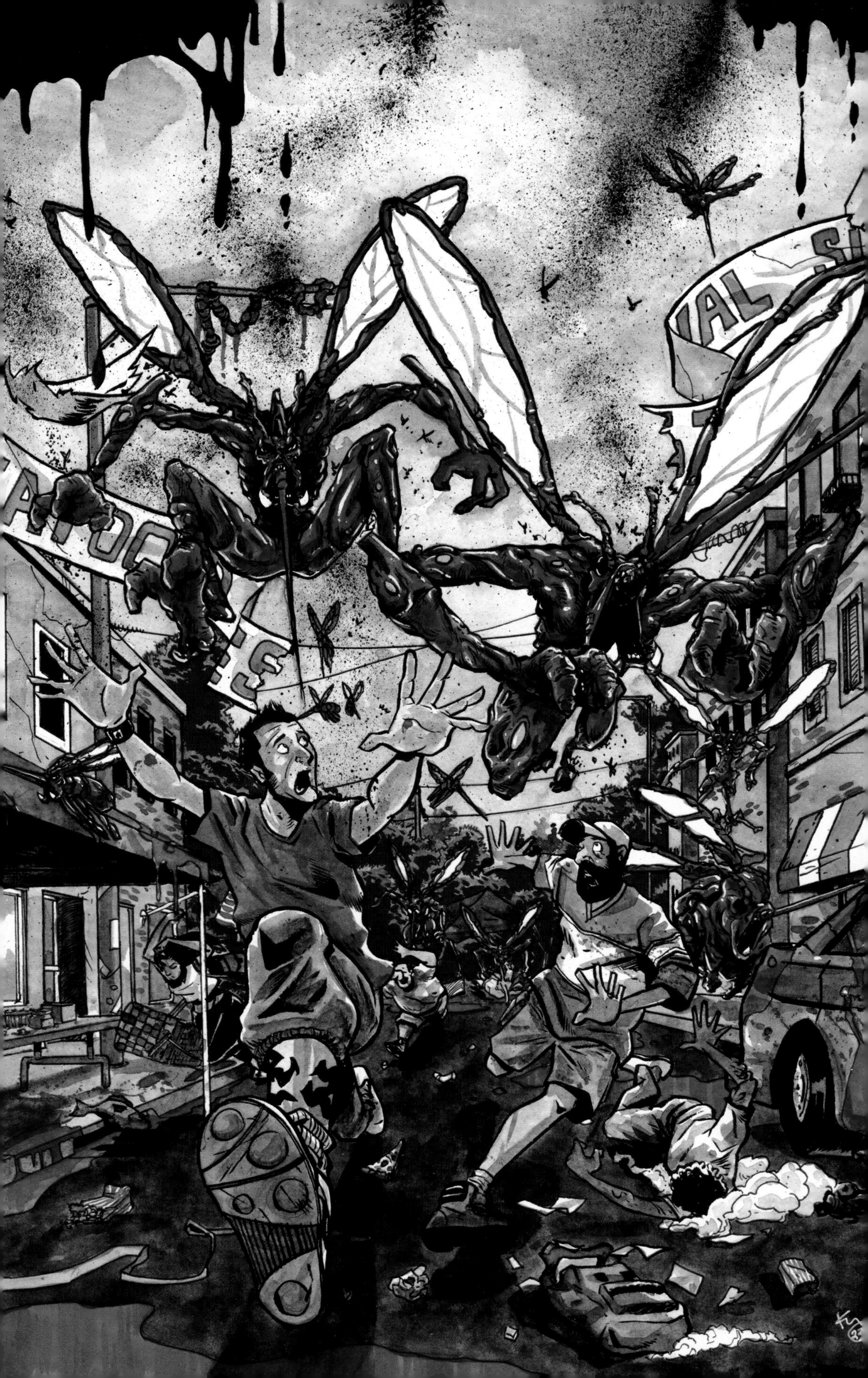

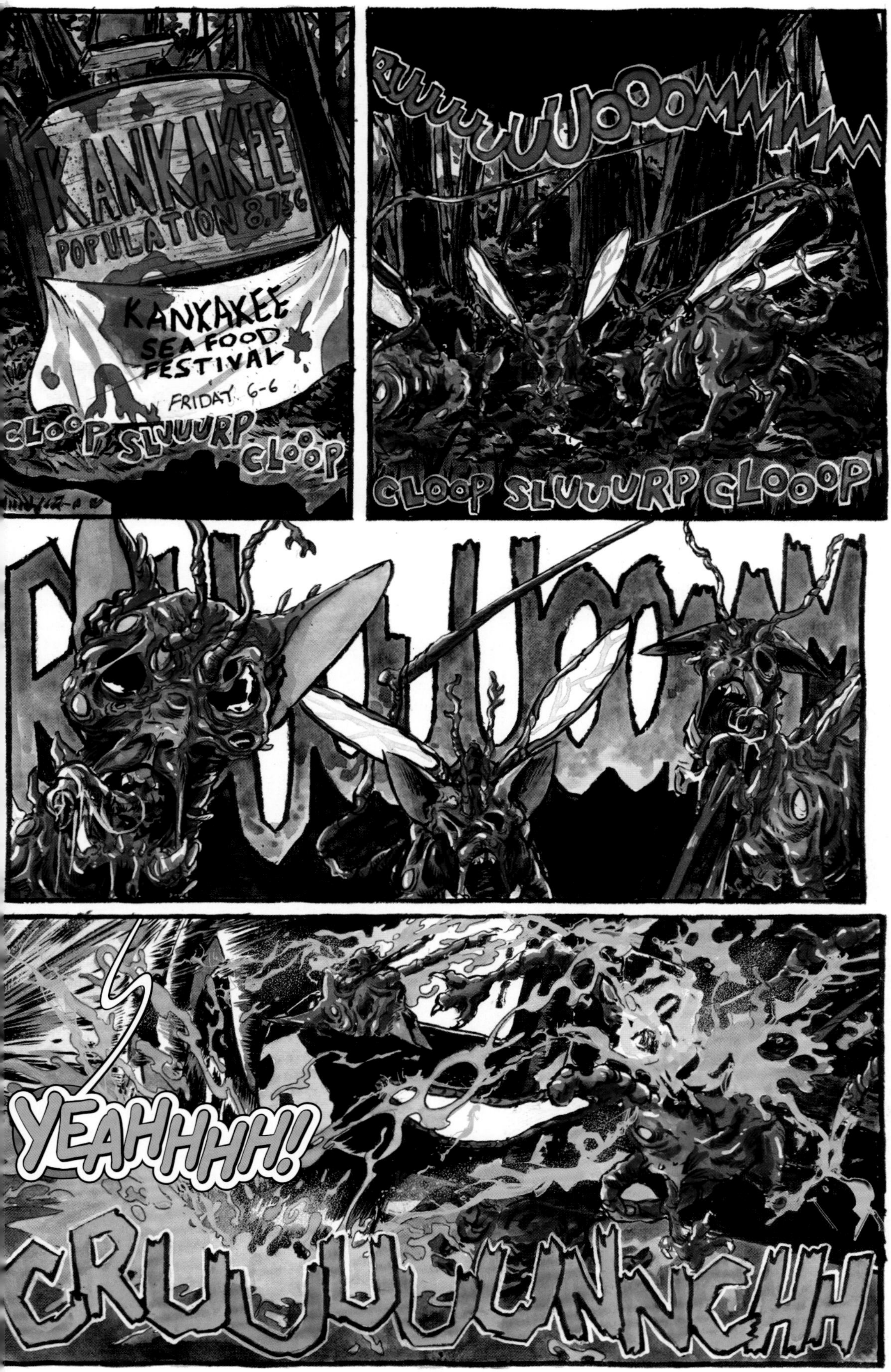
KANKAKEE
POPULATION 8,736
KANKAKEE SEA FOOD FESTIVAL
FRIDAY 6-6
CLOOP SLUUURP CLOOOP
RUUUUUUOOOOMMMMMM
CLOOP SLUUURP CLOOOP
YEAHHHH!
CRUUUUUNNCHH

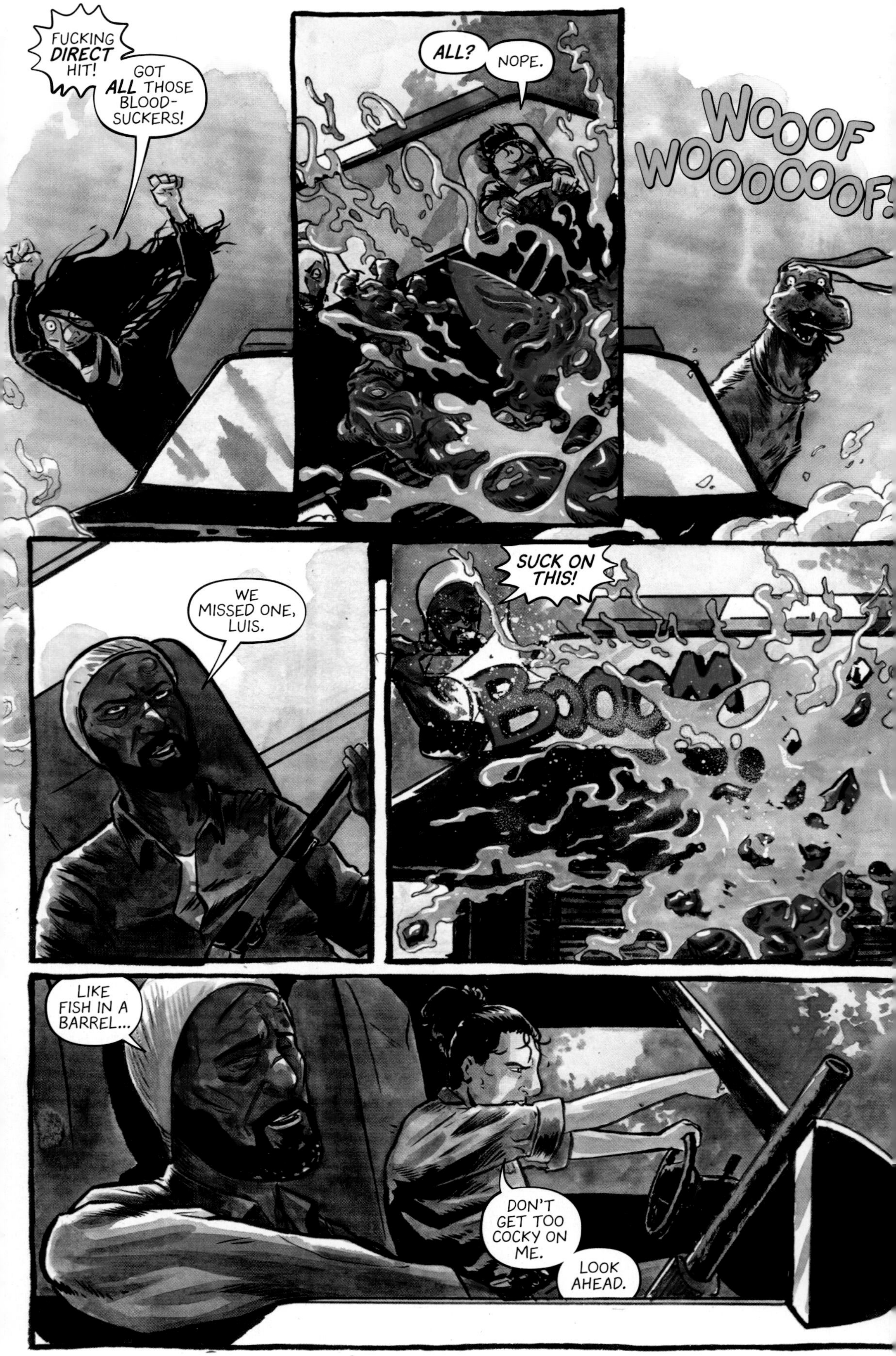
FUCKING DIRECT HIT!
GOT ALL THOSE BLOOD-SUCKERS!
ALL?
NOPE.
WOOOF WOOOOOOF!
WE MISSED ONE, LUIS.
SUCK ON THIS!
BOOOM
LIKE FISH IN A BARREL...
DON'T GET TOO COCKY ON ME.
LOOK AHEAD.

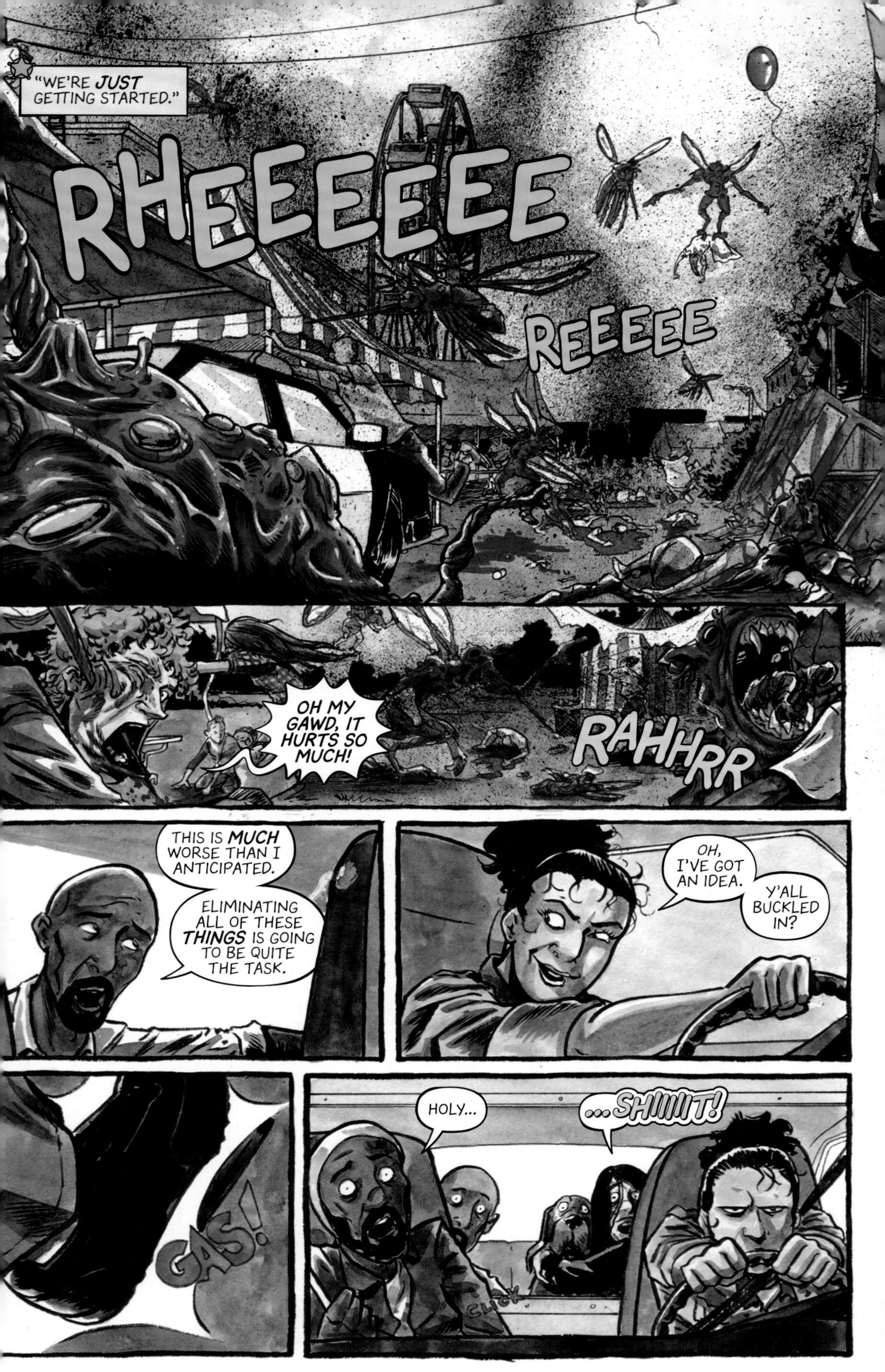
"WE'RE JUST GETTING STARTED."
RHEEEEEE
REEEEE
OH MY GAWD, IT HURTS SO MUCH!
RAHHRR
THIS IS MUCH WORSE THAN I ANTICIPATED.
ELIMINATING ALL OF THESE THINGS IS GOING TO BE QUITE THE TASK.
OH, I'VE GOT AN IDEA.
Y'ALL BUCKLED IN?
GAS!
HOLY...
...SHIIIIIT!

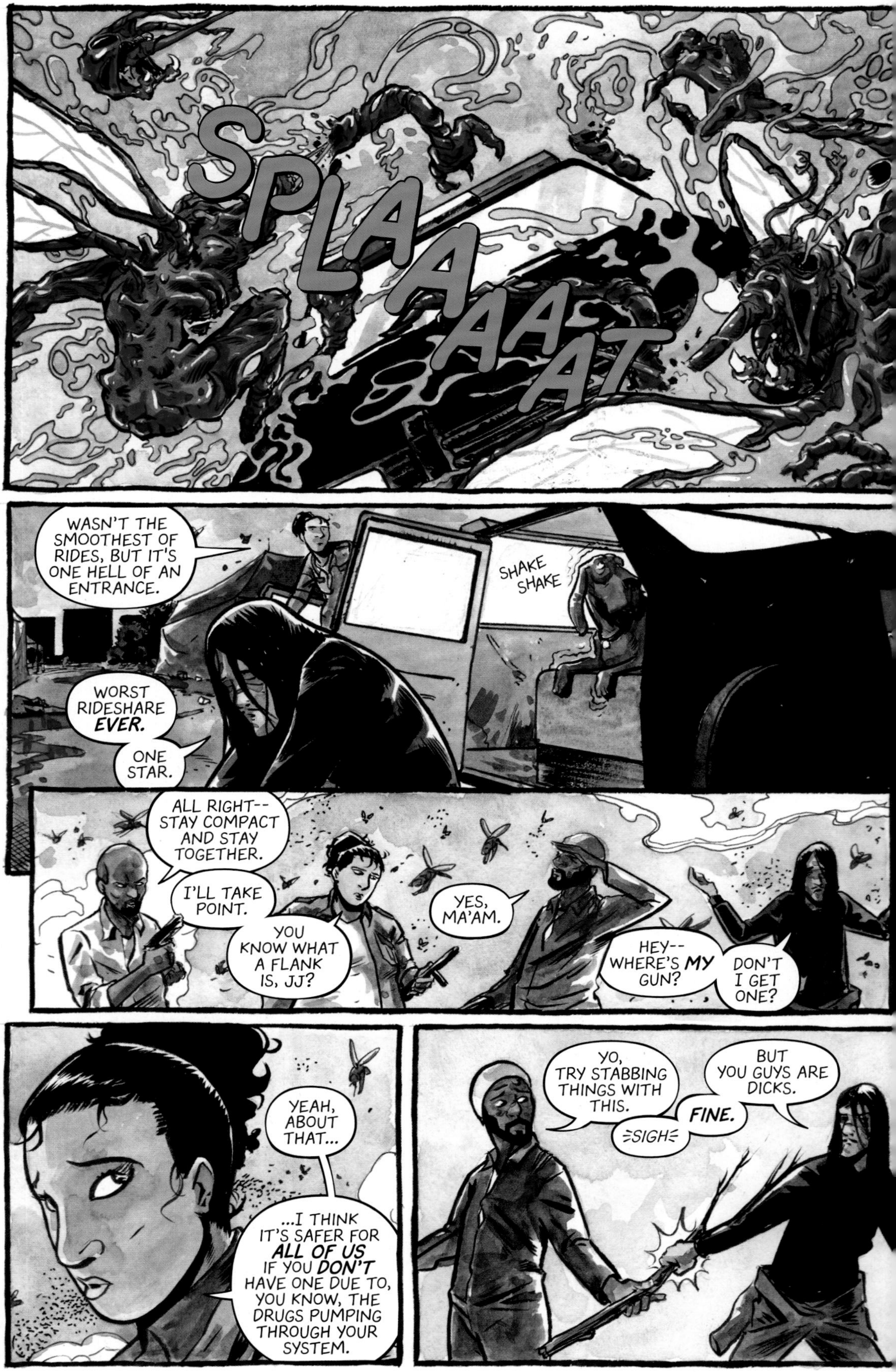
SPLAAAAAT
WASN'T THE SMOOTHEST OF RIDES, BUT IT'S ONE HELL OF AN ENTRANCE.
SHAKE SHAKE
WORST RIDESHARE *EVER.*
ONE STAR.
ALL RIGHT-- STAY COMPACT AND STAY TOGETHER.
I'LL TAKE POINT.
YOU KNOW WHAT A FLANK IS, JJ?
YES, MA'AM.
HEY-- WHERE'S *MY* GUN?
DON'T I GET ONE?
YEAH, ABOUT THAT...
...I THINK IT'S SAFER FOR *ALL OF US* IF YOU *DON'T* HAVE ONE DUE TO, YOU KNOW, THE DRUGS PUMPING THROUGH YOUR SYSTEM.
YO, TRY STABBING THINGS WITH THIS.
SIGH
FINE.
BUT YOU GUYS ARE DICKS.

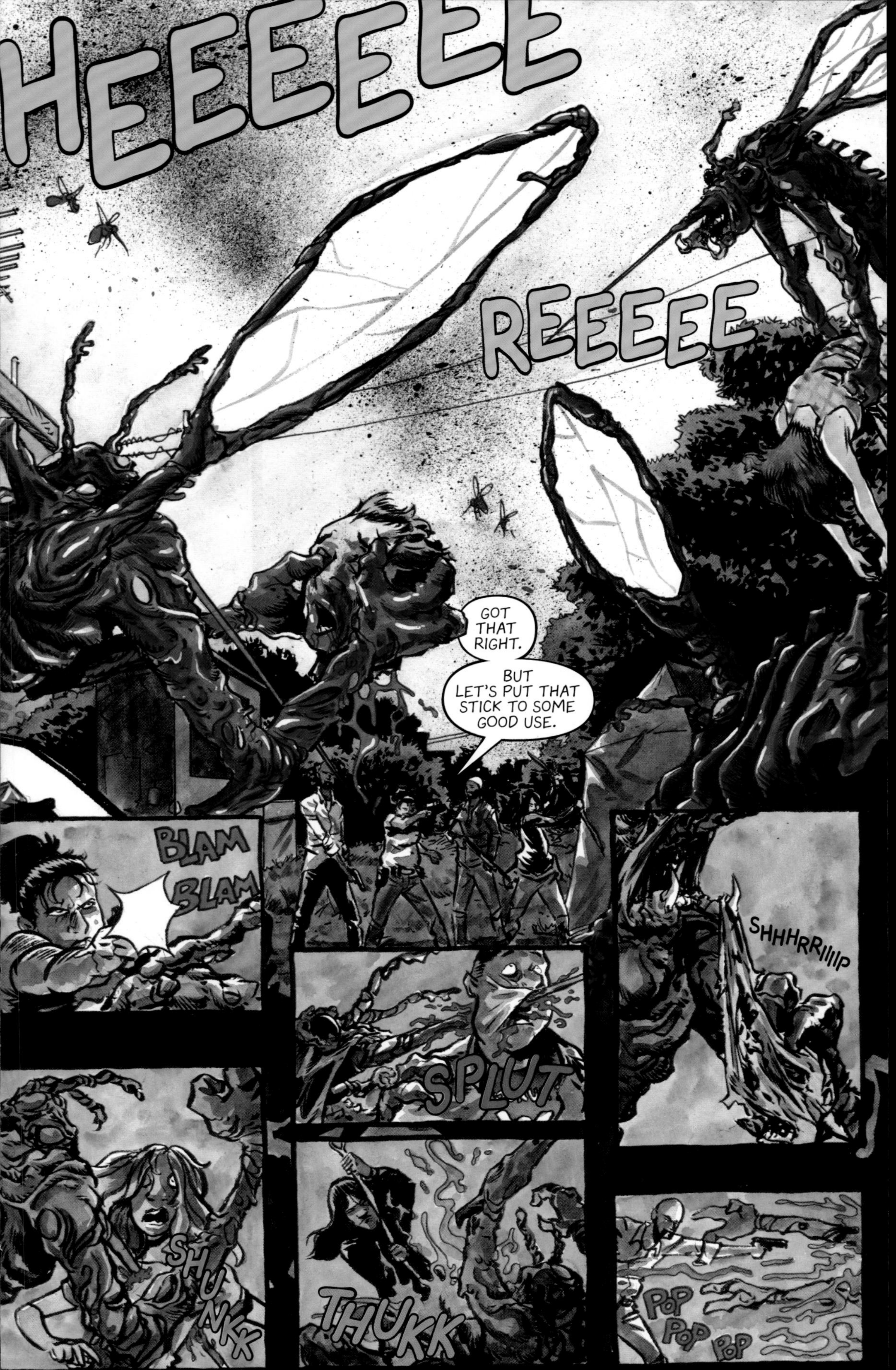
HEEEEEE
REEEEE
GOT THAT RIGHT.
BUT LET'S PUT THAT STICK TO SOME GOOD USE.
BLAM
BLAM
SPLUT
SHHHRRIIIIP
SHUNKK
THUKK
POP
POP
POP

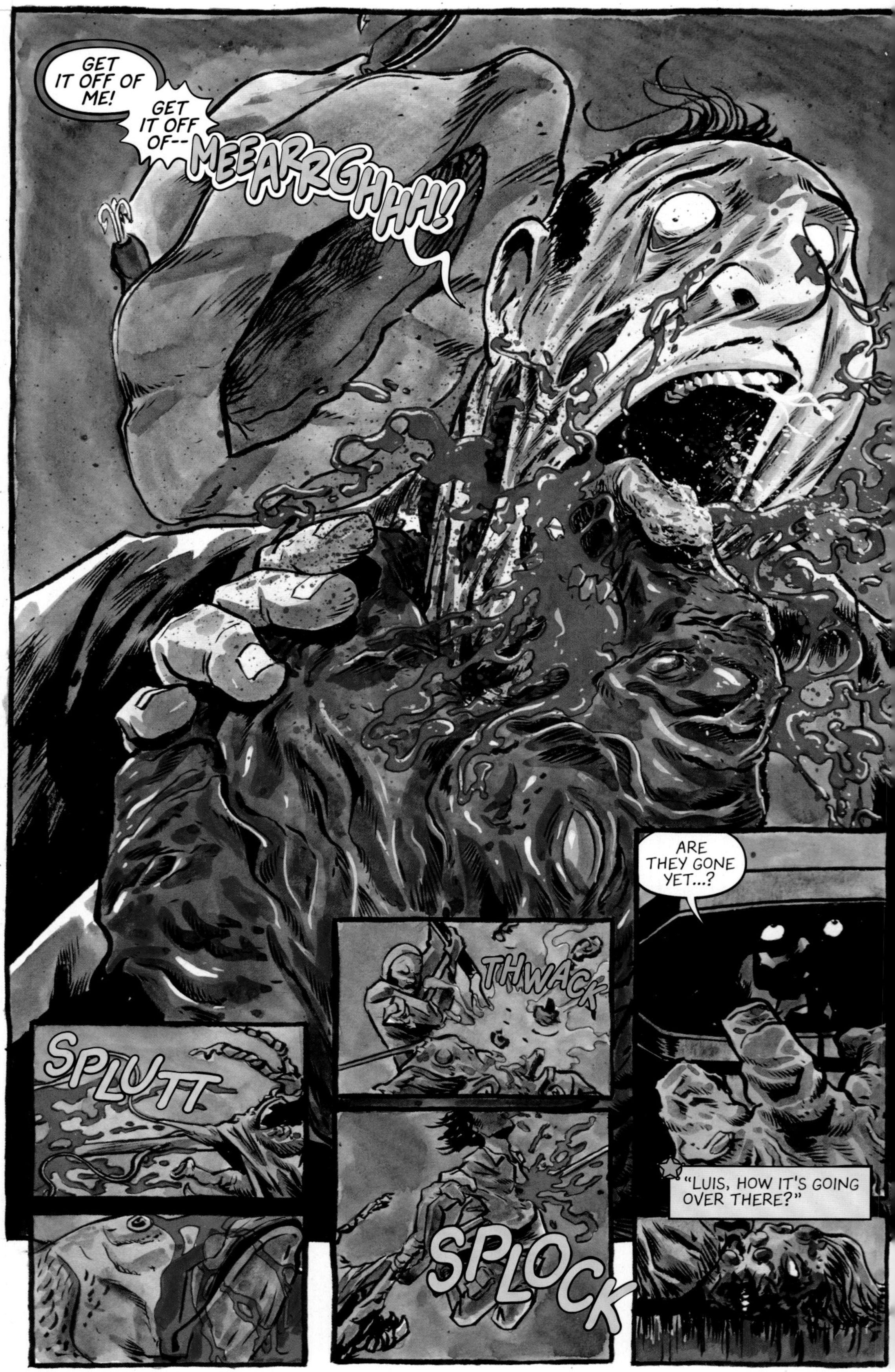
GET IT OFF OF ME!
GET IT OFF OF--
MEEARRGHHH!
SPLUTT
THWACK
SPLOCK
ARE THEY GONE YET...?
"LUIS, HOW IT'S GOING OVER THERE?"

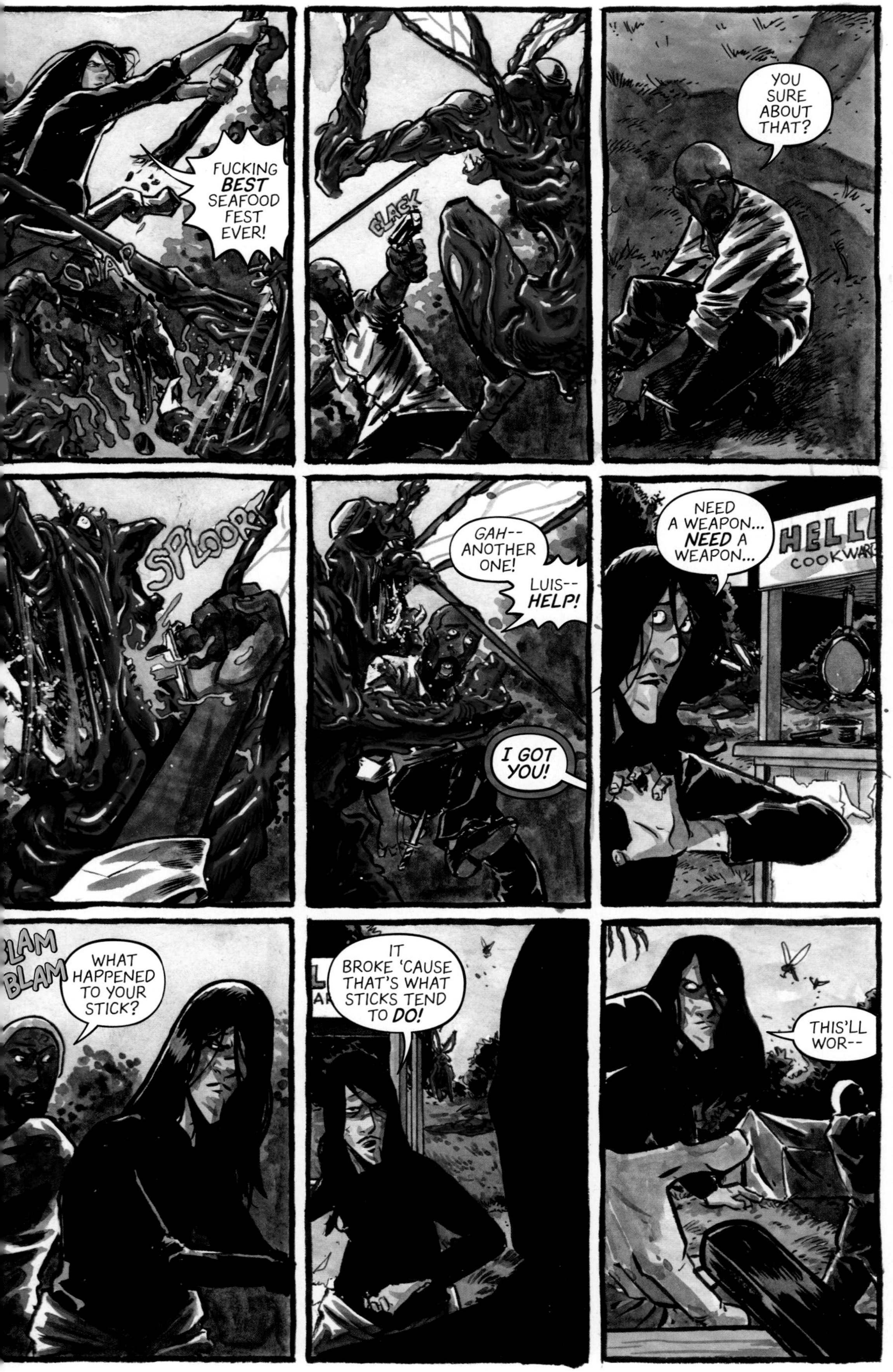
FUCKING BEST SEAFOOD FEST EVER!
SNAP
CLACK
YOU SURE ABOUT THAT?
SPLOORT
GAH-- ANOTHER ONE!
LUIS-- HELP!
I GOT YOU!
NEED A WEAPON... NEED A WEAPON...
HELL
COOKWARE
BLAM BLAM
WHAT HAPPENED TO YOUR STICK?
IT BROKE 'CAUSE THAT'S WHAT STICKS TEND TO DO!
THIS'LL WOR--

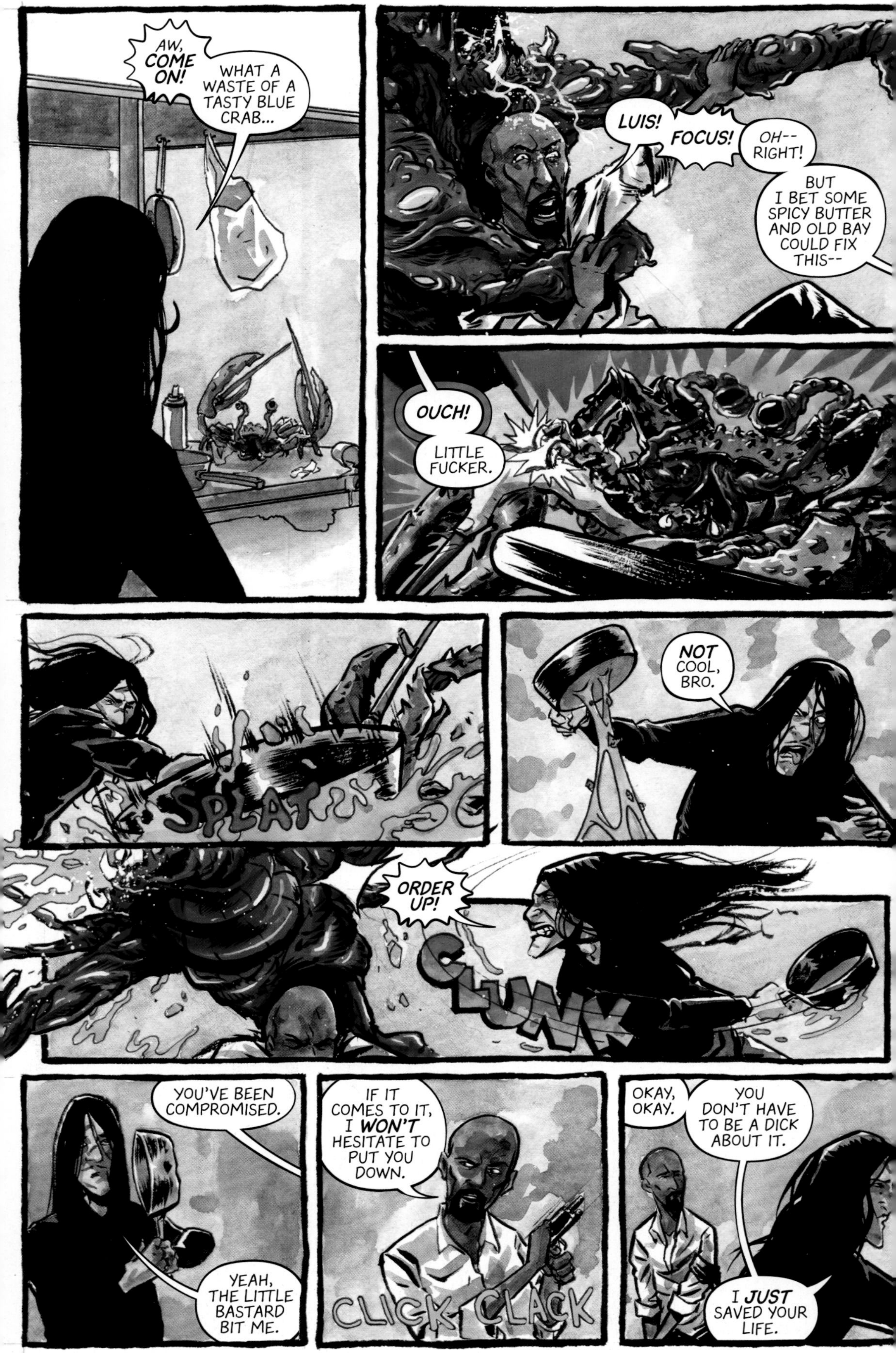
AW, COME ON!
WHAT A WASTE OF A TASTY BLUE CRAB...
LUIS!
FOCUS!
OH-- RIGHT!
BUT I BET SOME SPICY BUTTER AND OLD BAY COULD FIX THIS--
OUCH!
LITTLE FUCKER.
SPLAT
NOT COOL, BRO.
ORDER UP!
CLUNK
YOU'VE BEEN COMPROMISED.
YEAH, THE LITTLE BASTARD BIT ME.
IF IT COMES TO IT, I WON'T HESITATE TO PUT YOU DOWN.
CLICK CLACK
OKAY, OKAY.
YOU DON'T HAVE TO BE A DICK ABOUT IT.
I JUST SAVED YOUR LIFE.

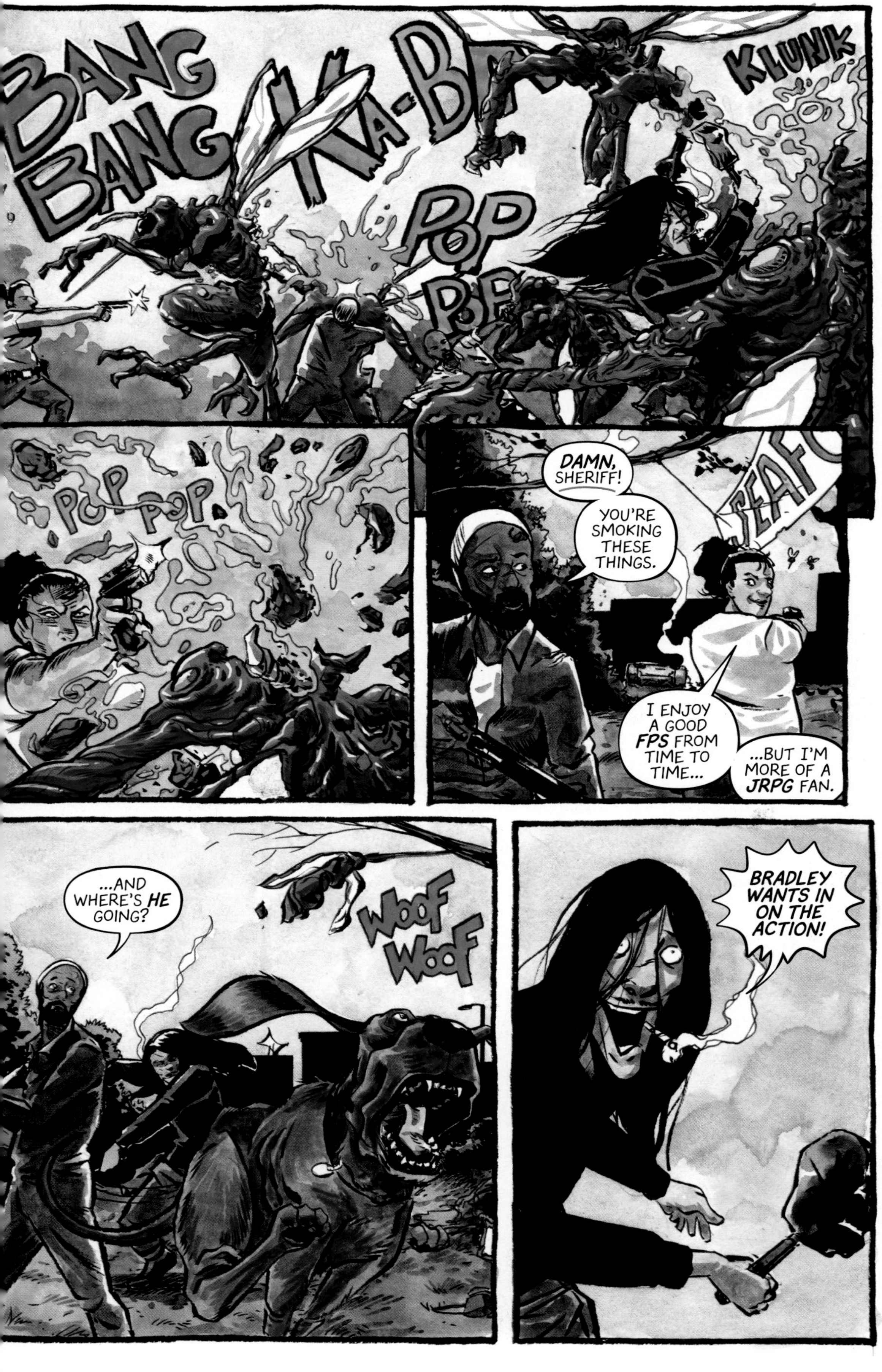
BANG BANG
KA-BL
KLUNK
POP POP
POP POP
DAMN, SHERIFF!
YOU'RE SMOKING THESE THINGS.
I ENJOY A GOOD FPS FROM TIME TO TIME...
...BUT I'M MORE OF A JRPG FAN.
...AND WHERE'S HE GOING?
WOOF WOOF
BRADLEY WANTS IN ON THE ACTION!

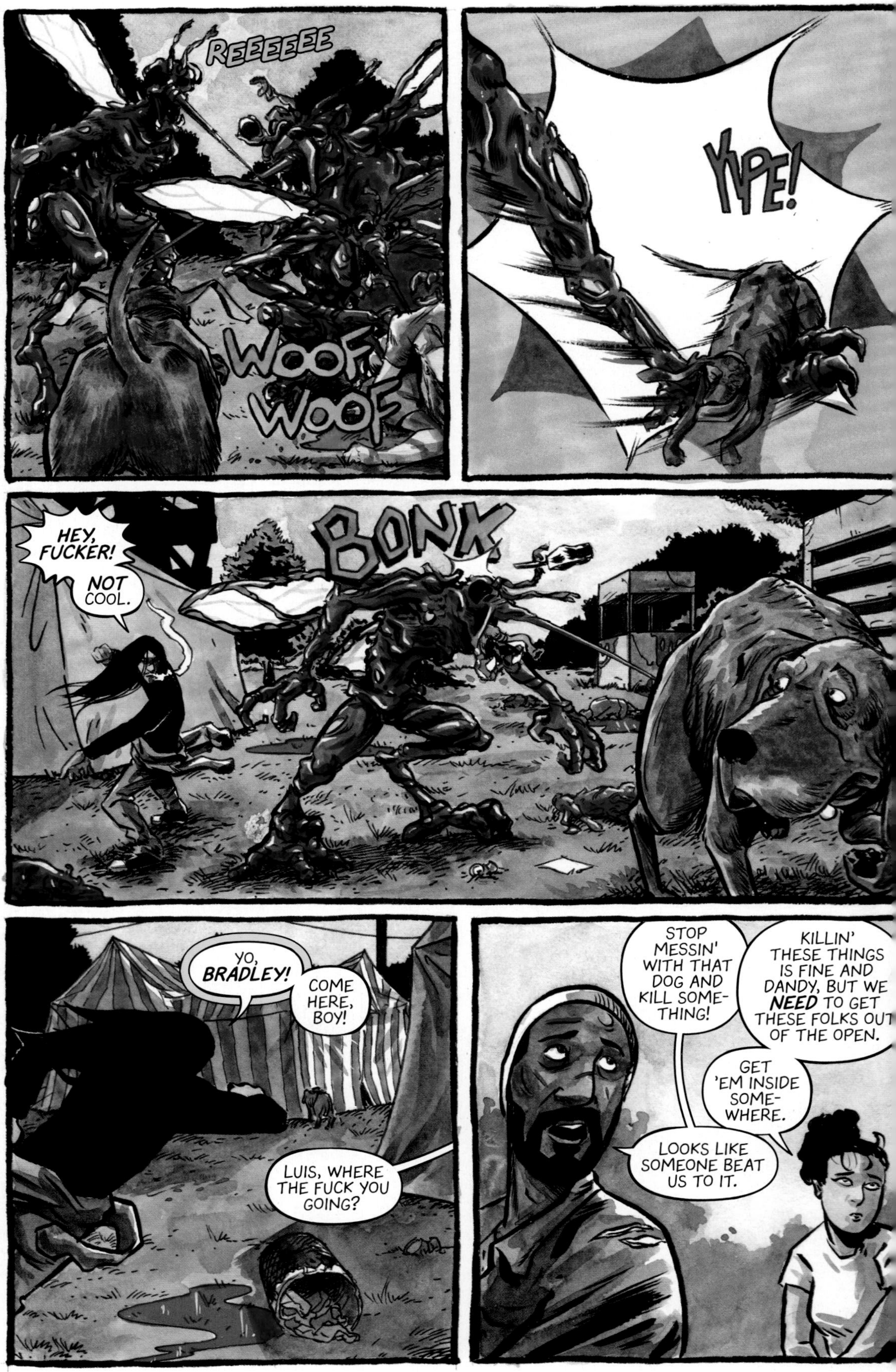
REEEEEE
WOOF WOOF
YIPE!
BONK
HEY, FUCKER!
NOT COOL.
YO, BRADLEY!
COME HERE, BOY!
LUIS, WHERE THE FUCK YOU GOING?
STOP MESSIN' WITH THAT DOG AND KILL SOME-THING!
KILLIN' THESE THINGS IS FINE AND DANDY, BUT WE NEED TO GET THESE FOLKS OUT OF THE OPEN.
GET 'EM INSIDE SOME-WHERE.
LOOKS LIKE SOMEONE BEAT US TO IT.

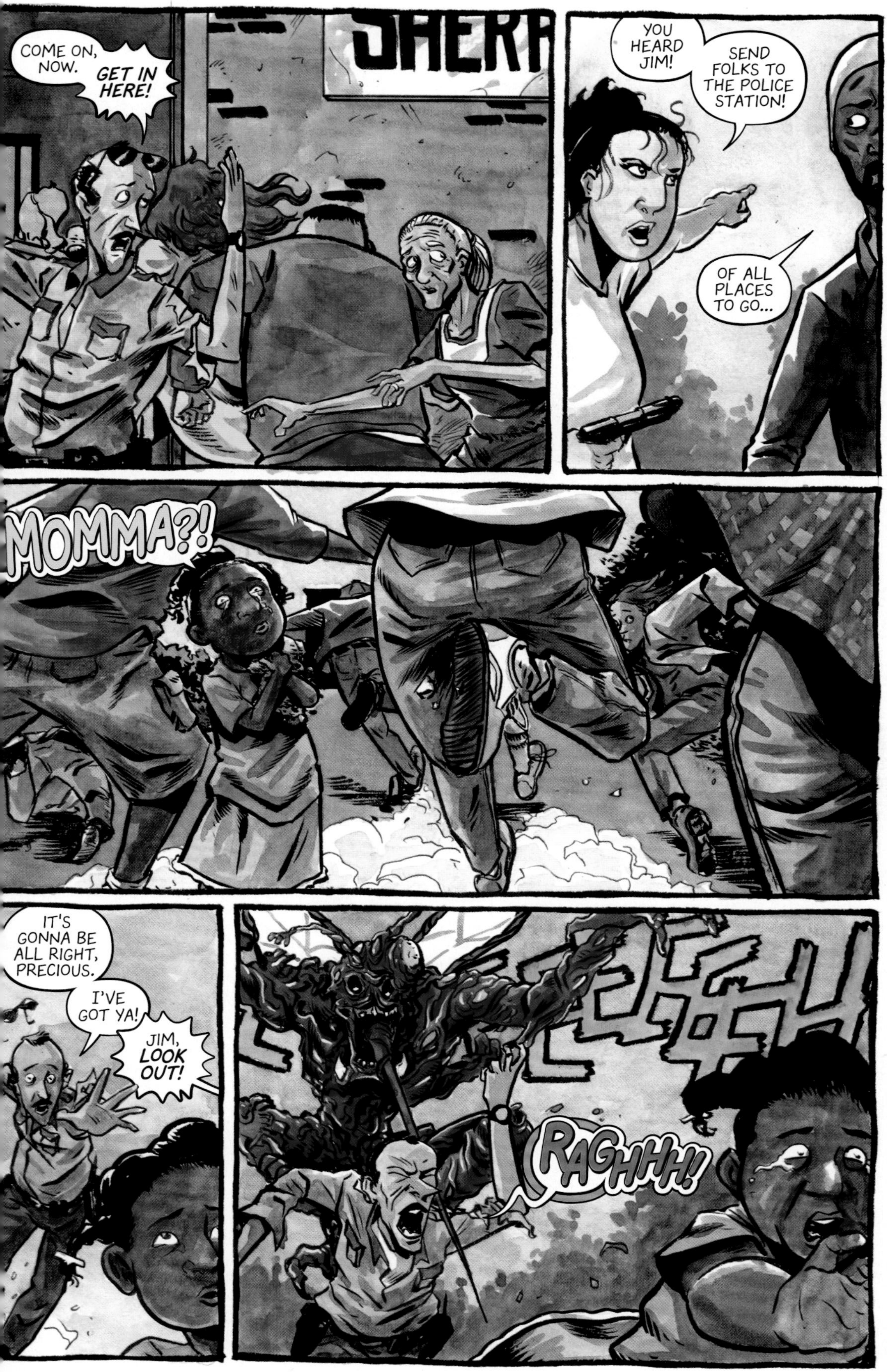

COME ON, NOW.
GET IN HERE!
YOU HEARD JIM!
SEND FOLKS TO THE POLICE STATION!
OF ALL PLACES TO GO...
MOMMA?!
IT'S GONNA BE ALL RIGHT, PRECIOUS.
I'VE GOT YA!
JIM, LOOK OUT!
RAGHHH!

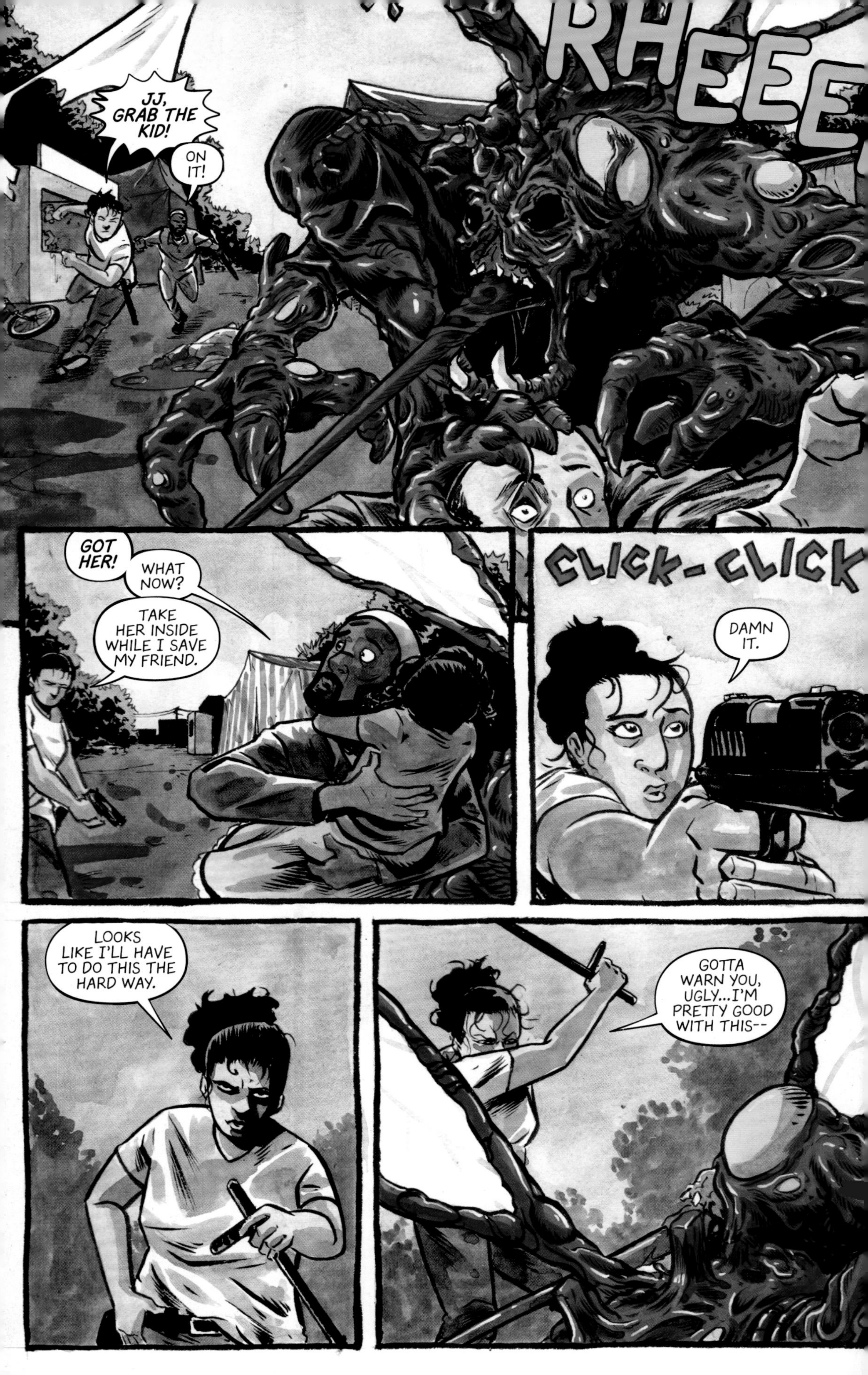
RHEEE
JJ, GRAB THE KID!
ON IT!
GOT HER!
WHAT NOW?
TAKE HER INSIDE WHILE I SAVE MY FRIEND.
CLICK-CLICK
DAMN IT.
LOOKS LIKE I'LL HAVE TO DO THIS THE HARD WAY.
GOTTA WARN YOU, UGLY...I'M PRETTY GOOD WITH THIS--

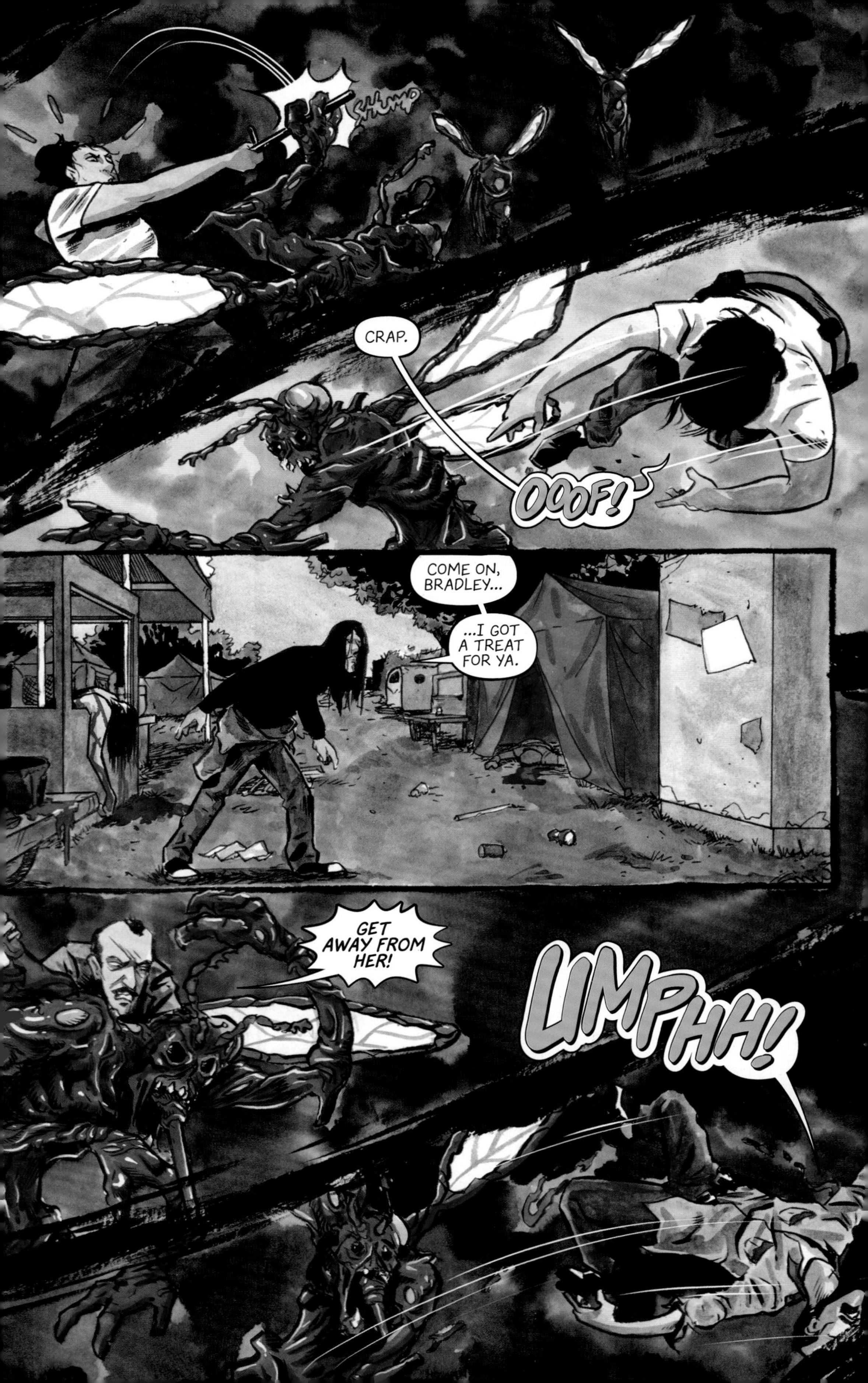
SHUMP
CRAP.
OOOF!
COME ON, BRADLEY...
...I GOT A TREAT FOR YA.
GET AWAY FROM HER!
UMPHH!

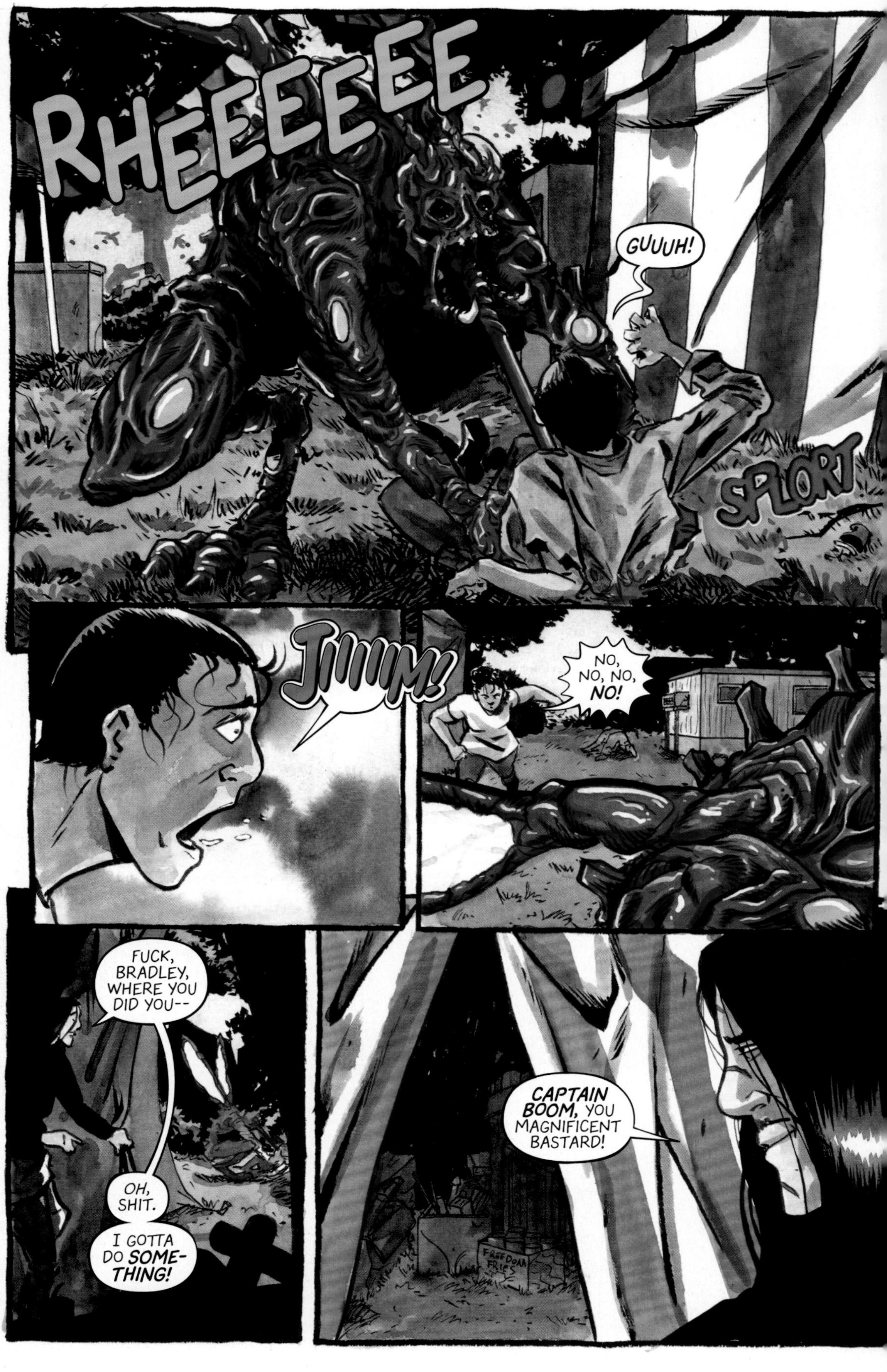
RHEEEEEEE
GUUUH!
SPLORT
JIIIIM!
NO, NO, NO, NO!
FUCK, BRADLEY, WHERE YOU DID YOU--
OH, SHIT.
I GOTTA DO SOMETHING!
CAPTAIN BOOM, YOU MAGNIFICENT BASTARD!
FREEDOM FRIES

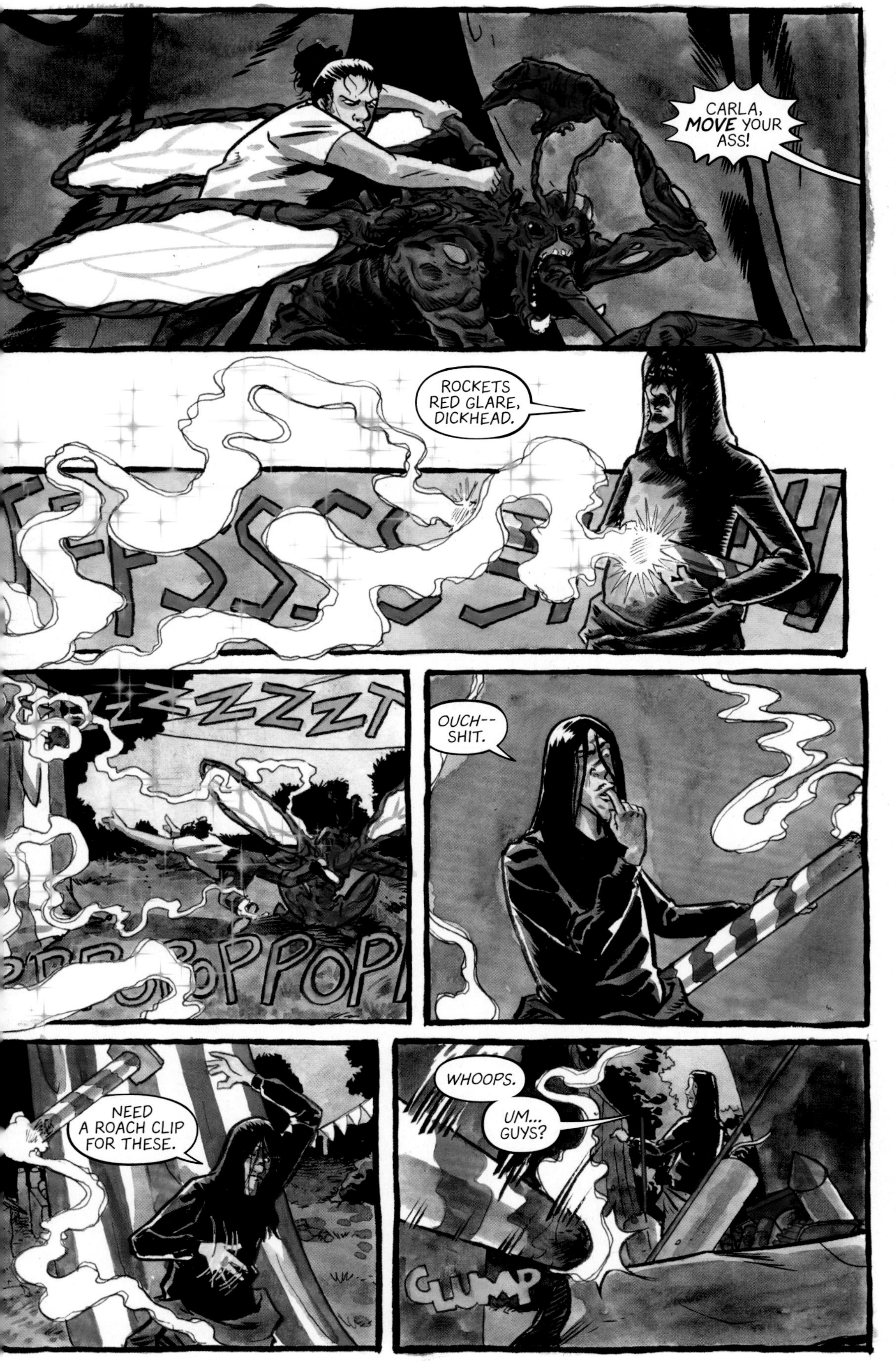
CARLA, MOVE YOUR ASS!
ROCKETS RED GLARE, DICKHEAD.
ZZZZZT
OUCH-- SHIT.
NEED A ROACH CLIP FOR THESE.
WHOOPS.
UM... GUYS?
GLUMP

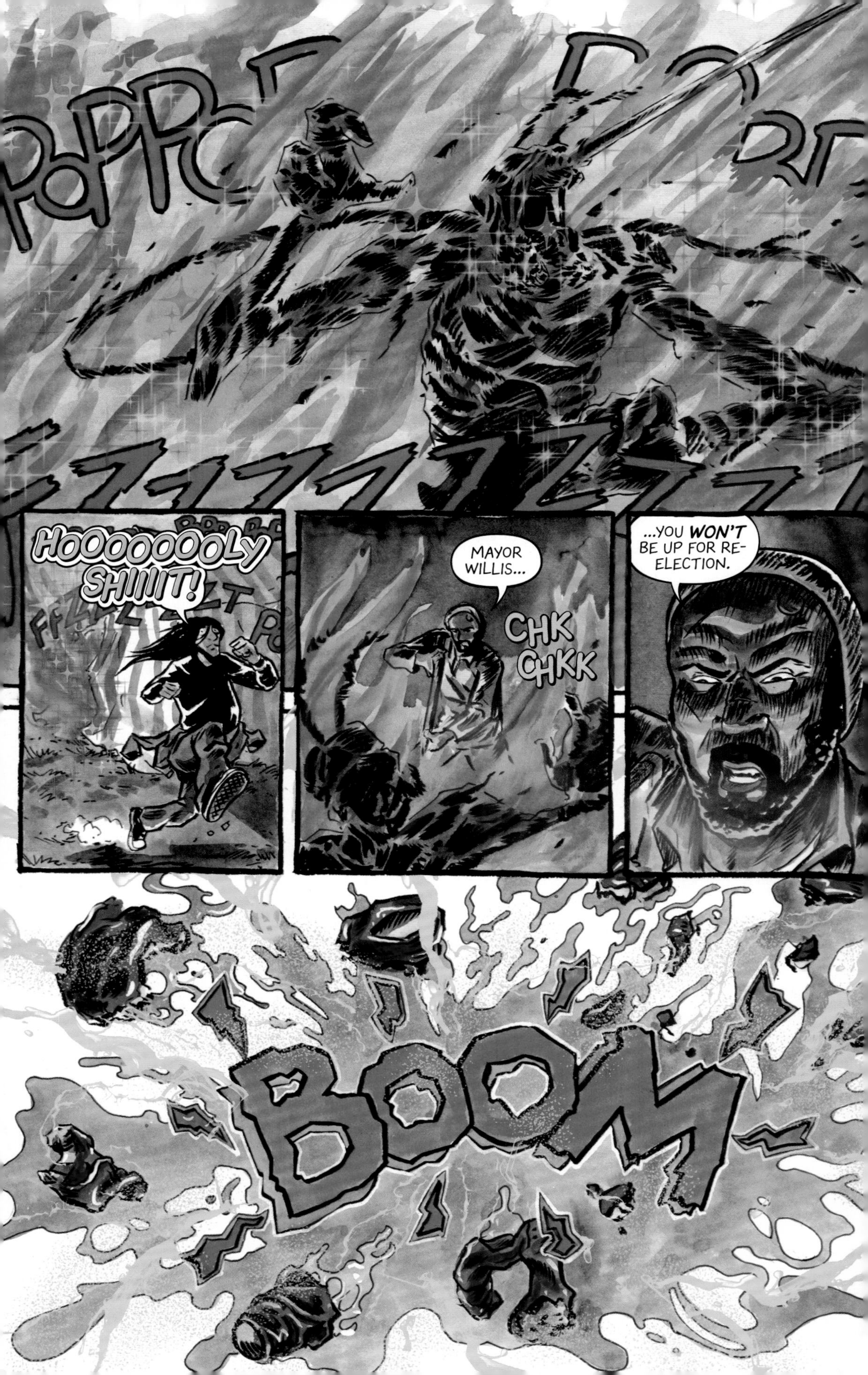
HOOOOOOOLY SHIIIIT!
MAYOR WILLIS...
CHK CHKK
...YOU WON'T BE UP FOR RE-ELECTION.
BOOM

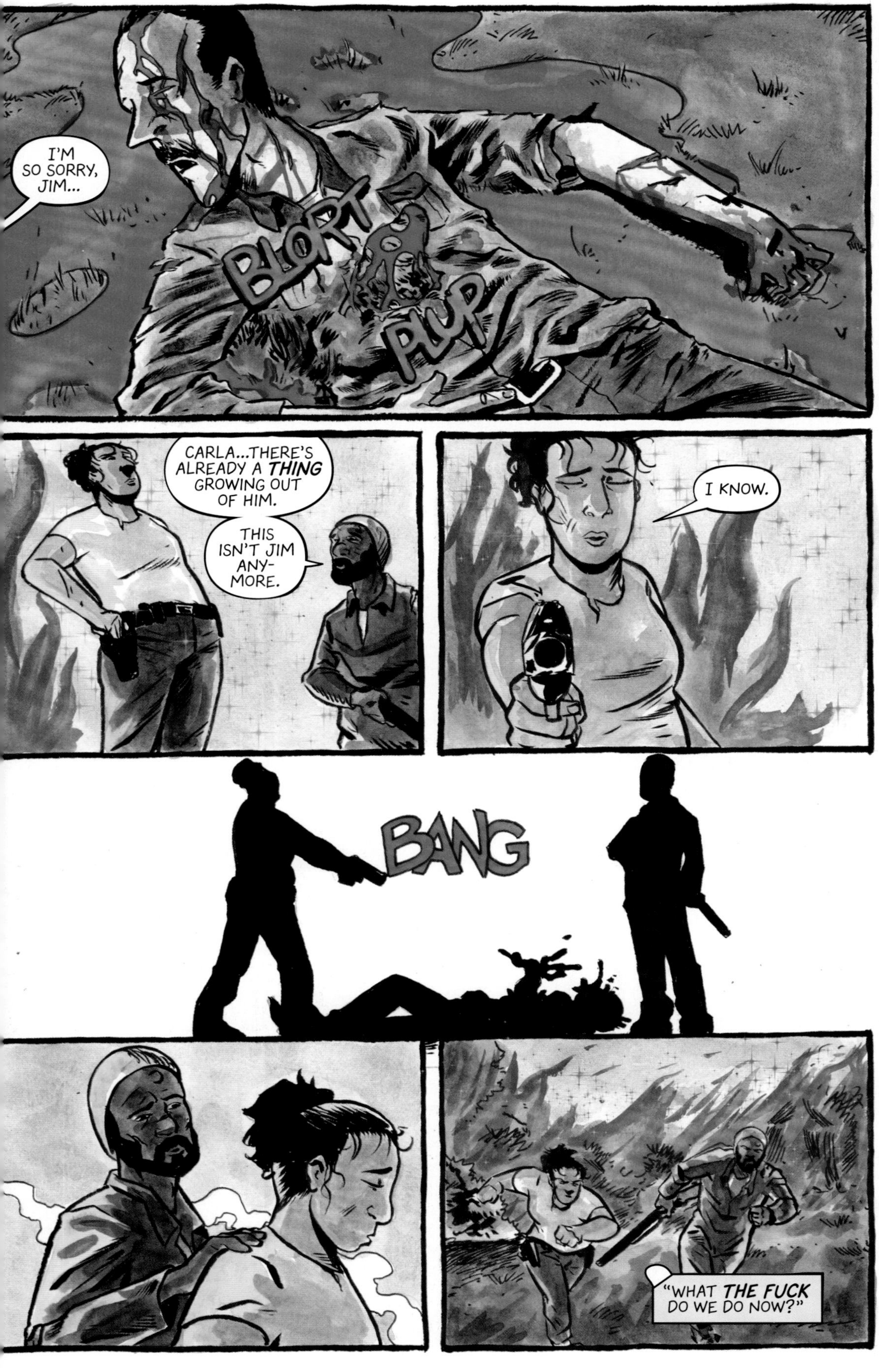
I'M SO SORRY, JIM...
BLORT
PLIP
CARLA...THERE'S ALREADY A *THING* GROWING OUT OF HIM.
THIS ISN'T JIM ANY-MORE.
I KNOW.
BANG
"WHAT *THE FUCK* DO WE DO NOW?"

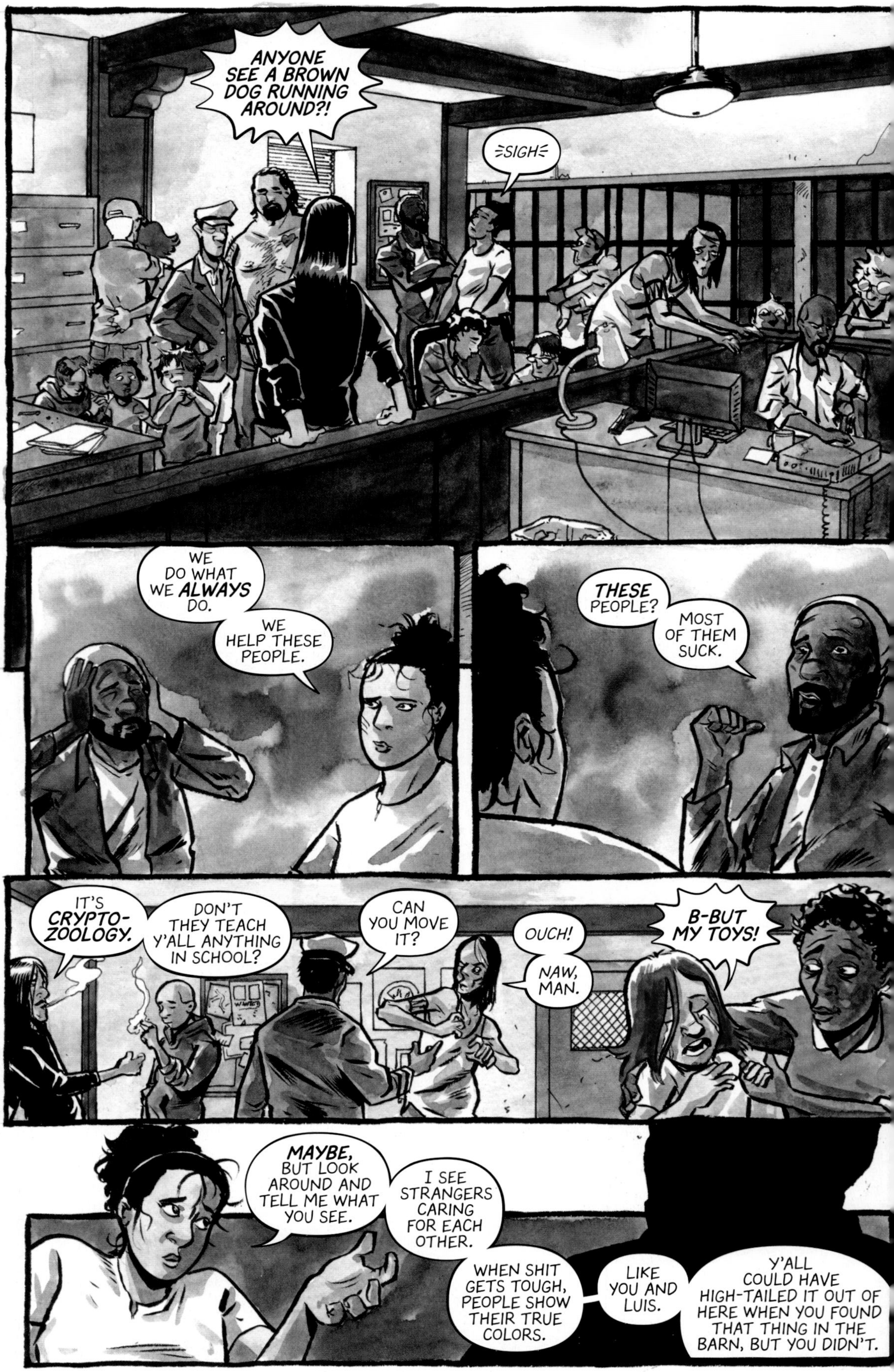
ANYONE SEE A BROWN DOG RUNNING AROUND?!
SIGH
WE DO WHAT WE ALWAYS DO.
WE HELP THESE PEOPLE.
THESE PEOPLE?
MOST OF THEM SUCK.
IT'S CRYPTO-ZOOLOGY.
DON'T THEY TEACH Y'ALL ANYTHING IN SCHOOL?
CAN YOU MOVE IT?
OUCH!
NAW, MAN.
B-BUT MY TOYS!
MAYBE, BUT LOOK AROUND AND TELL ME WHAT YOU SEE.
I SEE STRANGERS CARING FOR EACH OTHER.
WHEN SHIT GETS TOUGH, PEOPLE SHOW THEIR TRUE COLORS.
LIKE YOU AND LUIS.
Y'ALL COULD HAVE HIGH-TAILED IT OUT OF HERE WHEN YOU FOUND THAT THING IN THE BARN, BUT YOU DIDN'T.

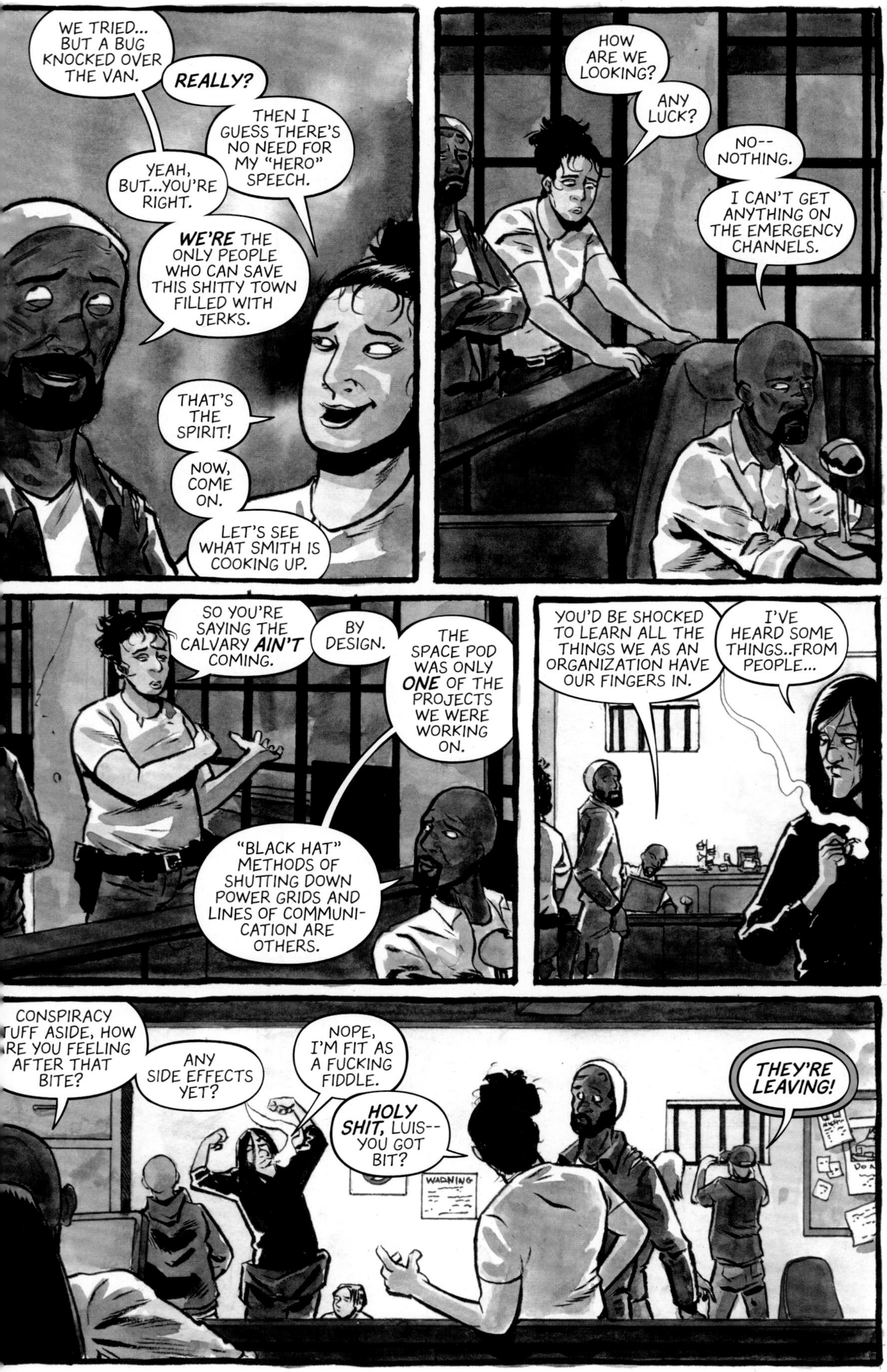
WE TRIED... BUT A BUG KNOCKED OVER THE VAN.
REALLY?
THEN I GUESS THERE'S NO NEED FOR MY "HERO" SPEECH.
YEAH, BUT...YOU'RE RIGHT.
WE'RE THE ONLY PEOPLE WHO CAN SAVE THIS SHITTY TOWN FILLED WITH JERKS.
THAT'S THE SPIRIT!
NOW, COME ON.
LET'S SEE WHAT SMITH IS COOKING UP.
HOW ARE WE LOOKING?
ANY LUCK?
NO-- NOTHING.
I CAN'T GET ANYTHING ON THE EMERGENCY CHANNELS.
SO YOU'RE SAYING THE CALVARY AIN'T COMING.
BY DESIGN.
THE SPACE POD WAS ONLY ONE OF THE PROJECTS WE WERE WORKING ON.
"BLACK HAT" METHODS OF SHUTTING DOWN POWER GRIDS AND LINES OF COMMUNI-CATION ARE OTHERS.
YOU'D BE SHOCKED TO LEARN ALL THE THINGS WE AS AN ORGANIZATION HAVE OUR FINGERS IN.
I'VE HEARD SOME THINGS..FROM PEOPLE...
CONSPIRACY TUFF ASIDE, HOW RE YOU FEELING AFTER THAT BITE?
ANY SIDE EFFECTS YET?
NOPE, I'M FIT AS A FUCKING FIDDLE.
HOLY SHIT, LUIS-- YOU GOT BIT?
THEY'RE LEAVING!
WARNING

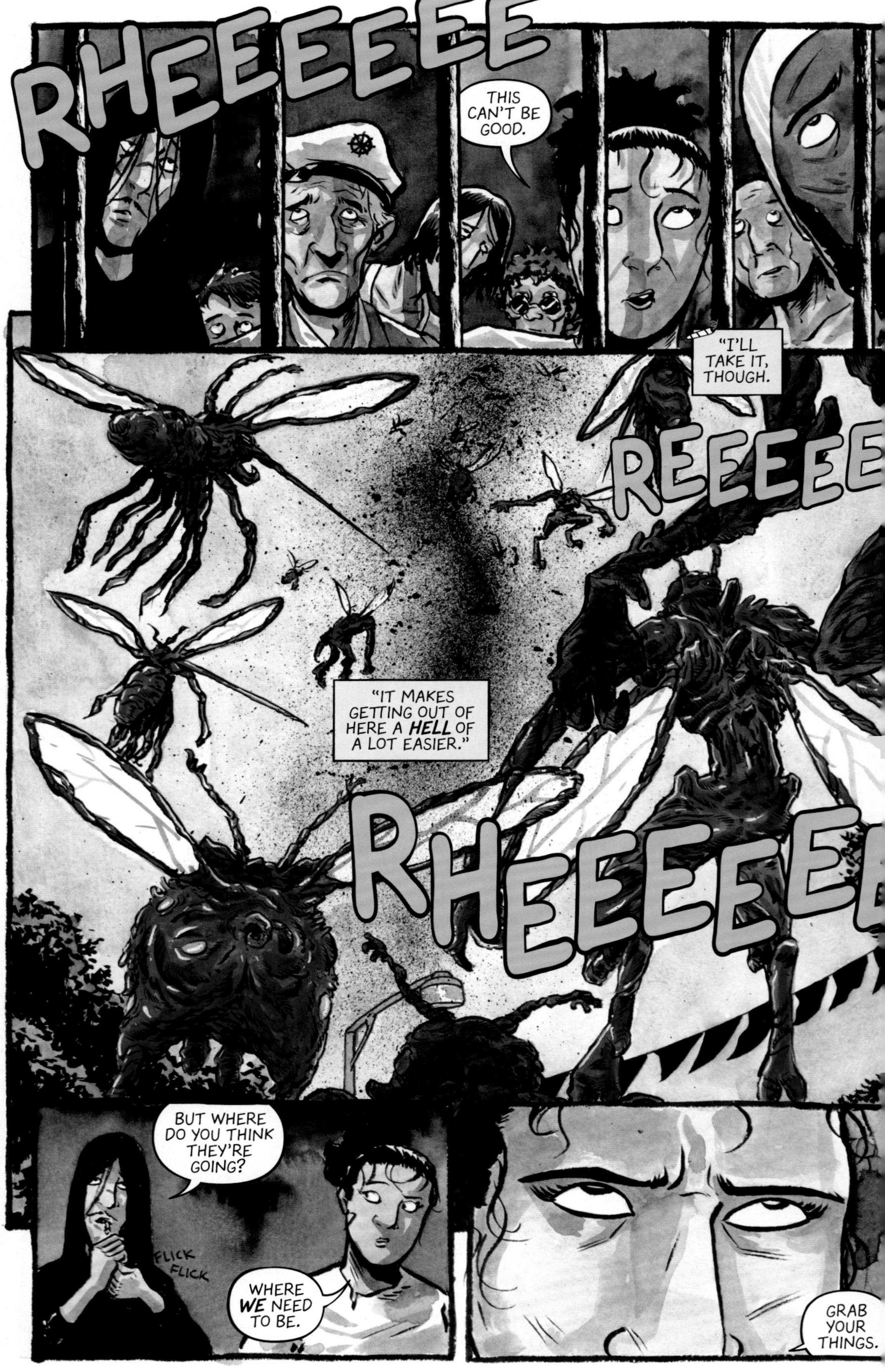
RHEEEEEE
THIS CAN'T BE GOOD.
"I'LL TAKE IT, THOUGH.
REEEEEE
"IT MAKES GETTING OUT OF HERE A ***HELL*** OF A LOT EASIER."
RHEEEEEE
BUT WHERE DO YOU THINK THEY'RE GOING?
FLICK FLICK
WHERE ***WE*** NEED TO BE.
GRAB YOUR THINGS.

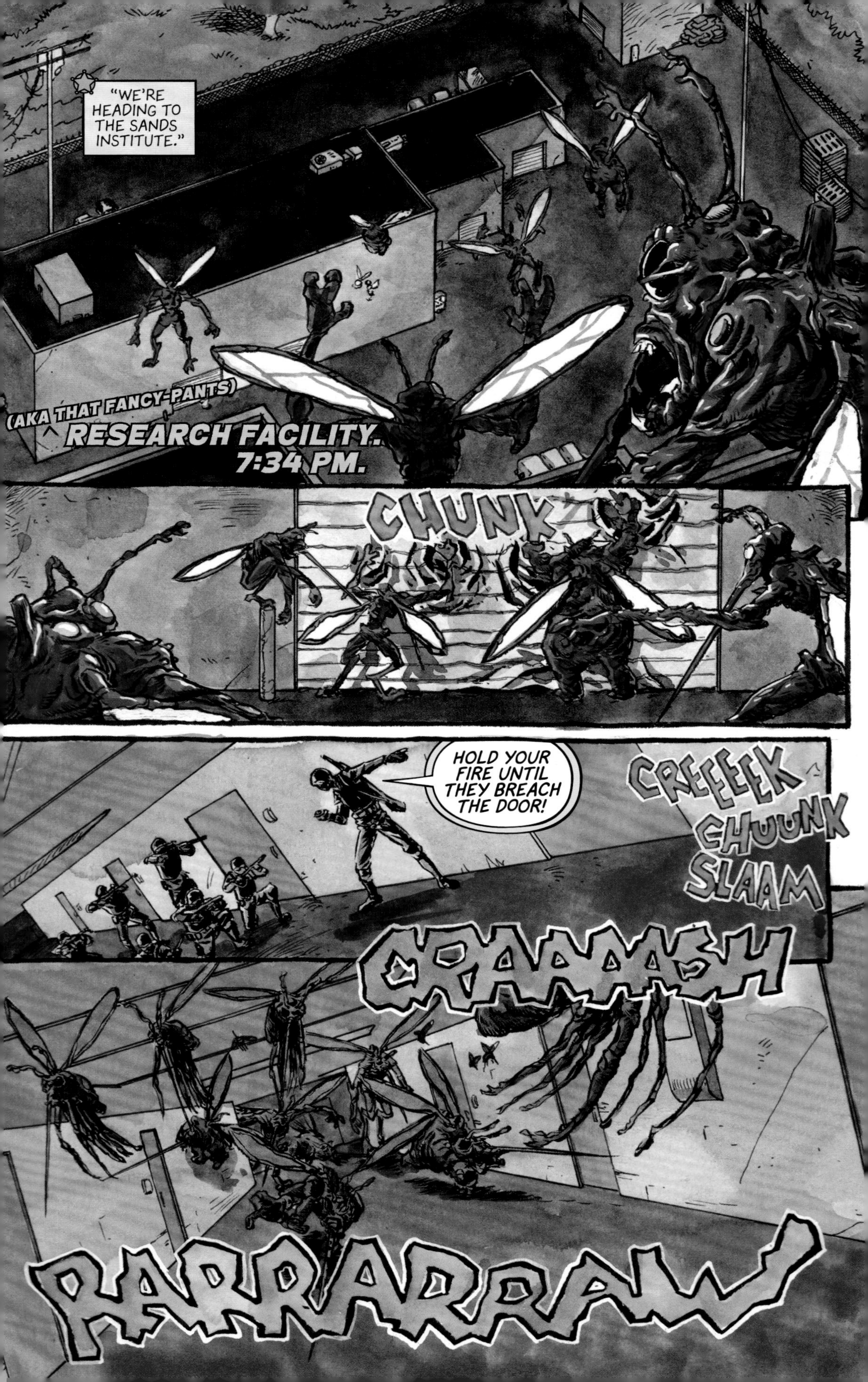

"WE'RE HEADING TO THE SANDS INSTITUTE."
(AKA THAT FANCY-PANTS)
RESEARCH FACILITY.
7:34 PM.
CHUNK
HOLD YOUR FIRE UNTIL THEY BREACH THE DOOR!
CREEEEK
CHUUNK
SLAAM
CRAAAASH
RARRARRAW

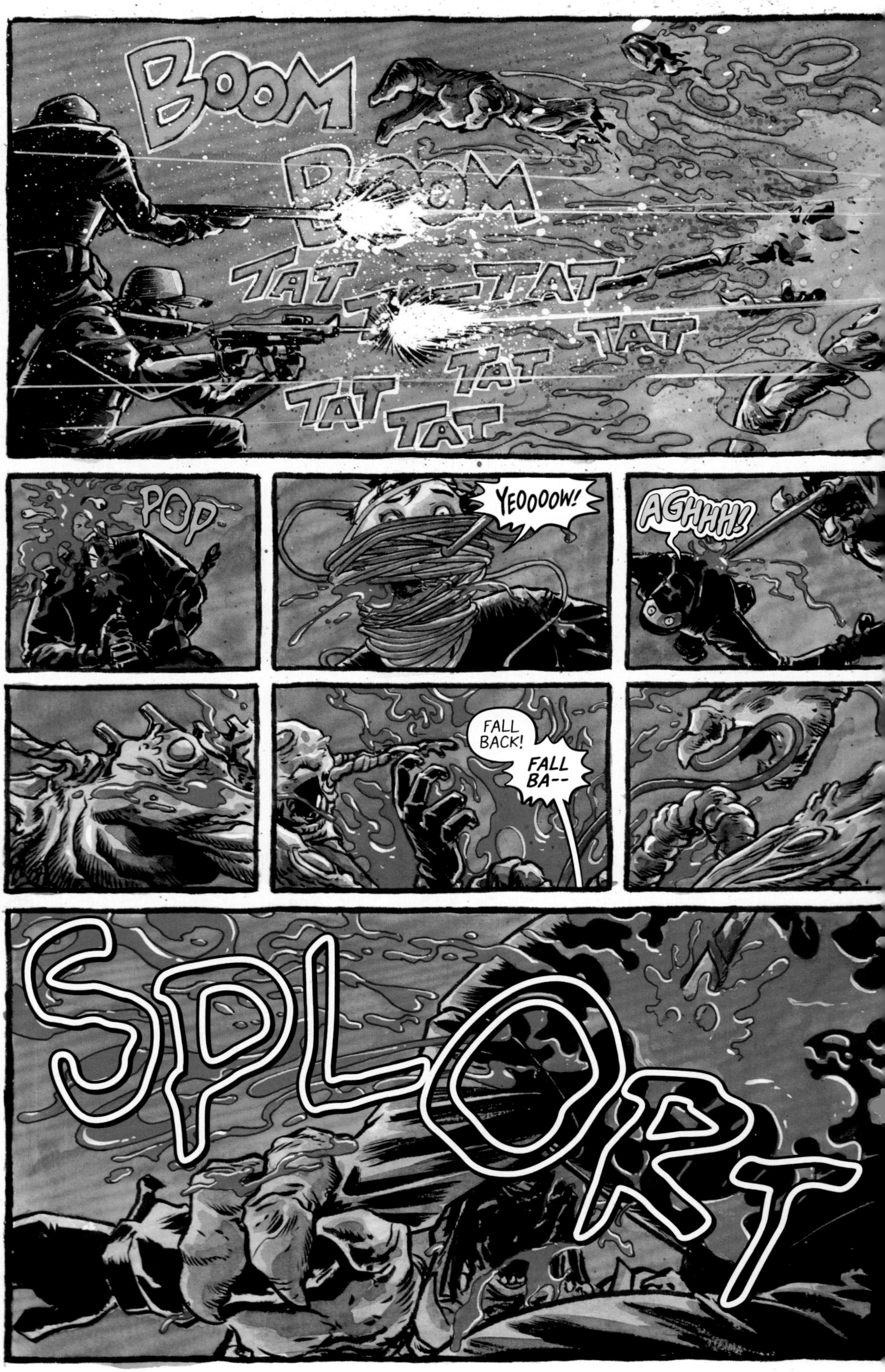
BOOM
BOOM
TAT TAT
TAT TAT
TAT TAT
POP
YEOOOOW!
AGHHH!
FALL BACK!
FALL BA--
SPLORT

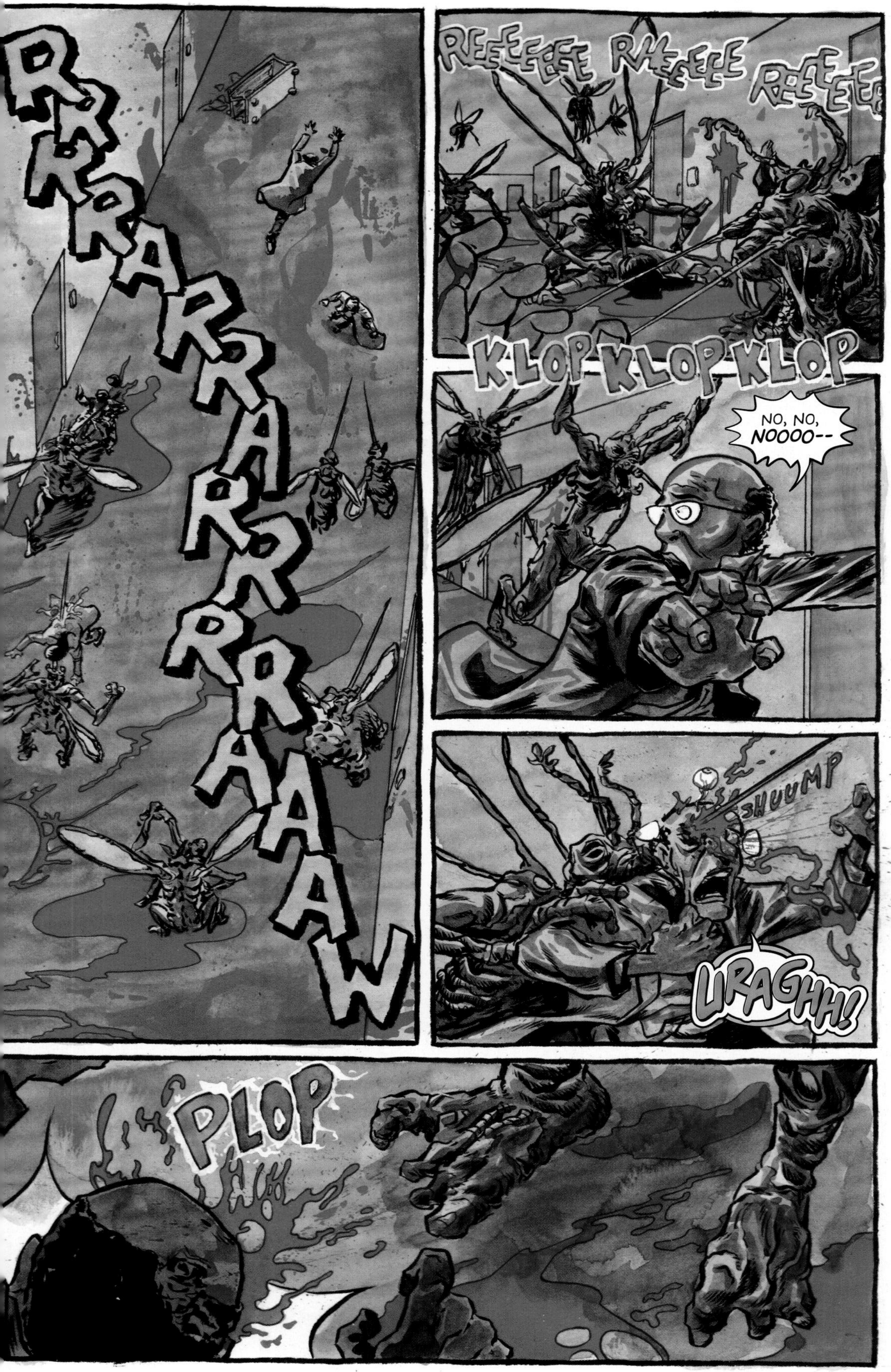
RRRRARRARRRARRRRAAAW
REEEEEEE RHEEEEE REEEEEEE
KLOP KLOP KLOP
NO, NO, NOOOO--
SHUUMP
URAGHH!
PLOP

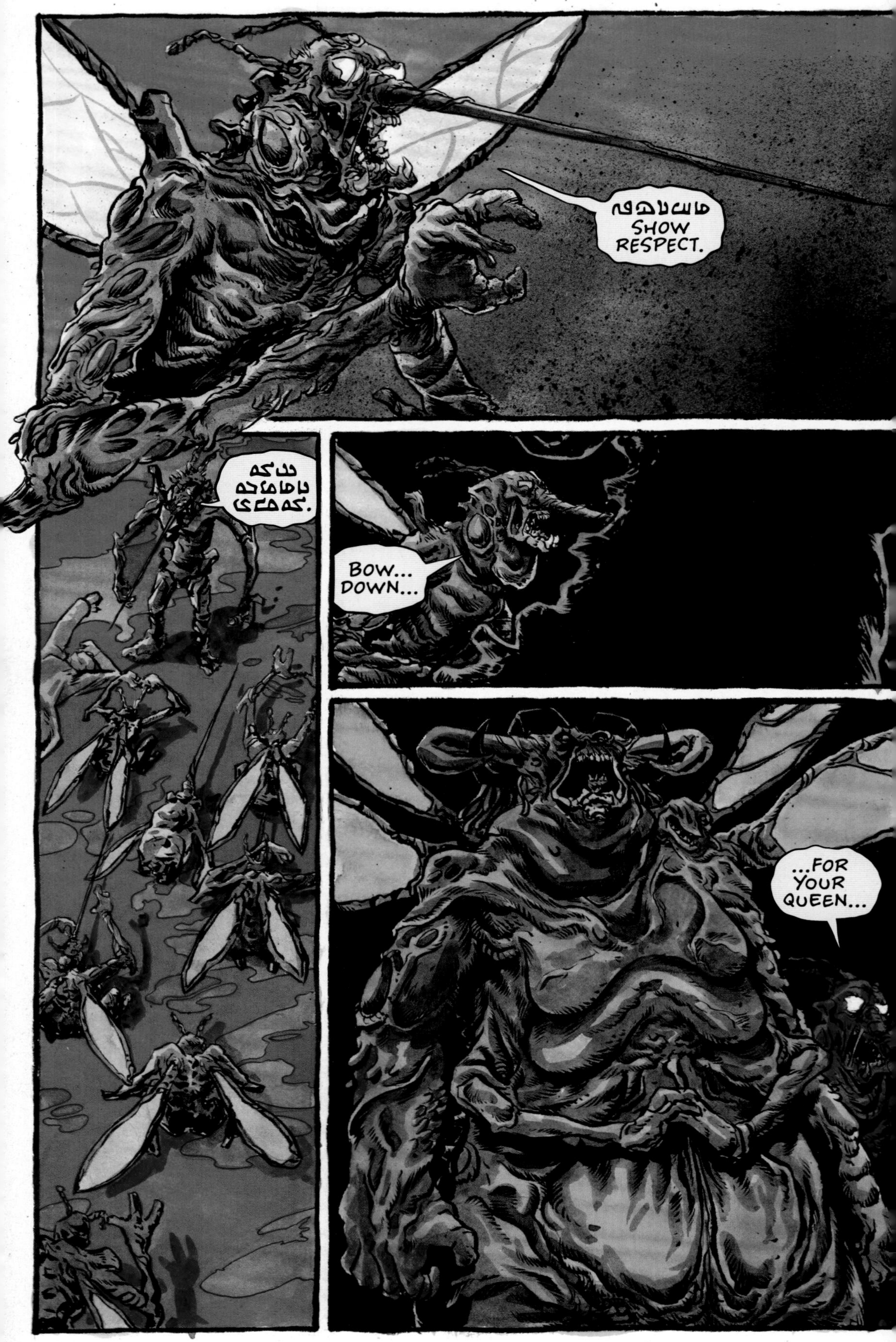
SHOW RESPECT.
BOW... DOWN...
...FOR YOUR QUEEN...

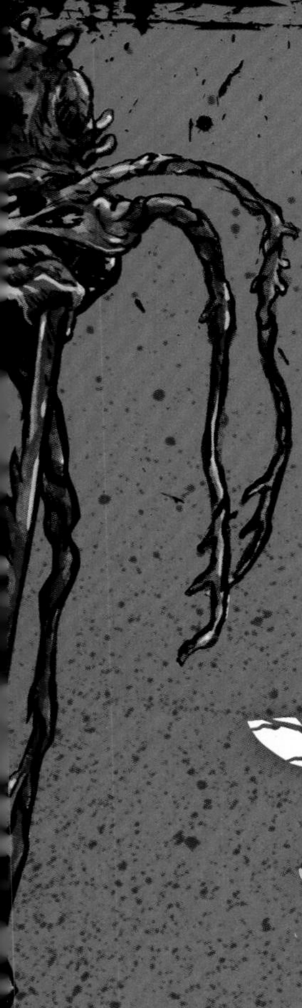

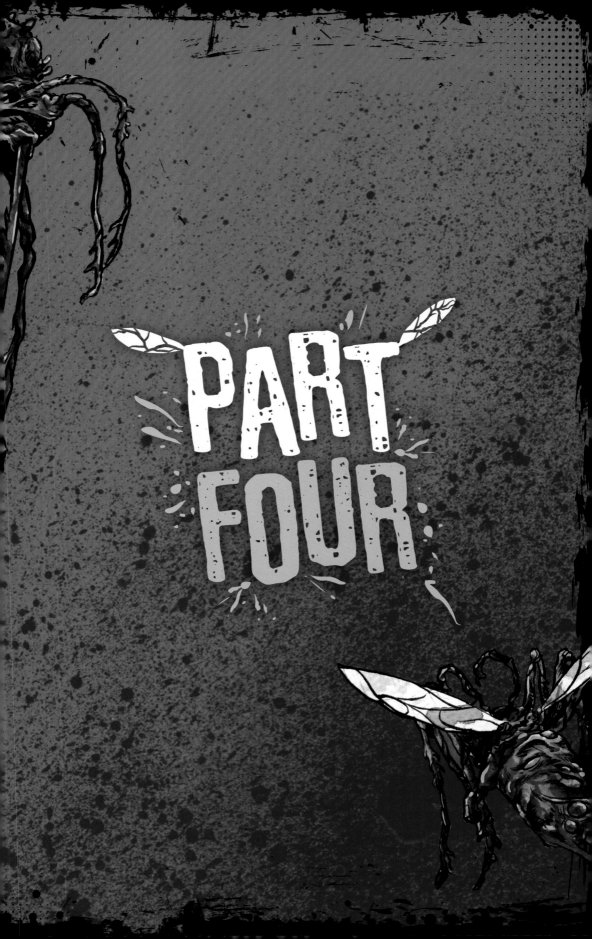

PART FOUR

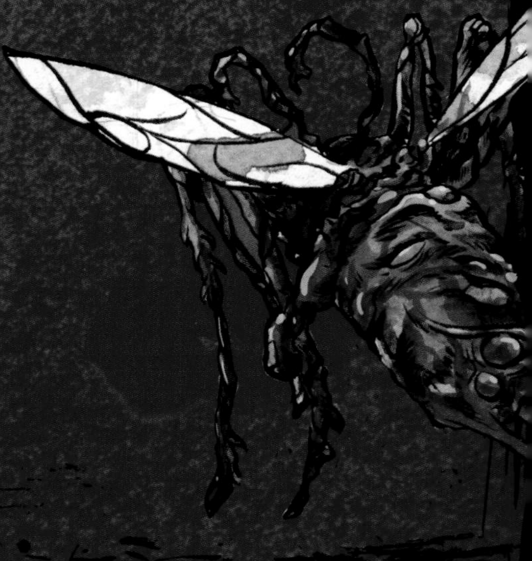

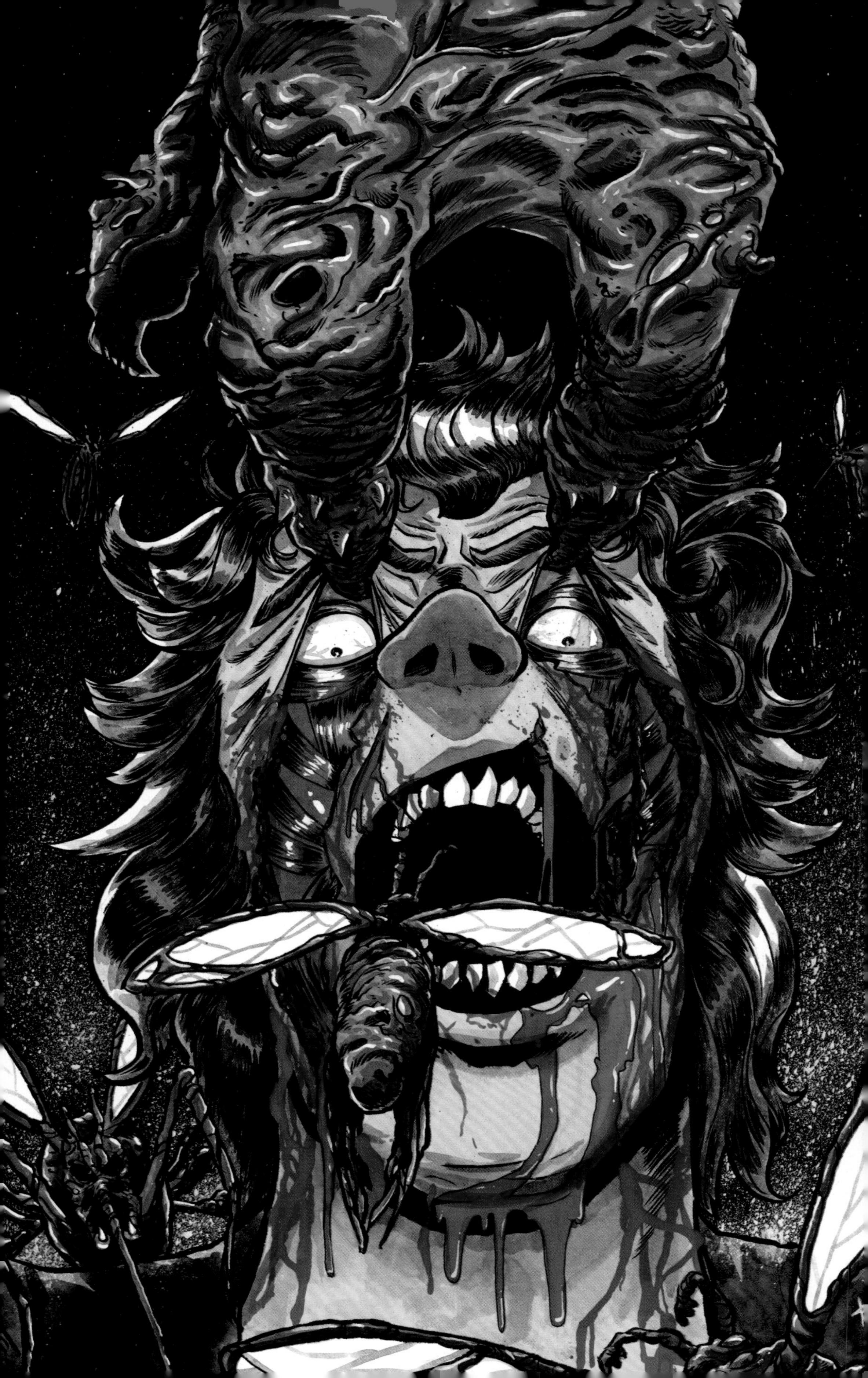

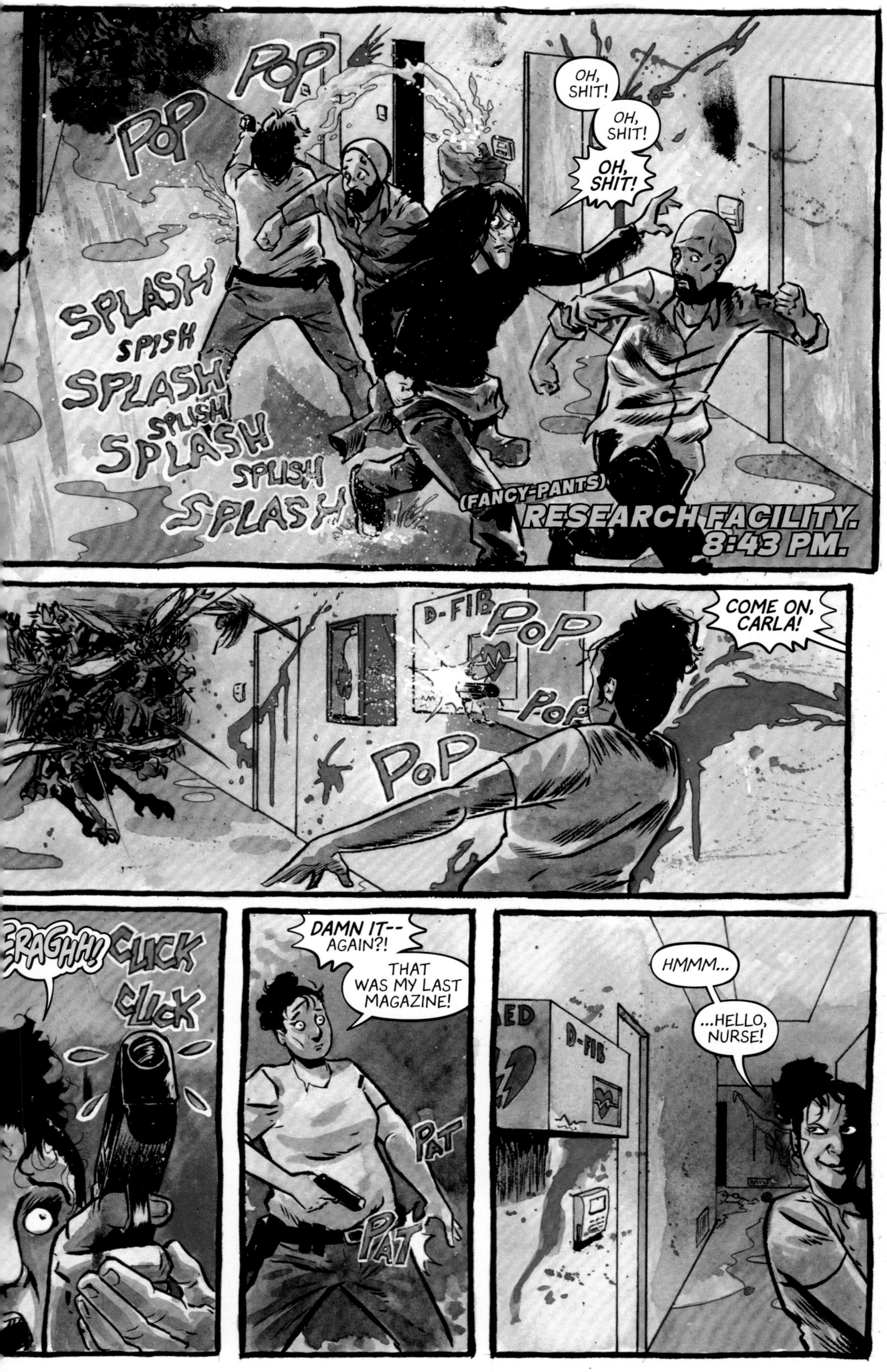
POP
POP
OH, SHIT!
OH, SHIT!
OH, SHIT!
SPLASH
SPISH
SPLASH
SPLISH
SPLASH
SPLISH
SPLASH
(FANCY-PANTS) RESEARCH FACILITY. 8:43 PM.
D-FIB
POP
COME ON, CARLA!
POP
POP
ERAGHH!
CLICK
CLICK
DAMN IT-- AGAIN?!
THAT WAS MY LAST MAGAZINE!
PAT
PAT
HMMM...
...HELLO, NURSE!
D-FIB

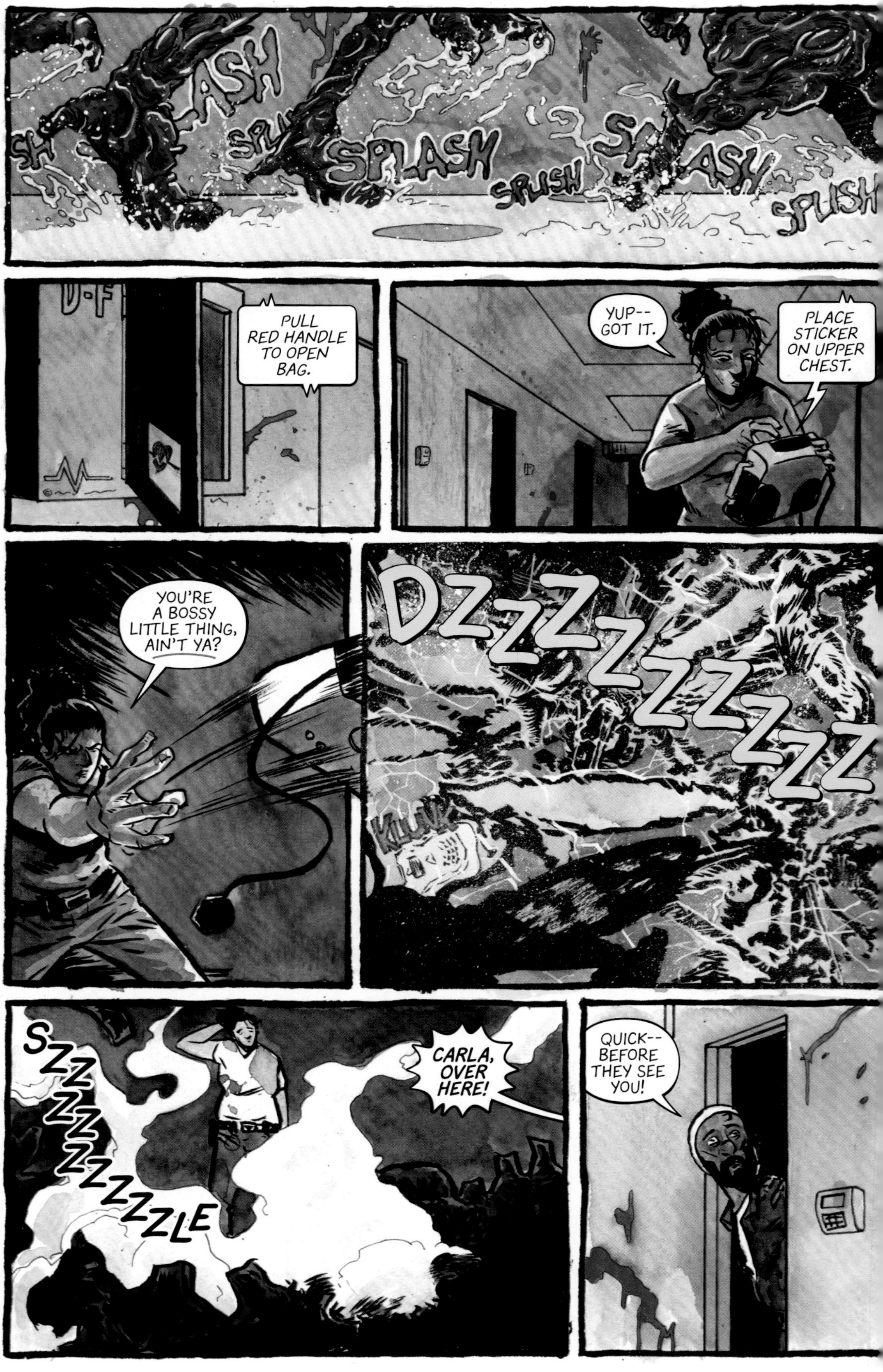
SPLASH
SPLASH
SPLASH
SPLISH
SPLASH
SPLISH
PULL RED HANDLE TO OPEN BAG.
YUP-- GOT IT.
PLACE STICKER ON UPPER CHEST.
YOU'RE A BOSSY LITTLE THING, AIN'T YA?
DZZZZZZZZZZ
KLUNK
SZZZZZZZZZZLE
CARLA, OVER HERE!
QUICK-- BEFORE THEY SEE YOU!

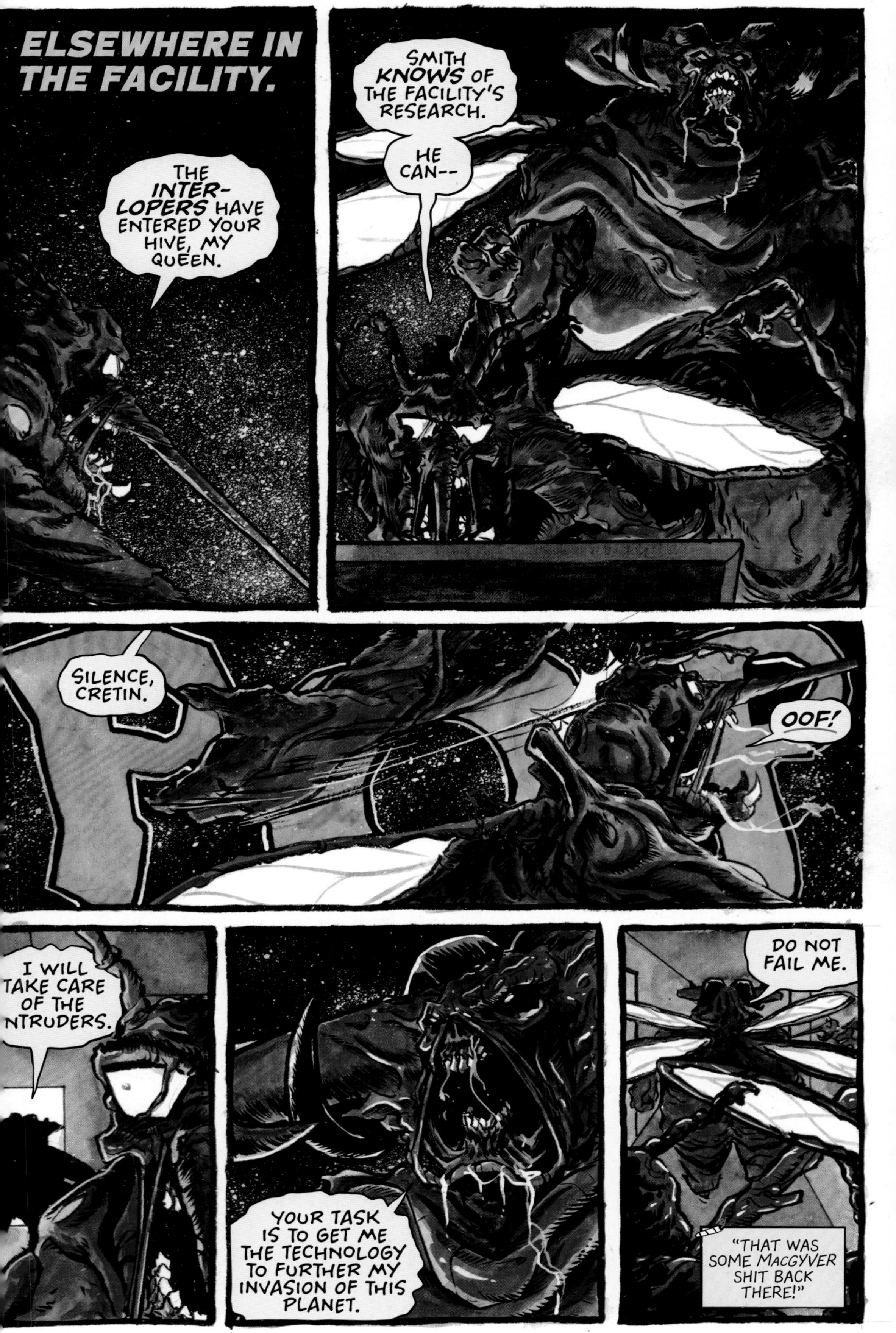
ELSEWHERE IN THE FACILITY.
THE INTER-LOPERS HAVE ENTERED YOUR HIVE, MY QUEEN.
SMITH KNOWS OF THE FACILITY'S RESEARCH.
HE CAN--
SILENCE, CRETIN.
OOF!
I WILL TAKE CARE OF THE NTRUDERS.
YOUR TASK IS TO GET ME THE TECHNOLOGY TO FURTHER MY INVASION OF THIS PLANET.
DO NOT FAIL ME.
"THAT WAS SOME MACGYVER SHIT BACK THERE!"

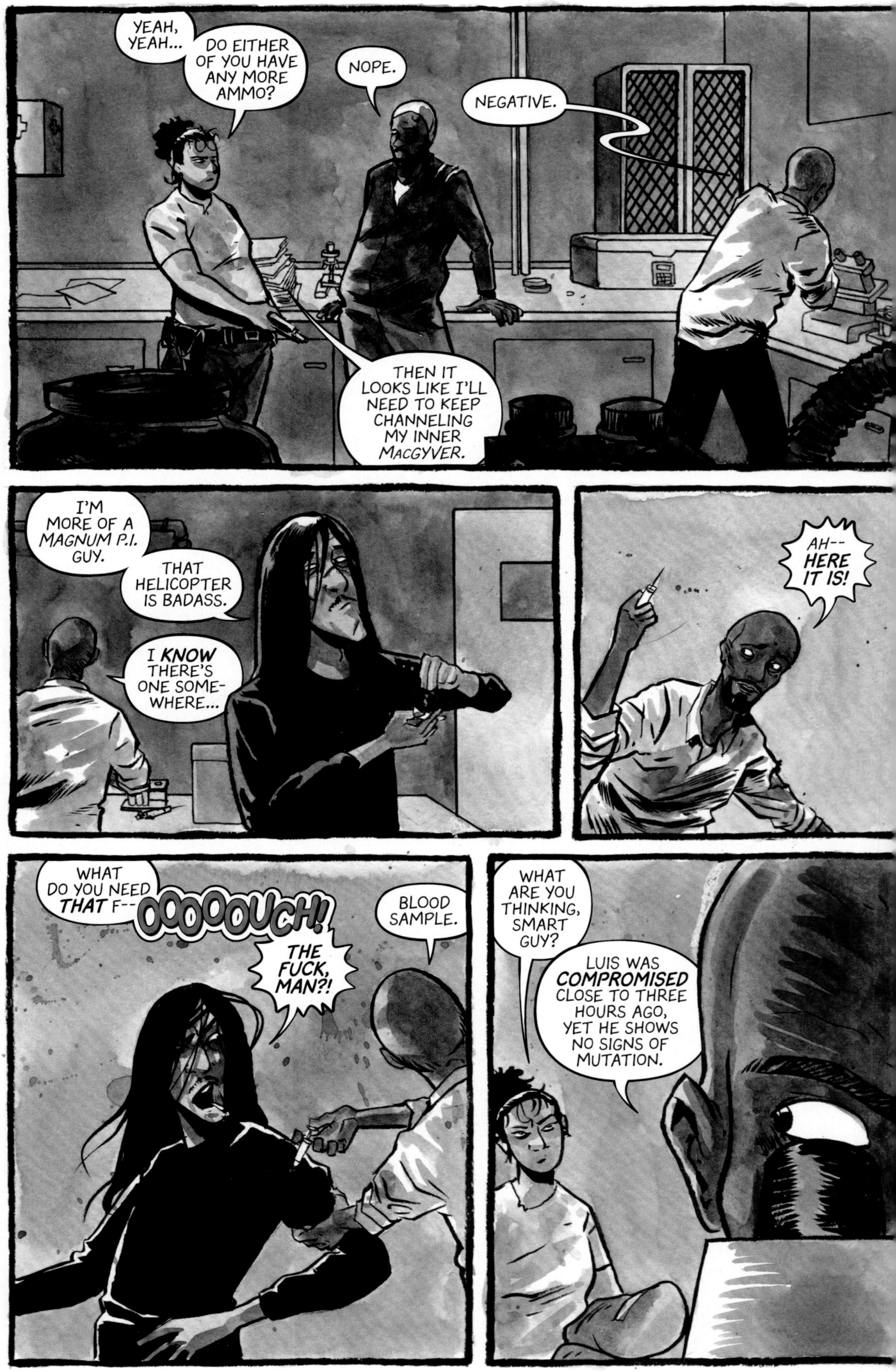
YEAH, YEAH...
DO EITHER OF YOU HAVE ANY MORE AMMO?
NOPE.
NEGATIVE.
THEN IT LOOKS LIKE I'LL NEED TO KEEP CHANNELING MY INNER *MacGYVER.*
I'M MORE OF A *MAGNUM P.I.* GUY.
THAT HELICOPTER IS BADASS.
I ***KNOW*** THERE'S ONE SOME-WHERE...
AH-- ***HERE IT IS!***
WHAT DO YOU NEED ***THAT*** F--
OOOOOOUCH!
THE FUCK, MAN?!
BLOOD SAMPLE.
WHAT ARE YOU THINKING, SMART GUY?
LUIS WAS **COMPROMISED** CLOSE TO THREE HOURS AGO, YET HE SHOWS NO SIGNS OF MUTATION.

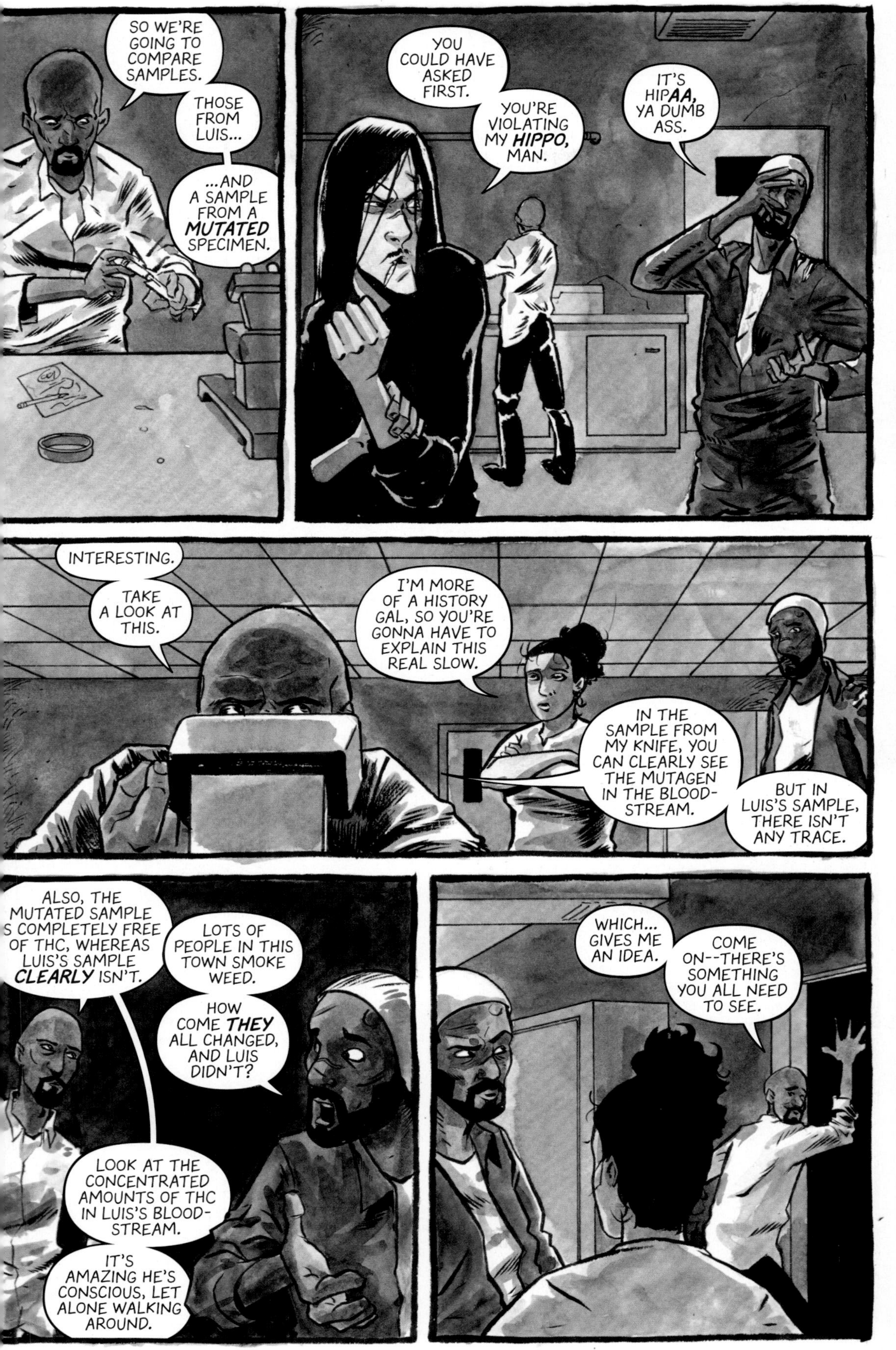
SO WE'RE GOING TO COMPARE SAMPLES.
THOSE FROM LUIS...
...AND A SAMPLE FROM A **MUTATED** SPECIMEN.
YOU COULD HAVE ASKED FIRST.
YOU'RE VIOLATING MY **HIPPO,** MAN.
IT'S HIP**AA,** YA DUMB ASS.
INTERESTING.
TAKE A LOOK AT THIS.
I'M MORE OF A HISTORY GAL, SO YOU'RE GONNA HAVE TO EXPLAIN THIS REAL SLOW.
IN THE SAMPLE FROM MY KNIFE, YOU CAN CLEARLY SEE THE MUTAGEN IN THE BLOOD-STREAM.
BUT IN LUIS'S SAMPLE, THERE ISN'T ANY TRACE.
ALSO, THE MUTATED SAMPLE S COMPLETELY FREE OF THC, WHEREAS LUIS'S SAMPLE **CLEARLY** ISN'T.
LOTS OF PEOPLE IN THIS TOWN SMOKE WEED.
HOW COME **THEY** ALL CHANGED, AND LUIS DIDN'T?
LOOK AT THE CONCENTRATED AMOUNTS OF THC IN LUIS'S BLOOD-STREAM.
IT'S AMAZING HE'S CONSCIOUS, LET ALONE WALKING AROUND.
WHICH... GIVES ME AN IDEA.
COME ON--THERE'S SOMETHING YOU ALL NEED TO SEE.

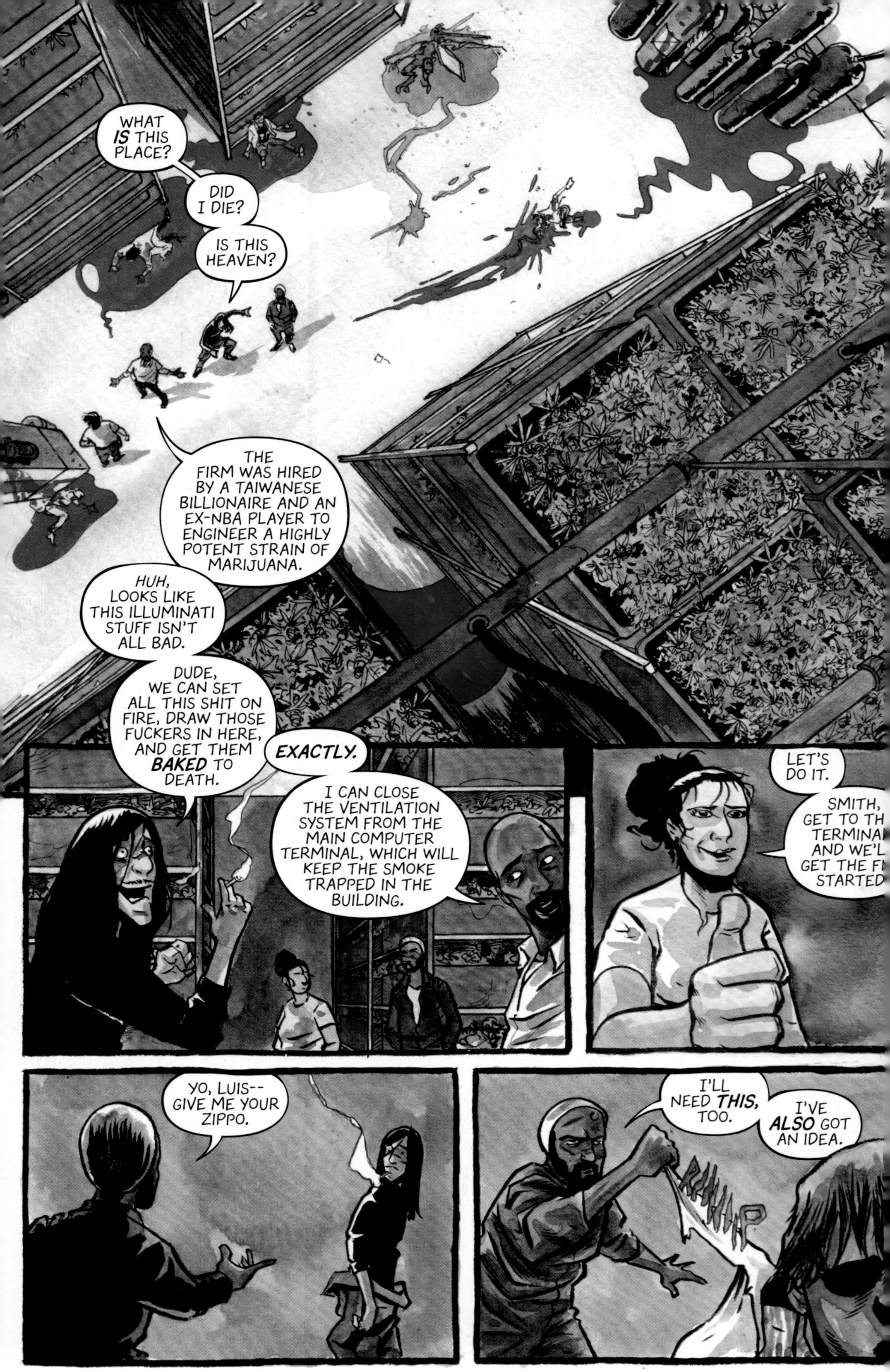
WHAT IS THIS PLACE?
DID I DIE?
IS THIS HEAVEN?
THE FIRM WAS HIRED BY A TAIWANESE BILLIONAIRE AND AN EX-NBA PLAYER TO ENGINEER A HIGHLY POTENT STRAIN OF MARIJUANA.
HUH, LOOKS LIKE THIS ILLUMINATI STUFF ISN'T ALL BAD.
DUDE, WE CAN SET ALL THIS SHIT ON FIRE, DRAW THOSE FUCKERS IN HERE, AND GET THEM BAKED TO DEATH.
EXACTLY.
I CAN CLOSE THE VENTILATION SYSTEM FROM THE MAIN COMPUTER TERMINAL, WHICH WILL KEEP THE SMOKE TRAPPED IN THE BUILDING.
LET'S DO IT.
YO, LUIS-- GIVE ME YOUR ZIPPO.
I'LL NEED THIS, TOO.
I'VE ALSO GOT AN IDEA.

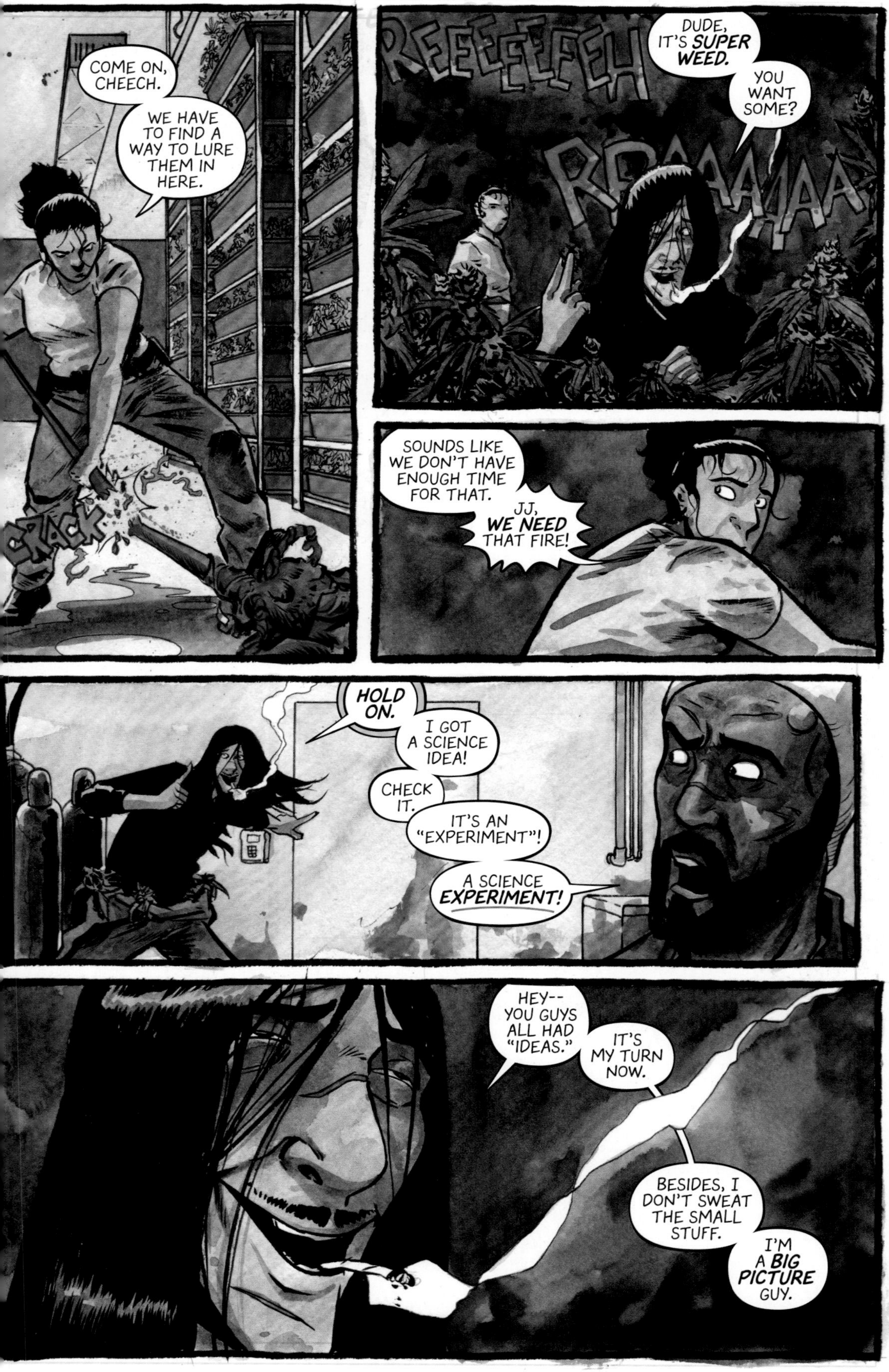
COME ON, CHEECH.
WE HAVE TO FIND A WAY TO LURE THEM IN HERE.
CRACK
REEEEEEEH
DUDE, IT'S **SUPER WEED.**
YOU WANT SOME?
RRAAAAAA
SOUNDS LIKE WE DON'T HAVE ENOUGH TIME FOR THAT.
JJ, **WE NEED** THAT FIRE!
HOLD ON.
I GOT A SCIENCE IDEA!
CHECK IT.
IT'S AN "EXPERIMENT"!
A SCIENCE **EXPERIMENT!**
HEY-- YOU GUYS ALL HAD "IDEAS."
IT'S MY TURN NOW.
BESIDES, I DON'T SWEAT THE SMALL STUFF.
I'M A **BIG PICTURE** GUY.

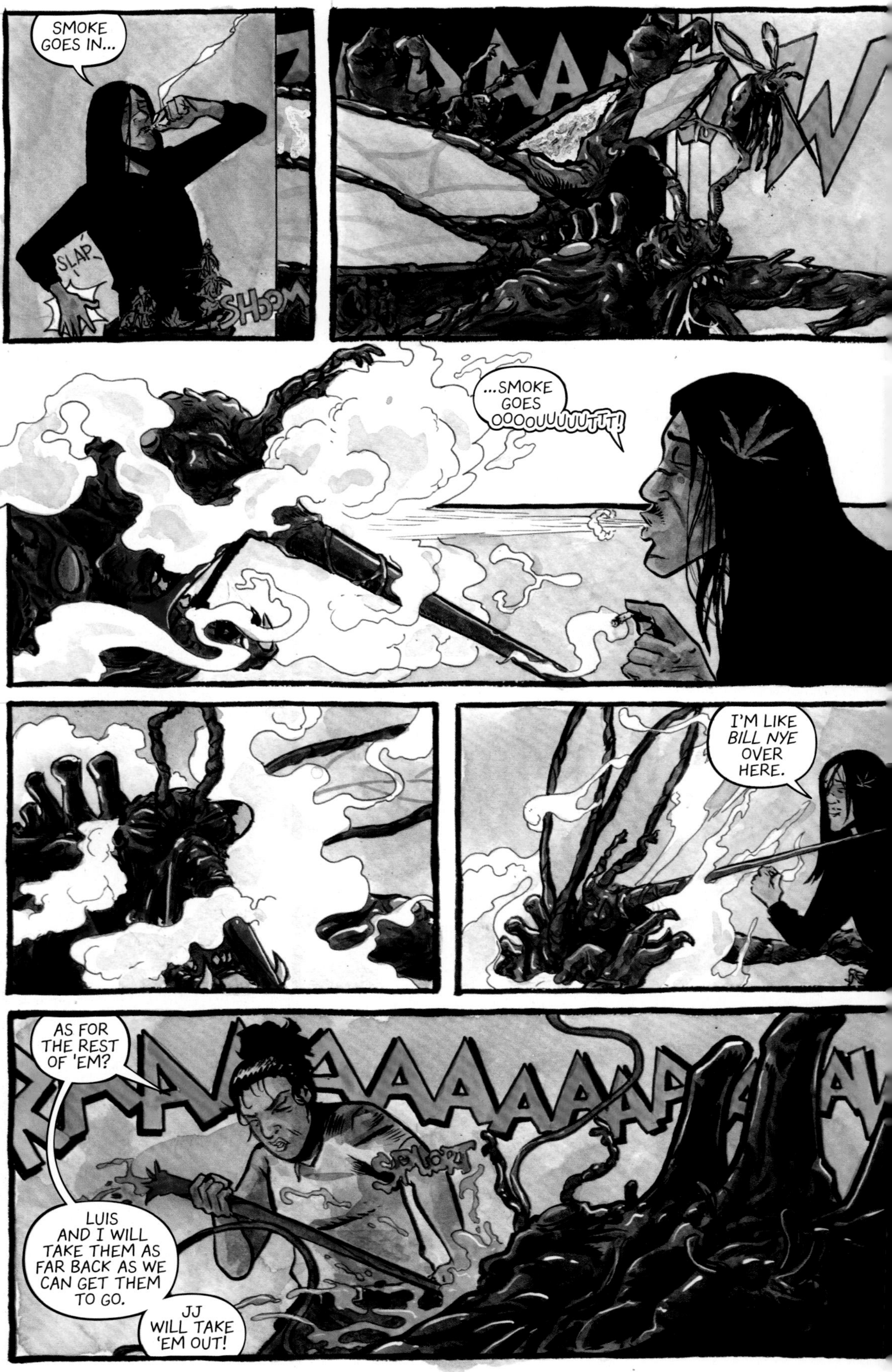
SMOKE GOES IN...
SLAP
SHOOM
...SMOKE GOES OOOOUUUUUTTTT!
I'M LIKE *BILL NYE* OVER HERE.
AS FOR THE REST OF 'EM?
LUIS AND I WILL TAKE THEM AS FAR BACK AS WE CAN GET THEM TO GO.
JJ WILL TAKE 'EM OUT!

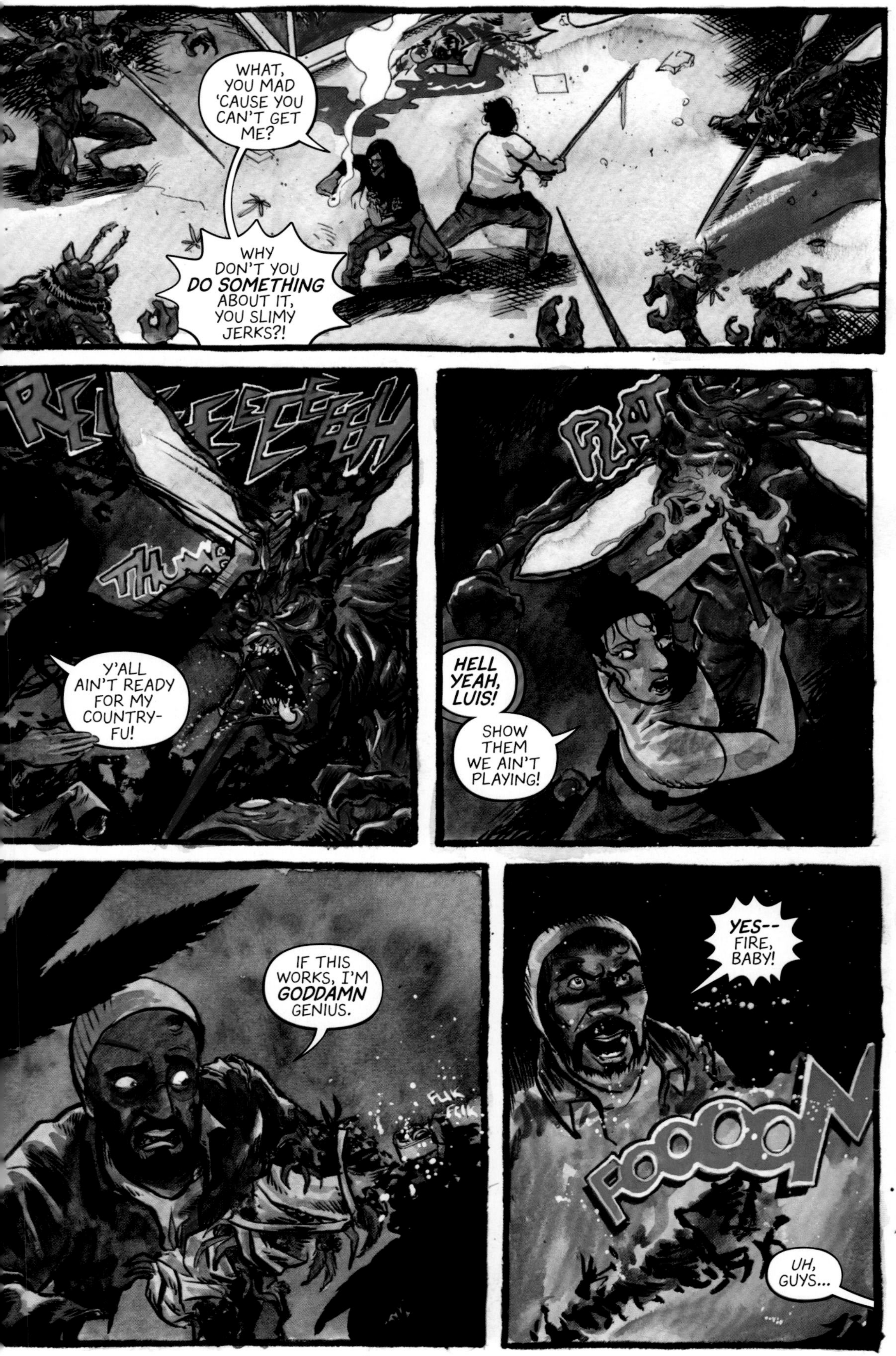
WHAT, YOU MAD 'CAUSE YOU CAN'T GET ME?
WHY DON'T YOU **DO SOMETHING** ABOUT IT, YOU SLIMY JERKS?!
Y'ALL AIN'T READY FOR MY COUNTRY-FU!
HELL YEAH, LUIS!
SHOW THEM WE AIN'T PLAYING!
IF THIS WORKS, I'M **GODDAMN** GENIUS.
YES-- FIRE, BABY!
UH, GUYS...

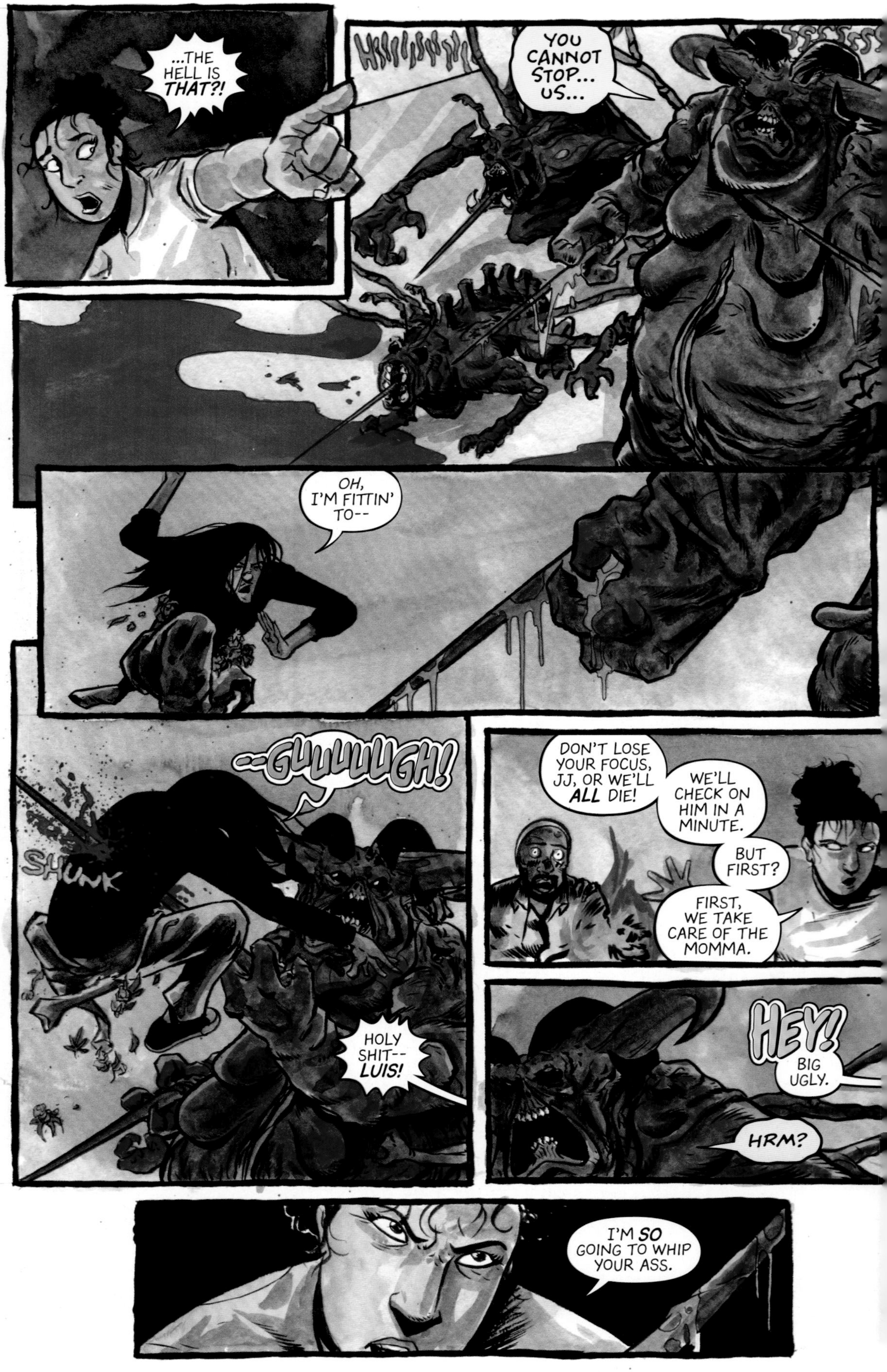
...THE HELL IS THAT?!
HHHHHHH
YOU CANNOT STOP... US...
SSSSSSS
OH, I'M FITTIN' TO--
--GUUUUUGH!
SHUNK
HOLY SHIT-- LUIS!
DON'T LOSE YOUR FOCUS, JJ, OR WE'LL ALL DIE!
WE'LL CHECK ON HIM IN A MINUTE.
BUT FIRST?
FIRST, WE TAKE CARE OF THE MOMMA.
HEY!
BIG UGLY.
HRM?
I'M SO GOING TO WHIP YOUR ASS.

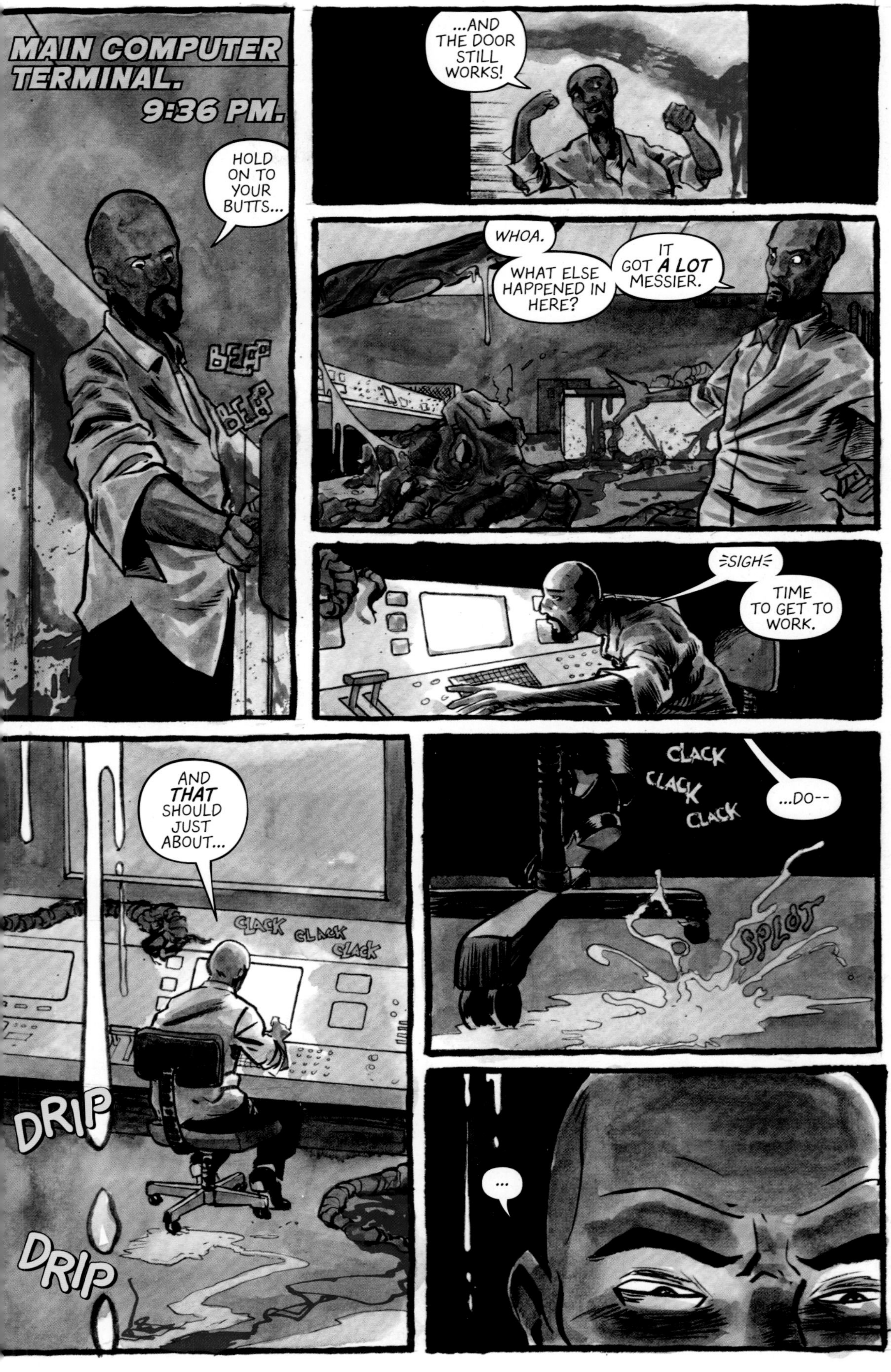
MAIN COMPUTER TERMINAL.
9:36 PM.
HOLD ON TO YOUR BUTTS...
BEEP
BEEP
...AND THE DOOR STILL WORKS!
WHOA.
WHAT ELSE HAPPENED IN HERE?
IT GOT A LOT MESSIER.
SIGH
TIME TO GET TO WORK.
AND THAT SHOULD JUST ABOUT...
CLACK CLACK CLACK
DRIP
DRIP
CLACK
CLACK
CLACK
...DO--
SPLOT
...

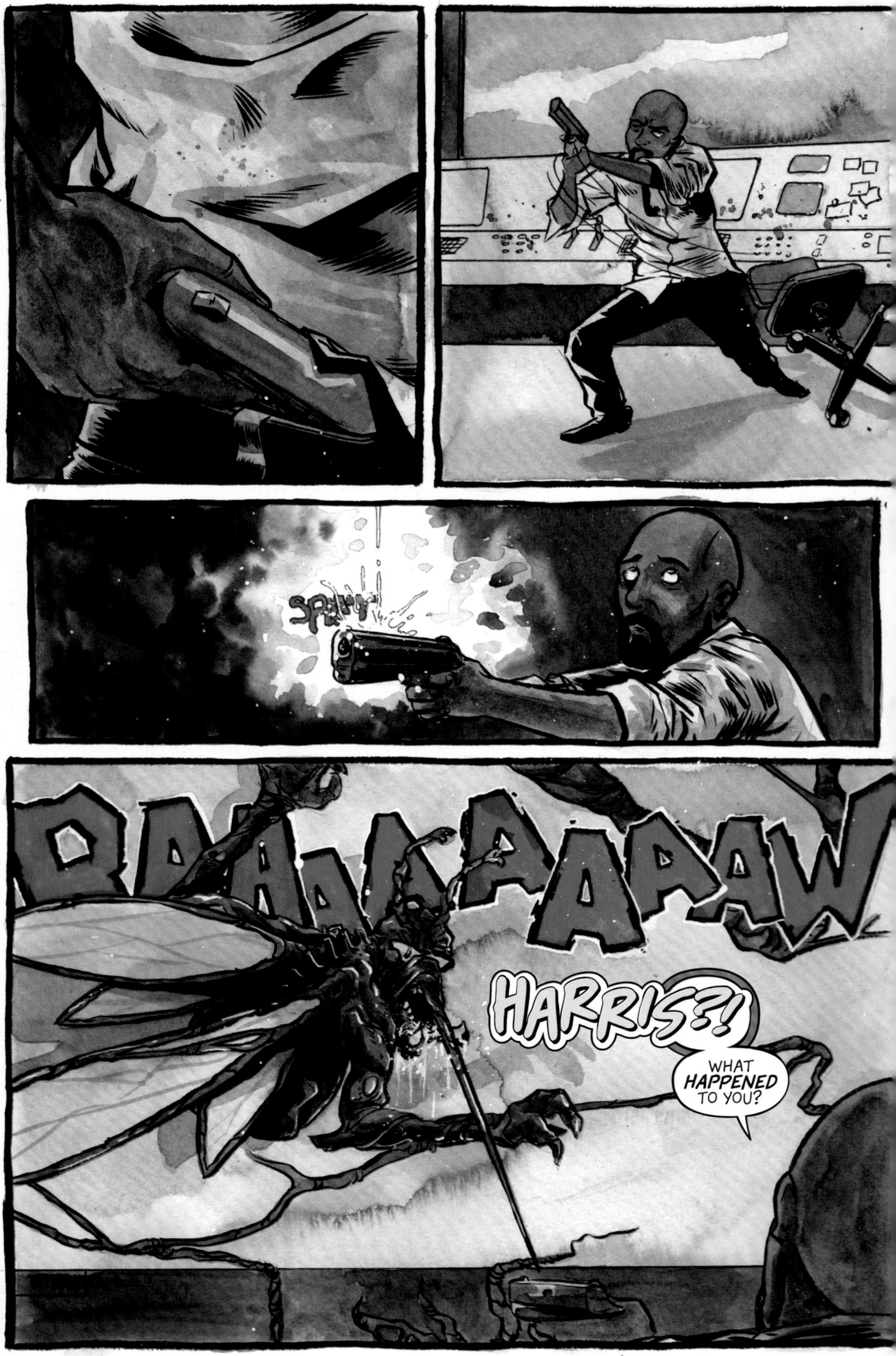
RAAAAAAAW
HARRIS?!
WHAT HAPPENED TO YOU?

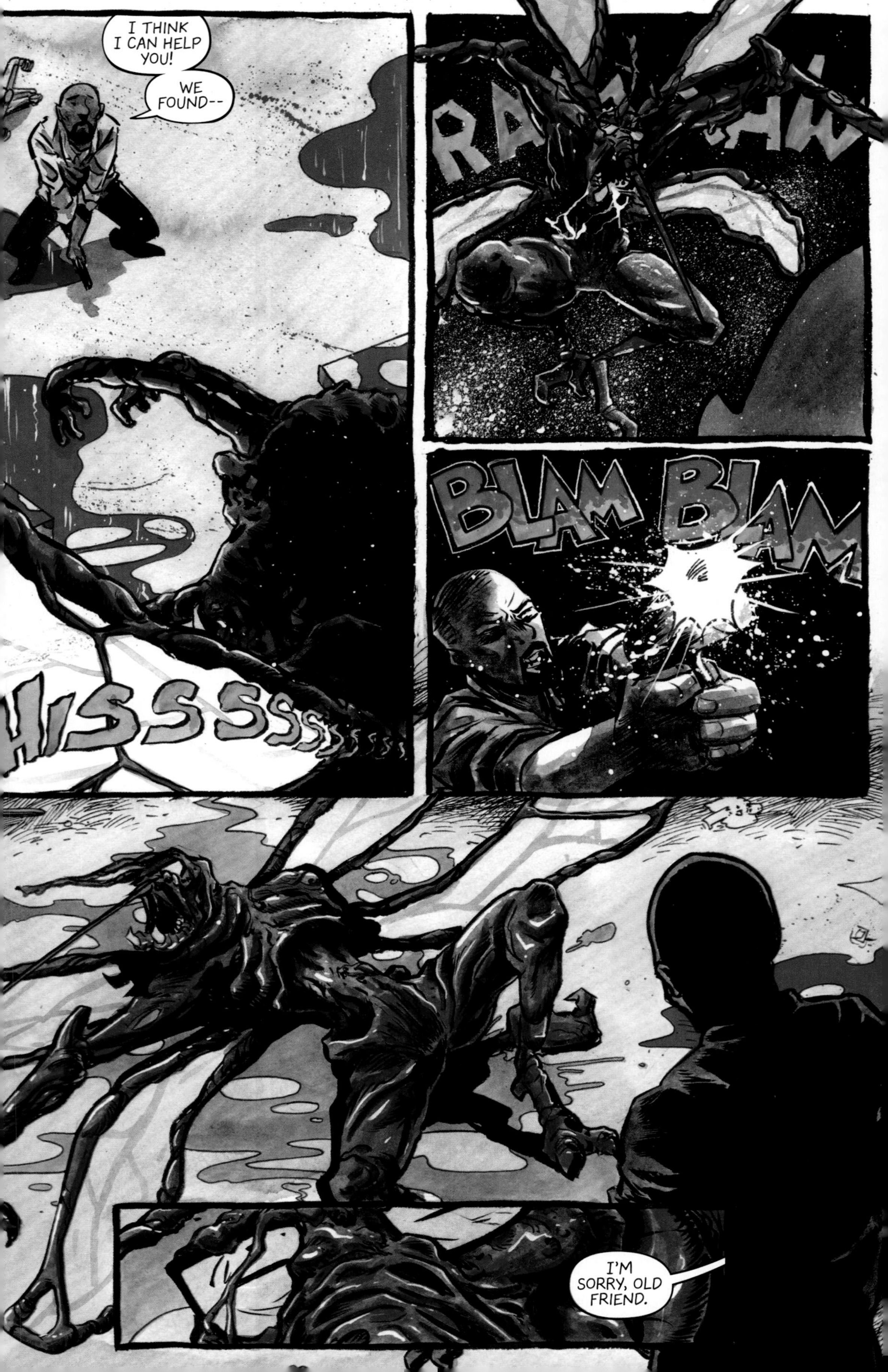
I THINK I CAN HELP YOU!
WE FOUND--
HISSSSS
RAWW
BLAM BLAM
I'M SORRY, OLD FRIEND.

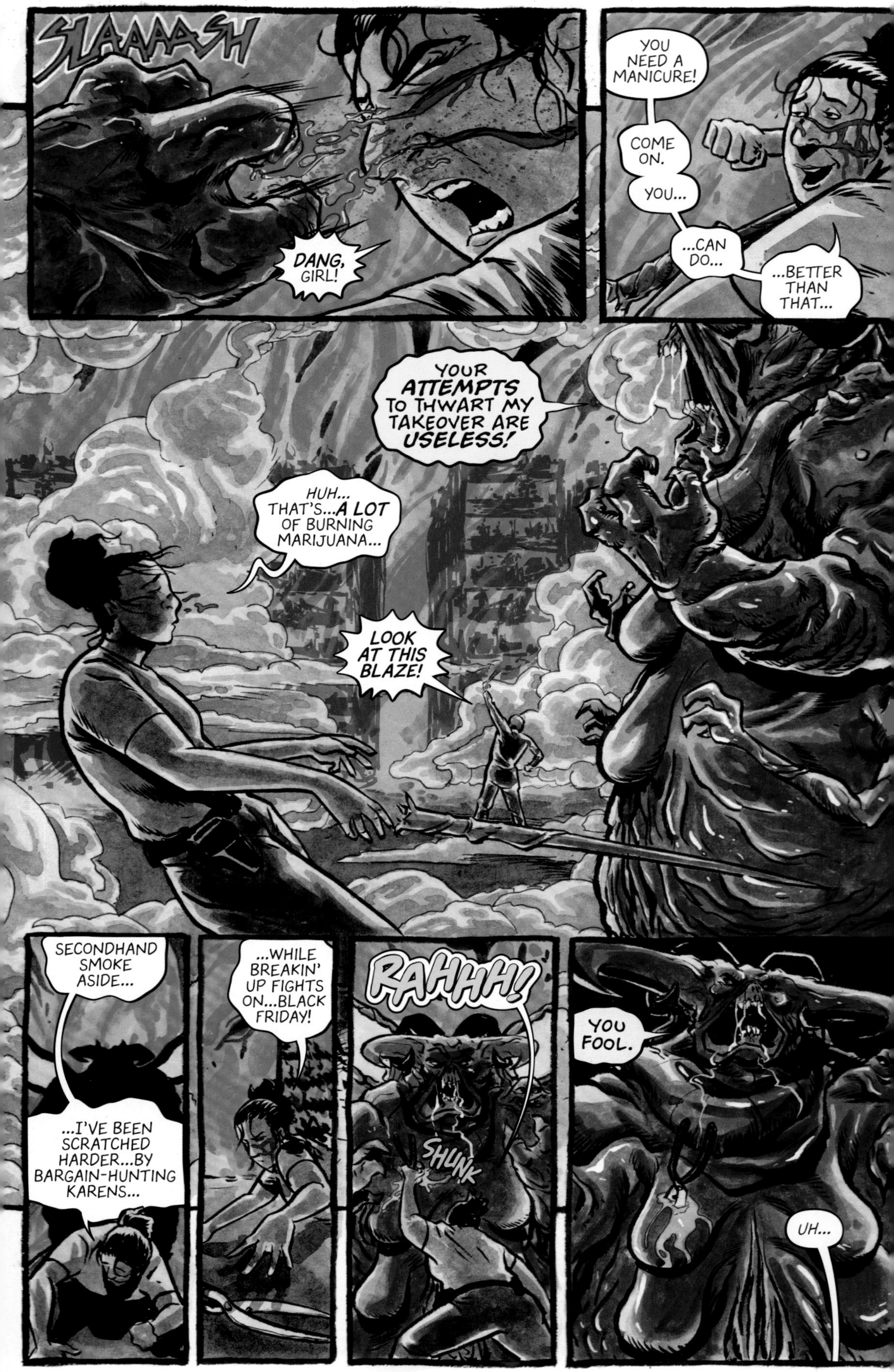
SLAAAASH
DANG, GIRL!
YOU NEED A MANICURE!
COME ON.
YOU...
...CAN DO...
...BETTER THAN THAT...
YOUR ATTEMPTS TO THWART MY TAKEOVER ARE USELESS!
HUH... THAT'S...A LOT OF BURNING MARIJUANA...
LOOK AT THIS BLAZE!
SECONDHAND SMOKE ASIDE...
...I'VE BEEN SCRATCHED HARDER...BY BARGAIN-HUNTING KARENS...
...WHILE BREAKIN' UP FIGHTS ON...BLACK FRIDAY!
RAHHH!
SHUNK
YOU FOOL.
UH...

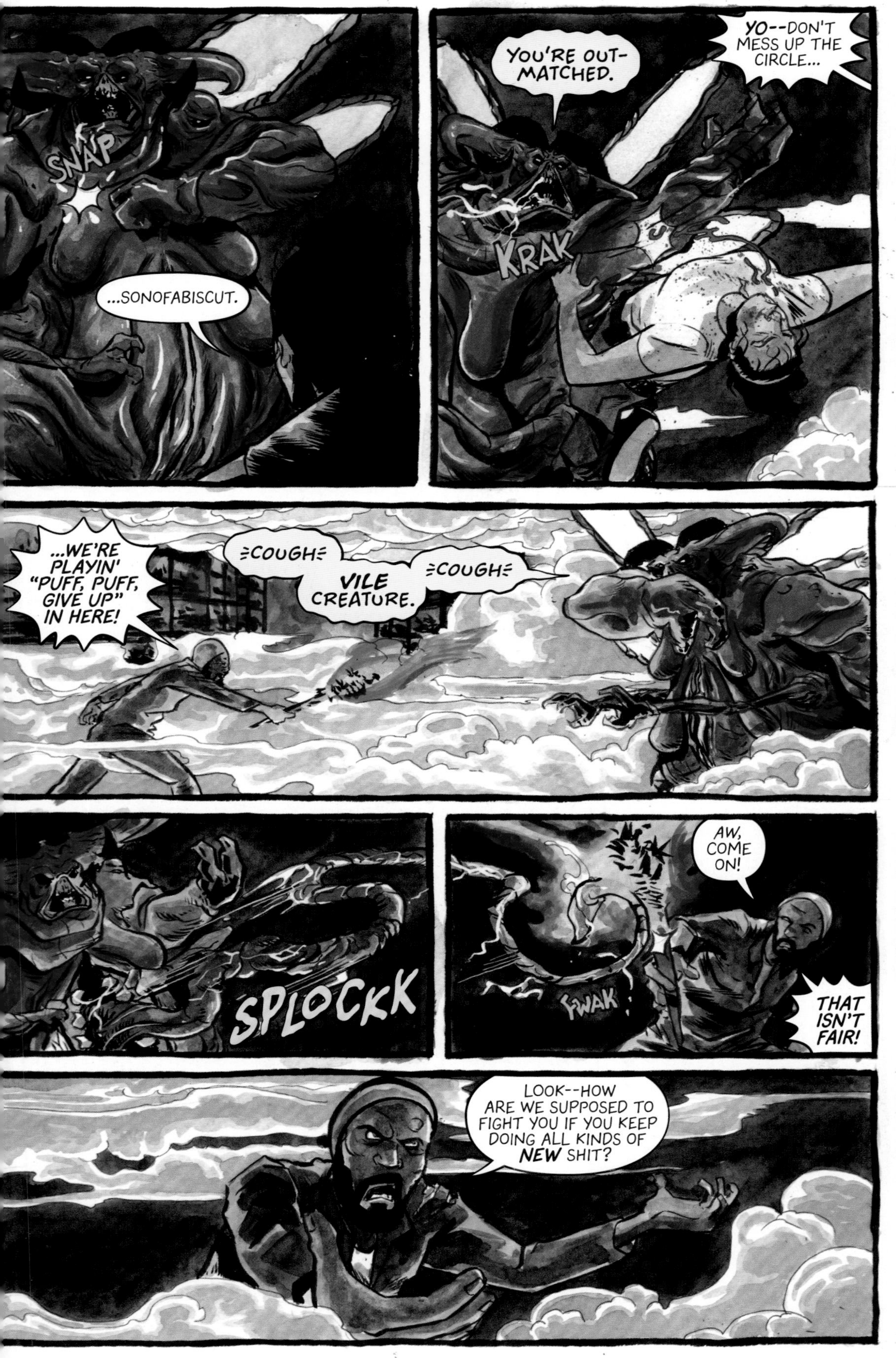
SNAP
...SONOFABISCUT.
YOU'RE OUT-MATCHED.
YO--DON'T MESS UP THE CIRCLE...
KRAK
...WE'RE PLAYIN' "PUFF, PUFF, GIVE UP" IN HERE!
COUGH
VILE CREATURE.
COUGH
SPLOCKK
FWAK
AW, COME ON!
THAT ISN'T FAIR!
LOOK--HOW ARE WE SUPPOSED TO FIGHT YOU IF YOU KEEP DOING ALL KINDS OF NEW SHIT?

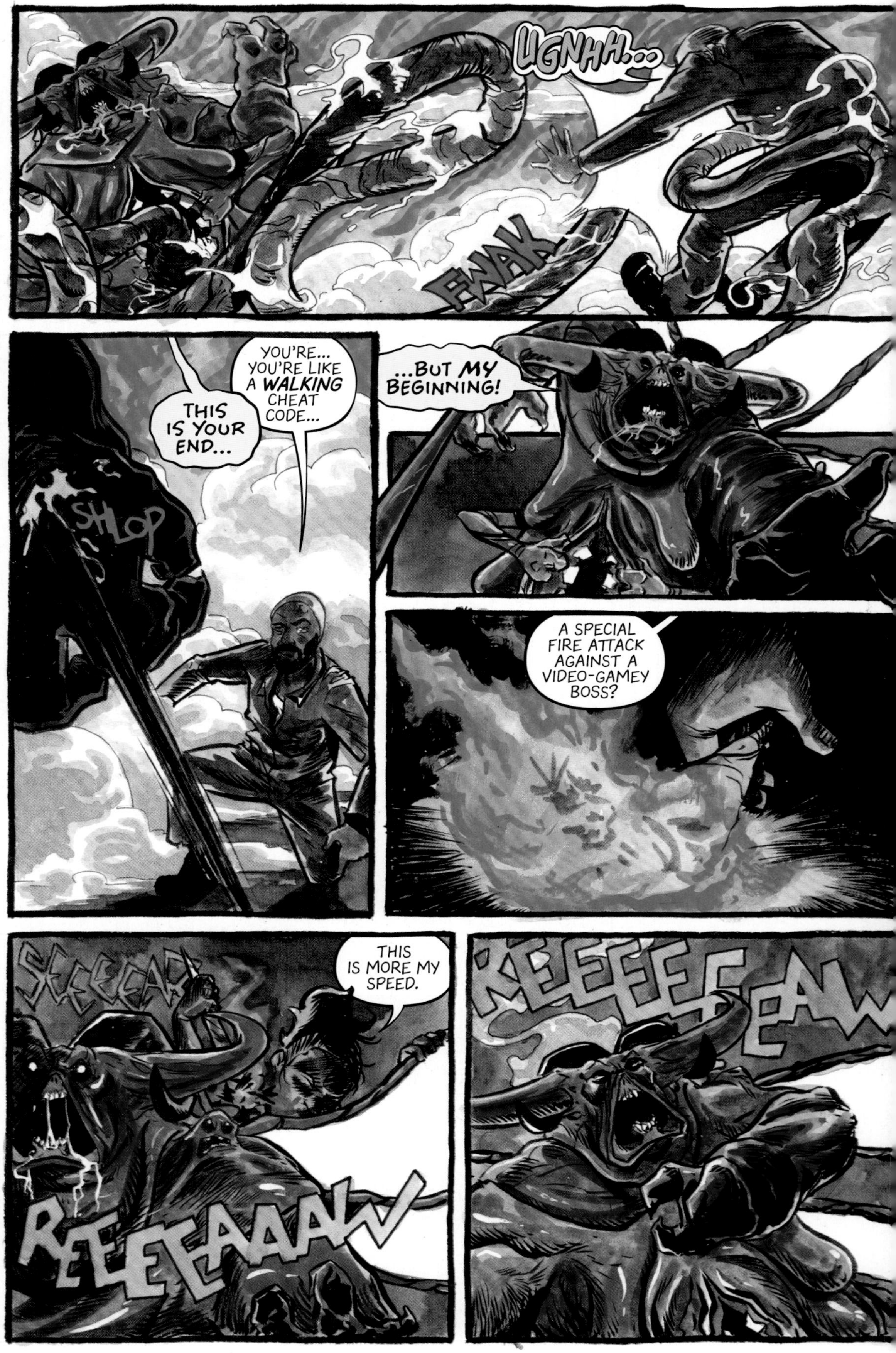
UGNHH...
FWAK
THIS IS YOUR END...
YOU'RE... YOU'RE LIKE A WALKING CHEAT CODE...
...BUT MY BEGINNING!
SHLOP
A SPECIAL FIRE ATTACK AGAINST A VIDEO-GAMEY BOSS?
THIS IS MORE MY SPEED.
REEEAAAW
REEEEEEAW

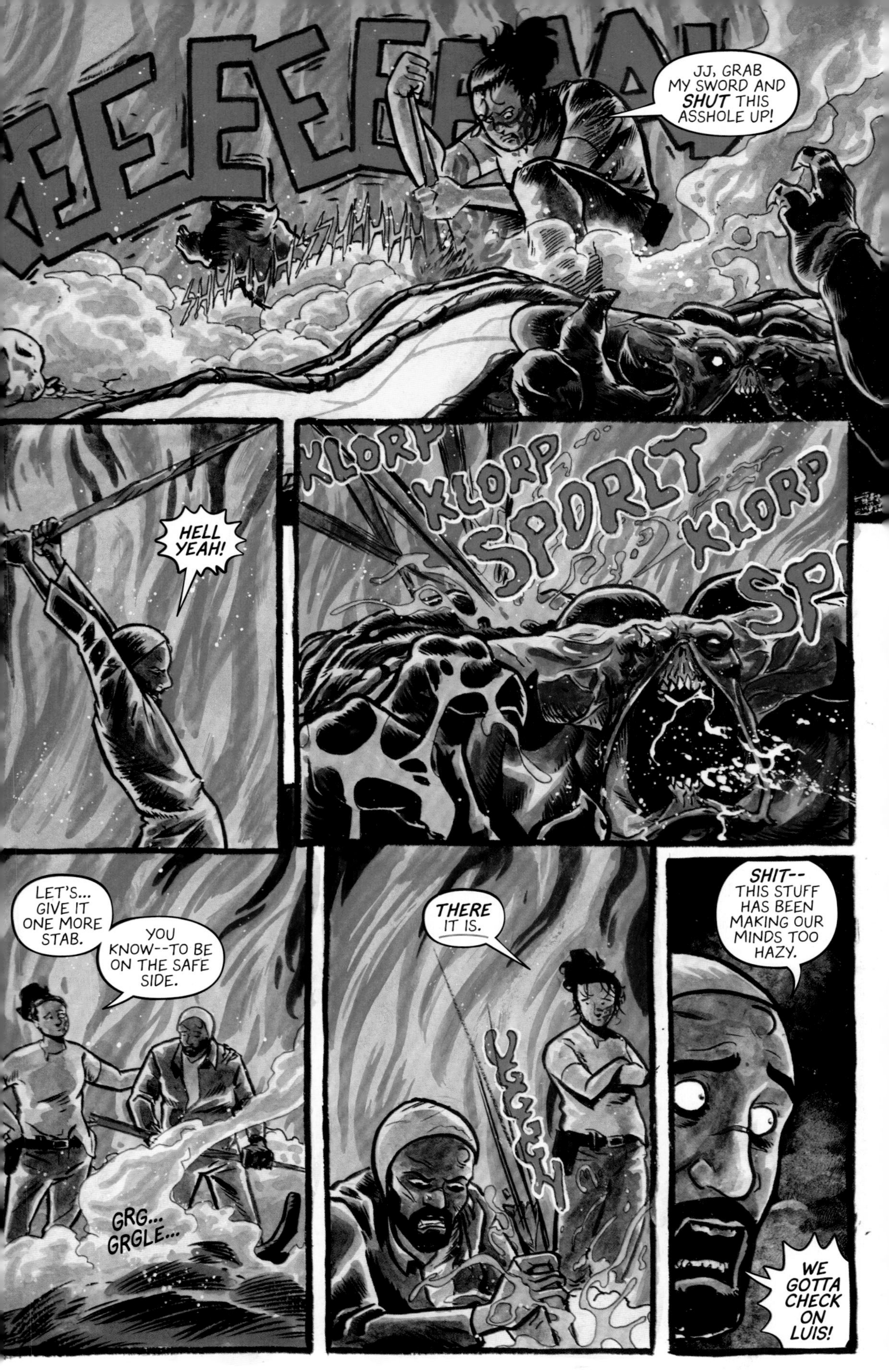
EEEEAA
JJ, GRAB MY SWORD AND SHUT THIS ASSHOLE UP!
SHHHHHSSHHHHH
HELL YEAH!
KLORP
KLORP
SPORLT
KLORP
SP
LET'S... GIVE IT ONE MORE STAB.
YOU KNOW--TO BE ON THE SAFE SIDE.
GRG... GRGLE...
THERE IT IS.
SHIT-- THIS STUFF HAS BEEN MAKING OUR MINDS TOO HAZY.
WE GOTTA CHECK ON LUIS!

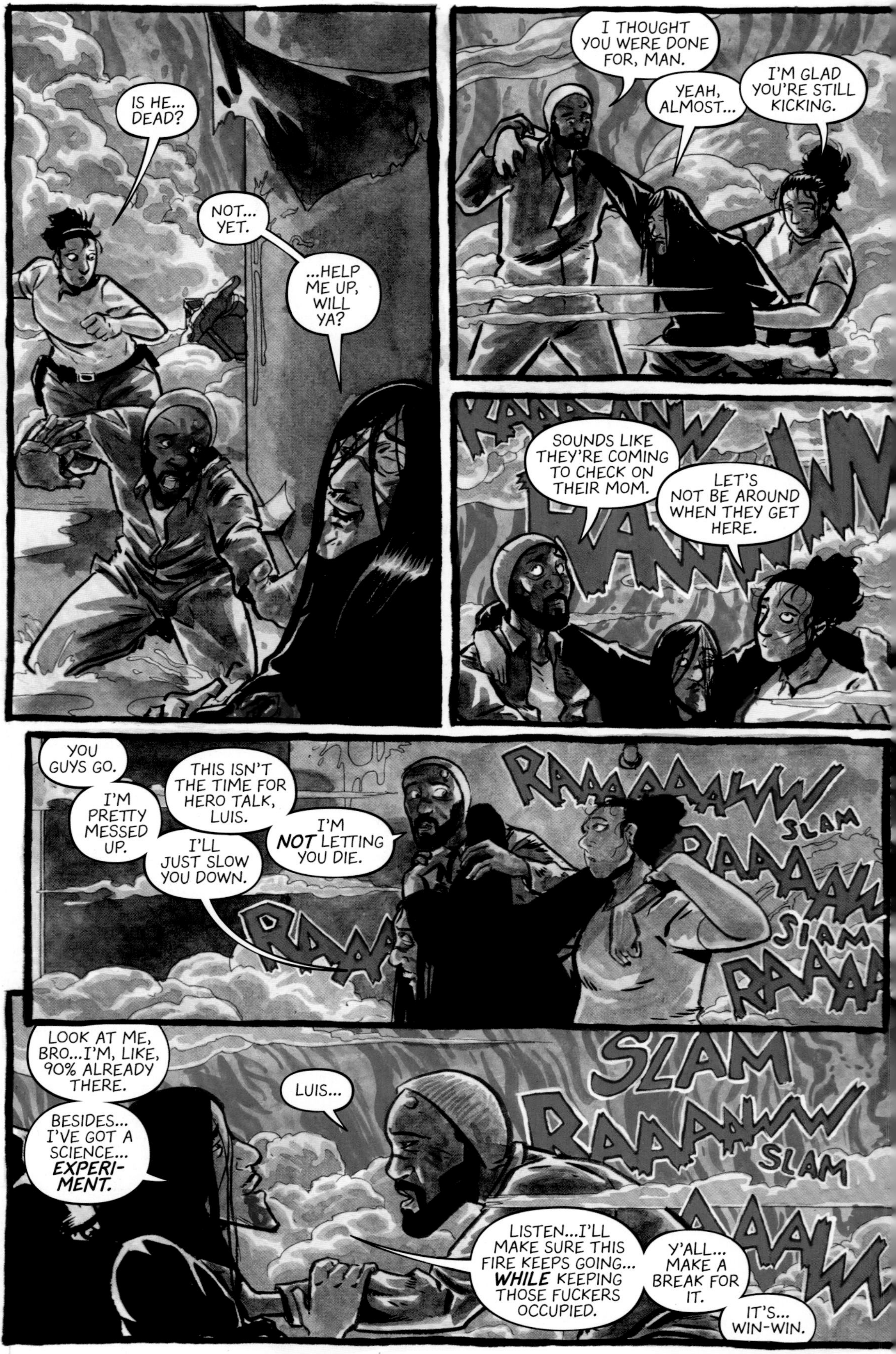
IS HE... DEAD?
NOT... YET.
...HELP ME UP, WILL YA?
I THOUGHT YOU WERE DONE FOR, MAN.
YEAH, ALMOST...
I'M GLAD YOU'RE STILL KICKING.
SOUNDS LIKE THEY'RE COMING TO CHECK ON THEIR MOM.
LET'S NOT BE AROUND WHEN THEY GET HERE.
YOU GUYS GO.
I'M PRETTY MESSED UP.
I'LL JUST SLOW YOU DOWN.
THIS ISN'T THE TIME FOR HERO TALK, LUIS.
I'M **NOT** LETTING YOU DIE.
RAAAAAWW
SLAM
SLAM
LOOK AT ME, BRO...I'M, LIKE, 90% ALREADY THERE.
BESIDES... I'VE GOT A SCIENCE... ***EXPERI-MENT.***
LUIS...
SLAM
RAAAAWW
SLAM
LISTEN...I'LL MAKE SURE THIS FIRE KEEPS GOING... ***WHILE*** KEEPING THOSE FUCKERS OCCUPIED.
Y'ALL... MAKE A BREAK FOR IT.
IT'S... WIN-WIN.

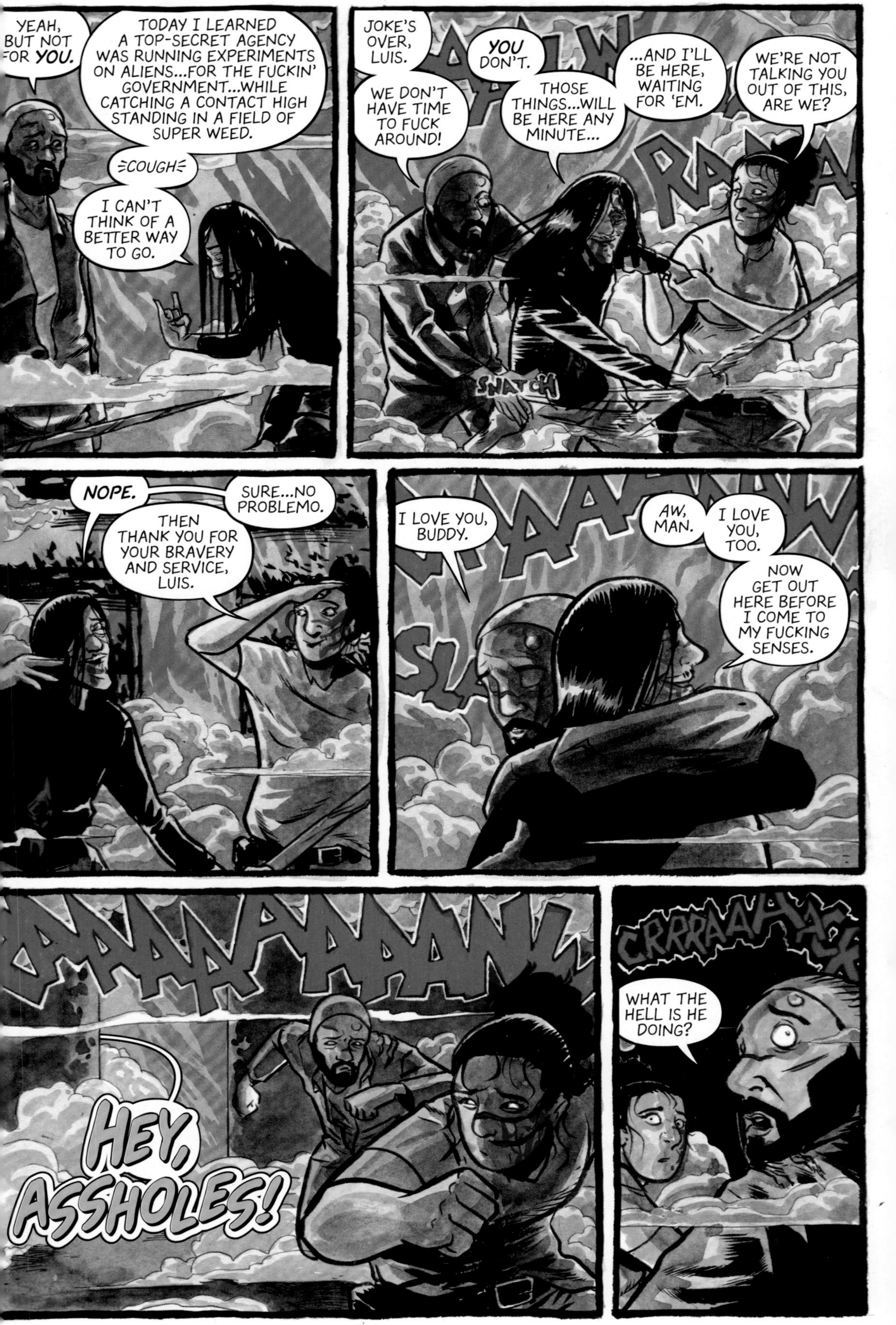
YEAH, BUT NOT FOR YOU.
TODAY I LEARNED A TOP-SECRET AGENCY WAS RUNNING EXPERIMENTS ON ALIENS...FOR THE FUCKIN' GOVERNMENT...WHILE CATCHING A CONTACT HIGH STANDING IN A FIELD OF SUPER WEED.
COUGH
I CAN'T THINK OF A BETTER WAY TO GO.
JOKE'S OVER, LUIS.
WE DON'T HAVE TIME TO FUCK AROUND!
YOU DON'T.
THOSE THINGS...WILL BE HERE ANY MINUTE...
...AND I'LL BE HERE, WAITING FOR 'EM.
WE'RE NOT TALKING YOU OUT OF THIS, ARE WE?
SNATCH
NOPE.
SURE...NO PROBLEMO.
THEN THANK YOU FOR YOUR BRAVERY AND SERVICE, LUIS.
I LOVE YOU, BUDDY.
AW, MAN.
I LOVE YOU, TOO.
NOW GET OUT HERE BEFORE I COME TO MY FUCKING SENSES.
HEY, ASSHOLES!
CRRRAAAACK
WHAT THE HELL IS HE DOING?

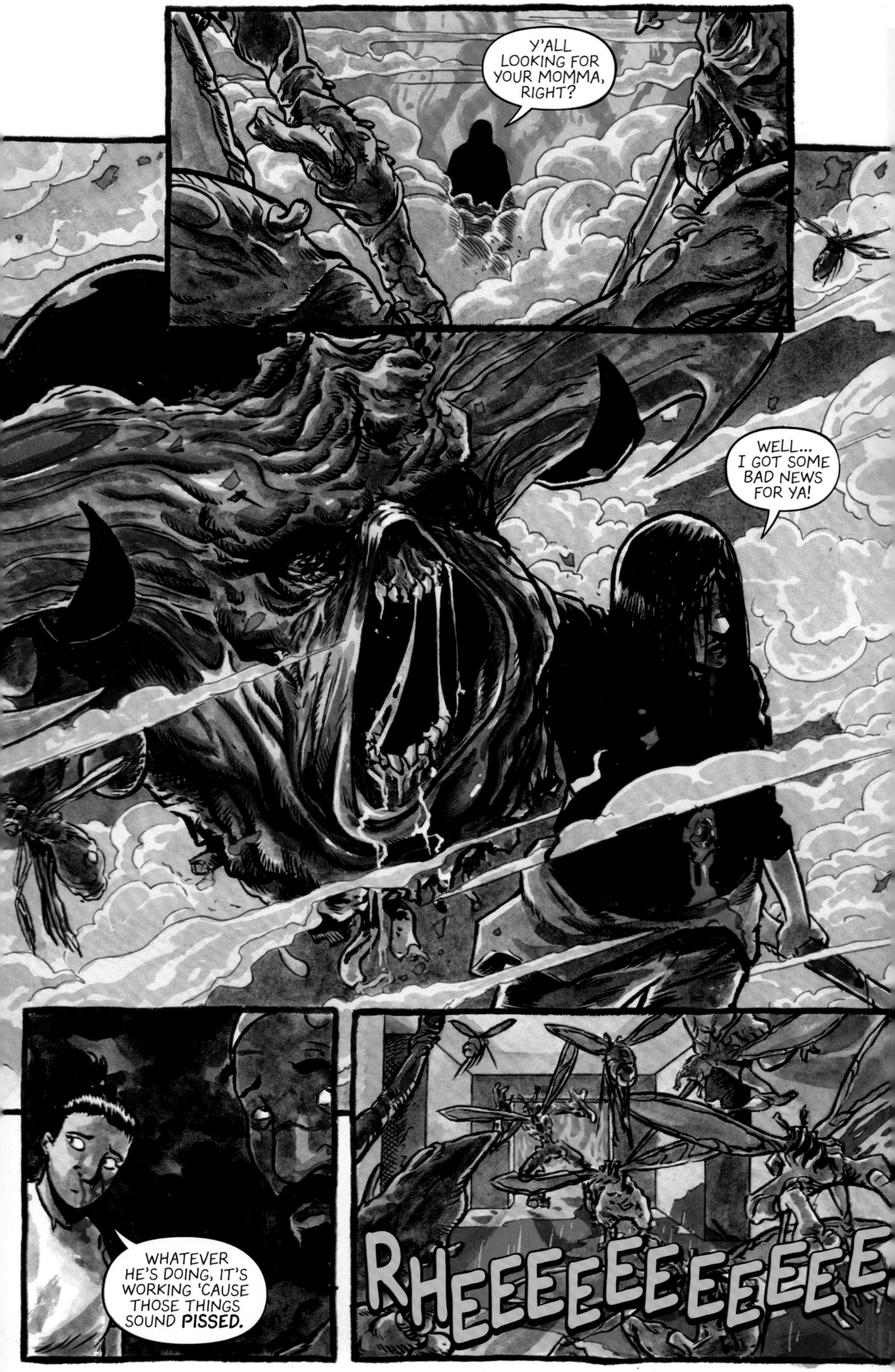
Y'ALL LOOKING FOR YOUR MOMMA, RIGHT?
WELL... I GOT SOME BAD NEWS FOR YA!
WHATEVER HE'S DOING, IT'S WORKING 'CAUSE THOSE THINGS SOUND **PISSED.**
RHEEEEEEEEEEEE

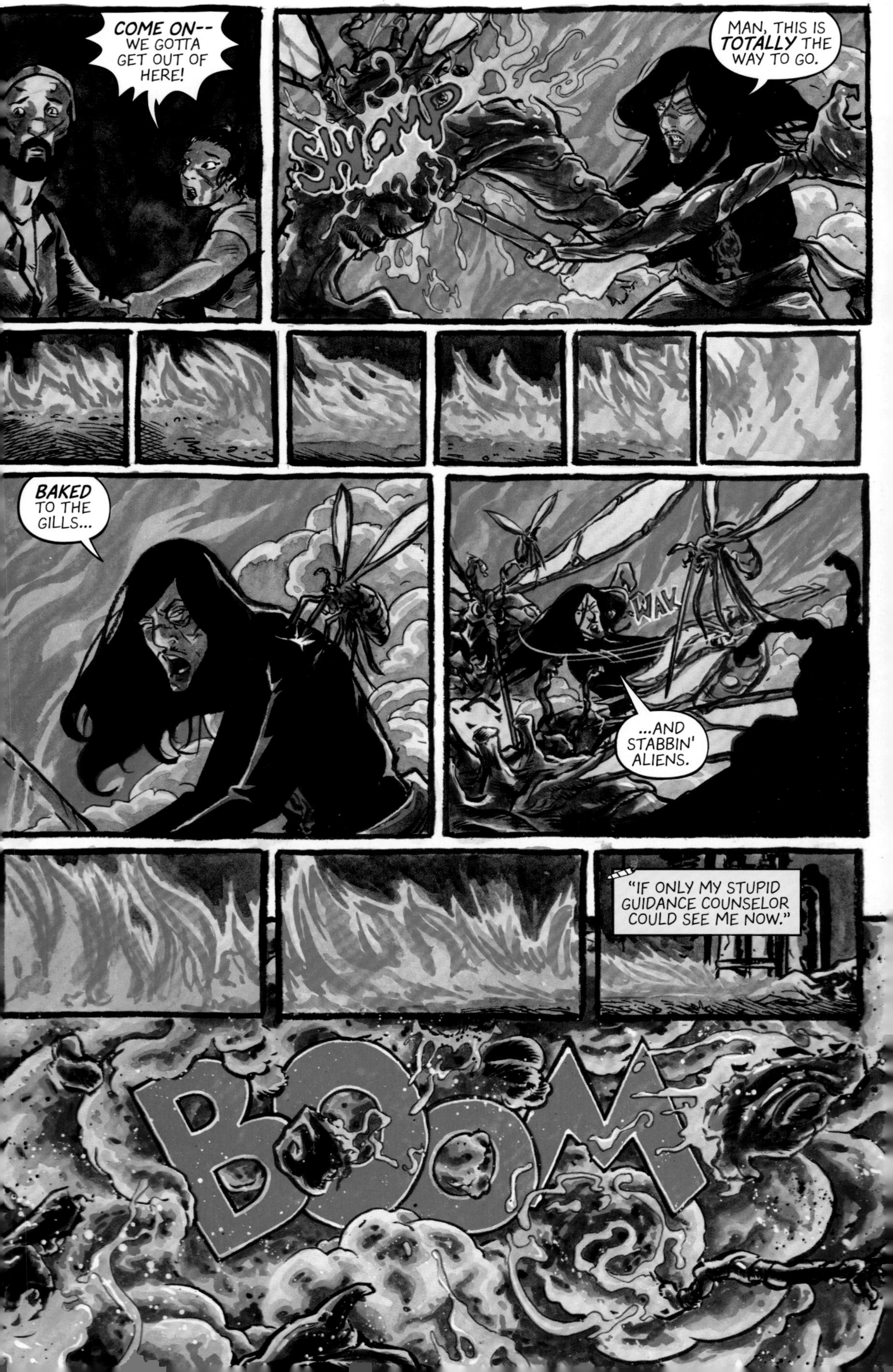
COME ON-- WE GOTTA GET OUT OF HERE!
MAN, THIS IS TOTALLY THE WAY TO GO.
SHOMP
BAKED TO THE GILLS...
WAK
...AND STABBIN' ALIENS.
"IF ONLY MY STUPID GUIDANCE COUNSELOR COULD SEE ME NOW."
BOOM

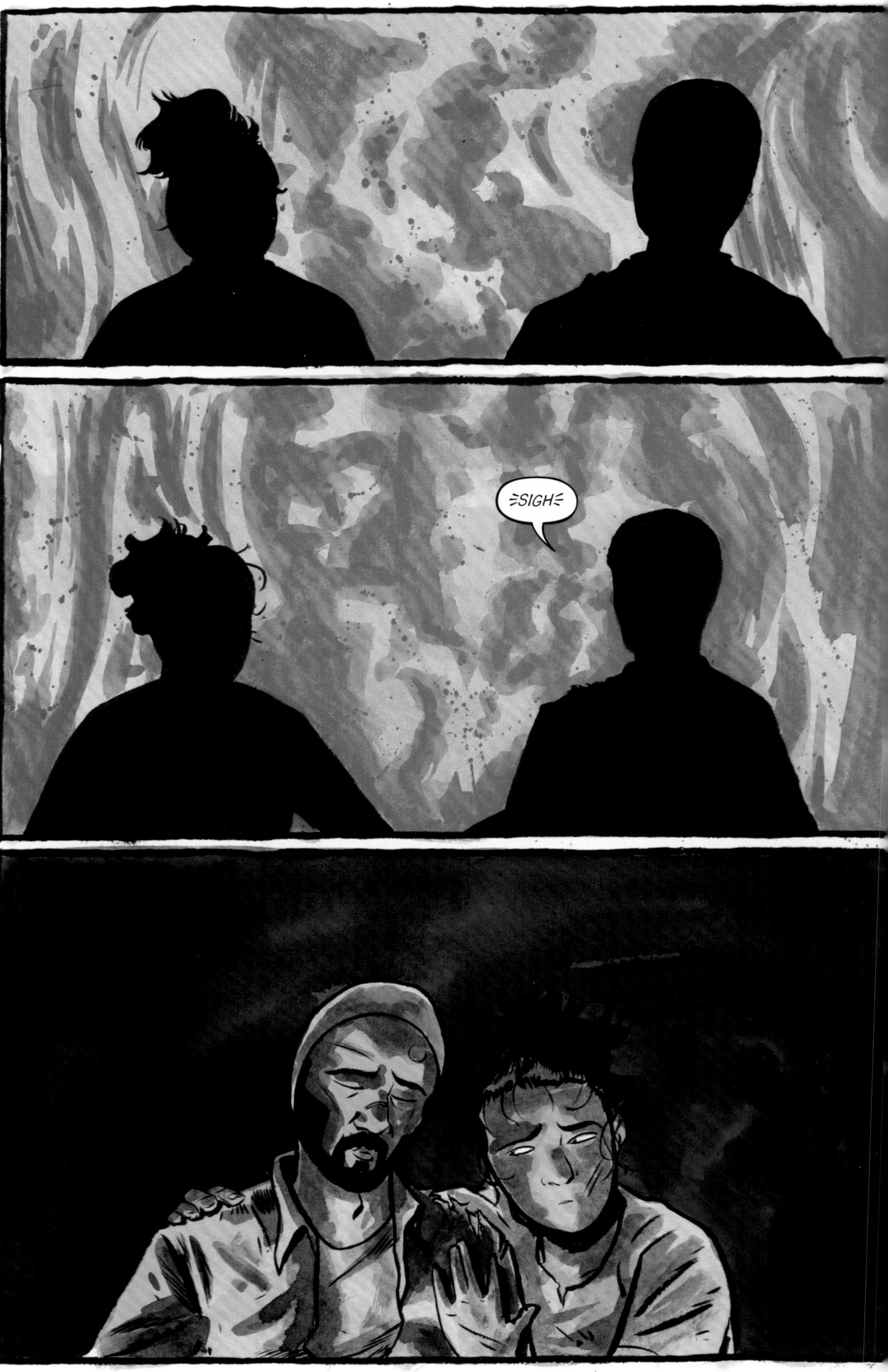
SIGH

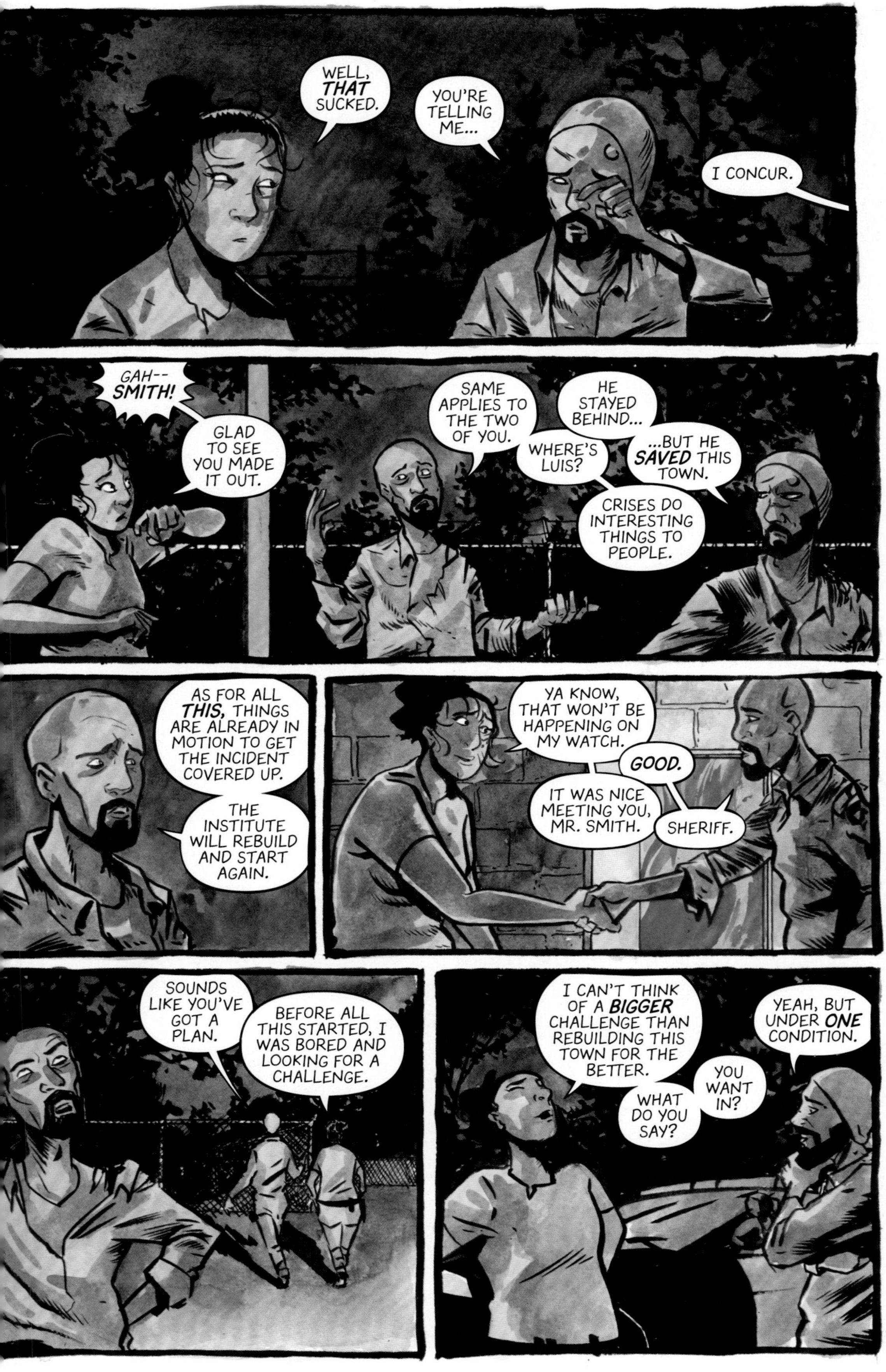
WELL, THAT SUCKED.
YOU'RE TELLING ME...
I CONCUR.
GAH-- SMITH!
GLAD TO SEE YOU MADE IT OUT.
SAME APPLIES TO THE TWO OF YOU.
WHERE'S LUIS?
HE STAYED BEHIND...
...BUT HE SAVED THIS TOWN.
CRISES DO INTERESTING THINGS TO PEOPLE.
AS FOR ALL THIS, THINGS ARE ALREADY IN MOTION TO GET THE INCIDENT COVERED UP.
THE INSTITUTE WILL REBUILD AND START AGAIN.
YA KNOW, THAT WON'T BE HAPPENING ON MY WATCH.
GOOD.
IT WAS NICE MEETING YOU, MR. SMITH.
SHERIFF.
SOUNDS LIKE YOU'VE GOT A PLAN.
BEFORE ALL THIS STARTED, I WAS BORED AND LOOKING FOR A CHALLENGE.
I CAN'T THINK OF A BIGGER CHALLENGE THAN REBUILDING THIS TOWN FOR THE BETTER.
WHAT DO YOU SAY?
YOU WANT IN?
YEAH, BUT UNDER ONE CONDITION.

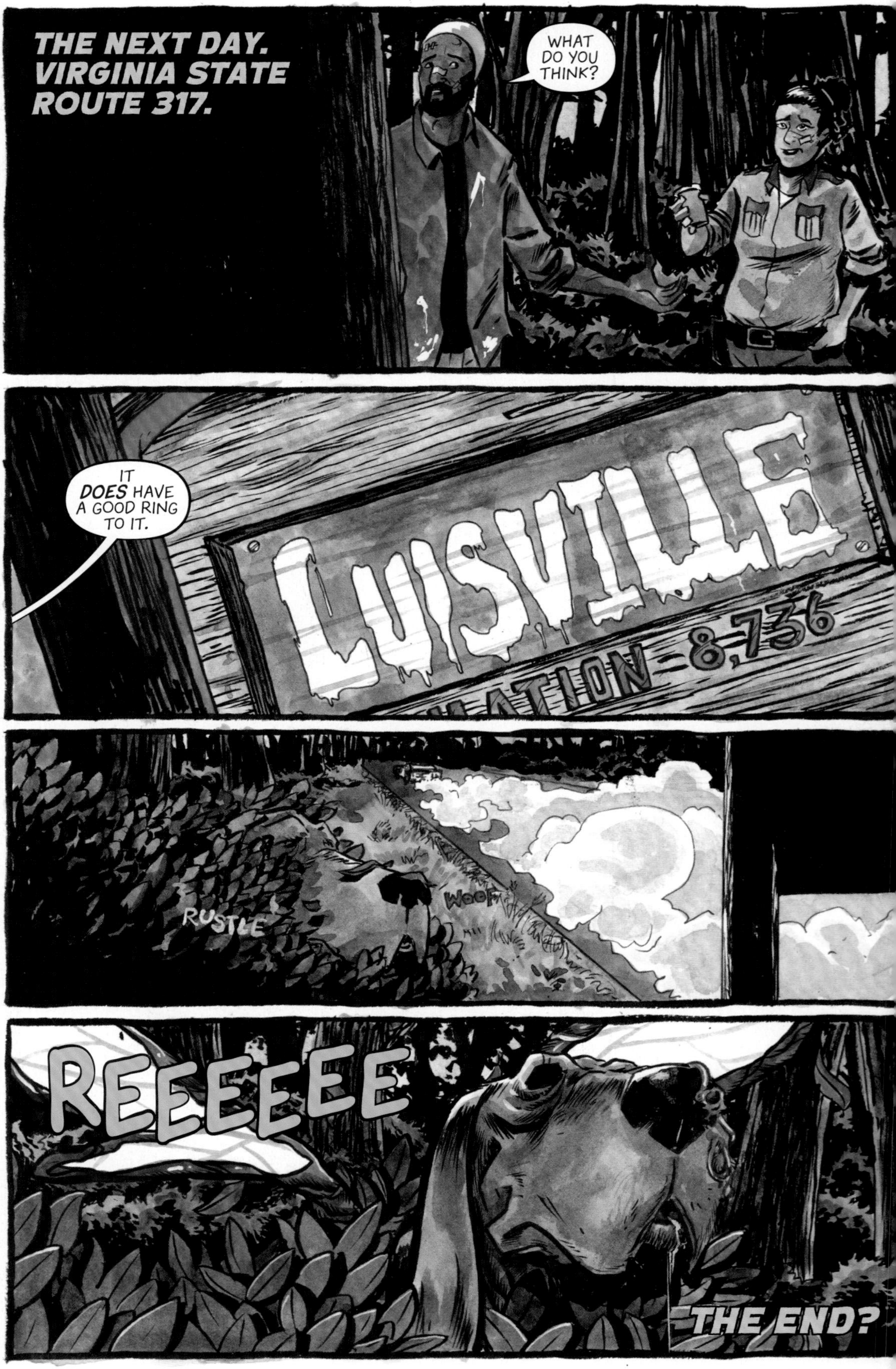
THE NEXT DAY. VIRGINIA STATE ROUTE 317.
WHAT DO YOU THINK?
IT DOES HAVE A GOOD RING TO IT.
LUISVILLE
...LATION 8,736
RUSTLE
WOOF
REEEEEE
THE END?

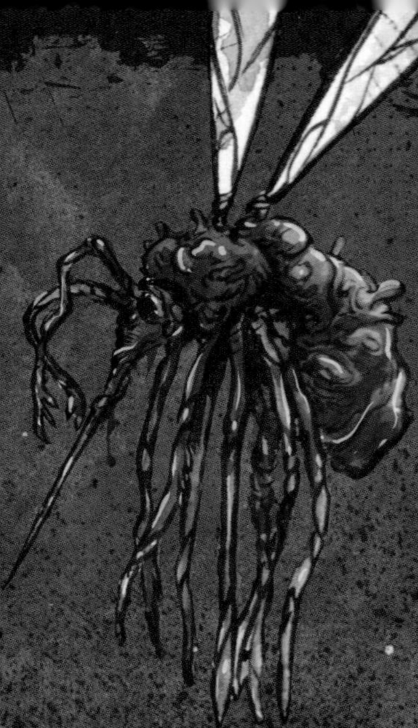

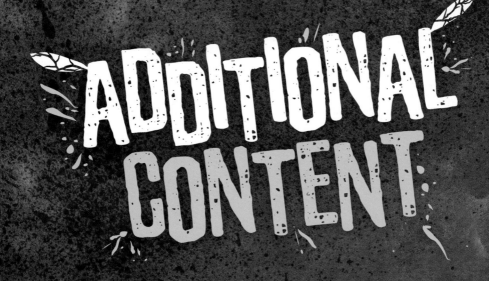

ADDITIONAL CONTENT

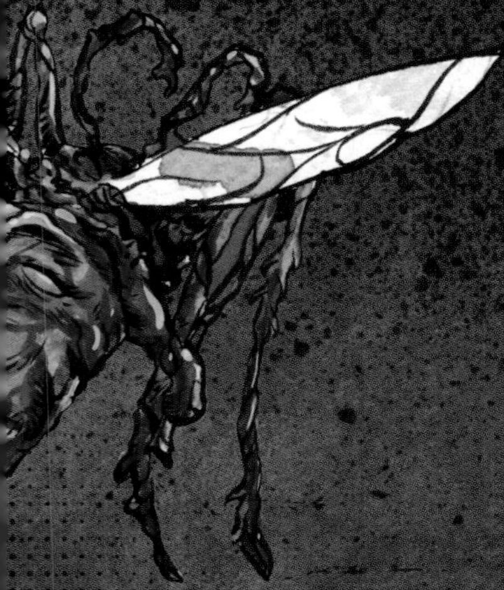

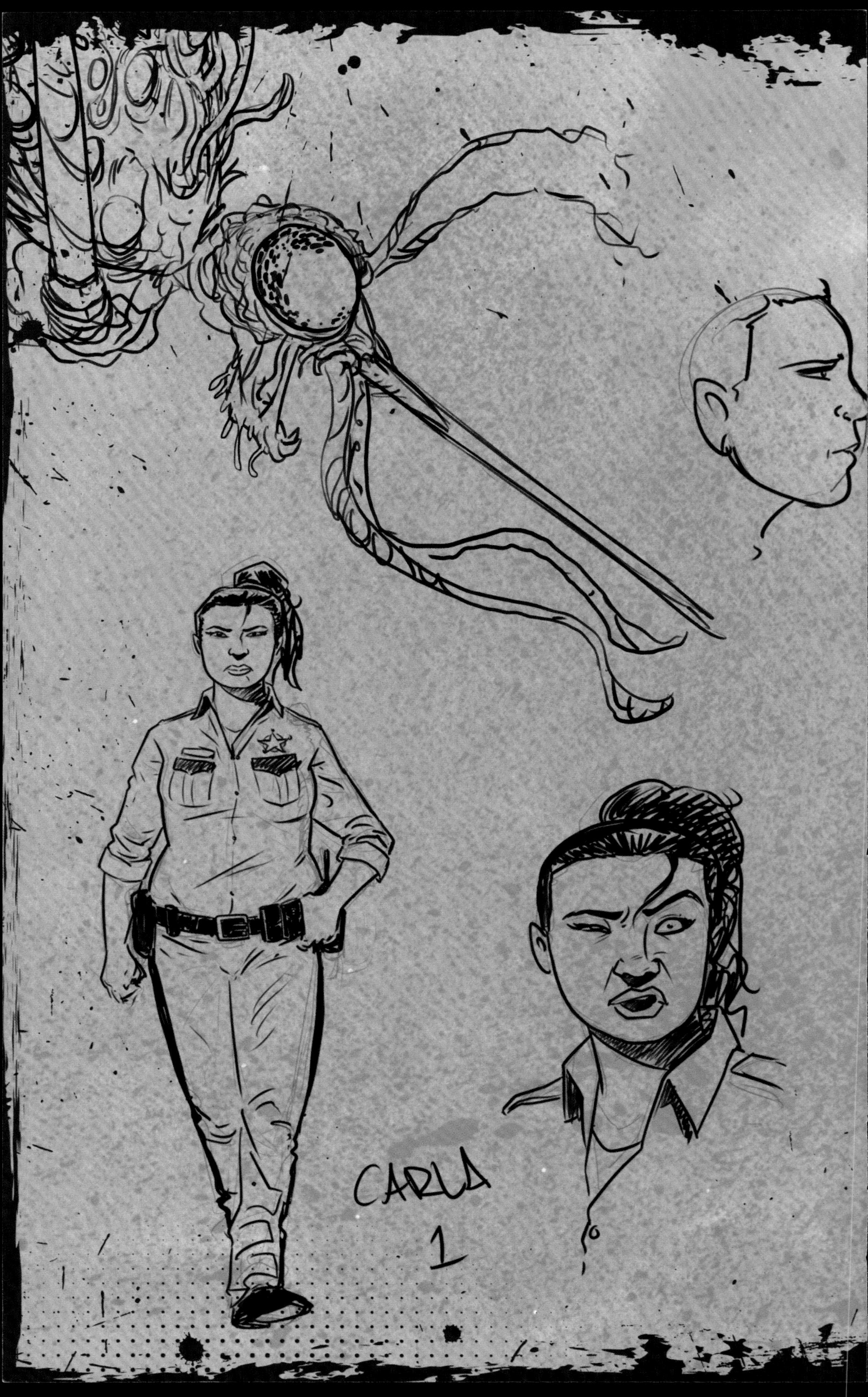
CARLA
1

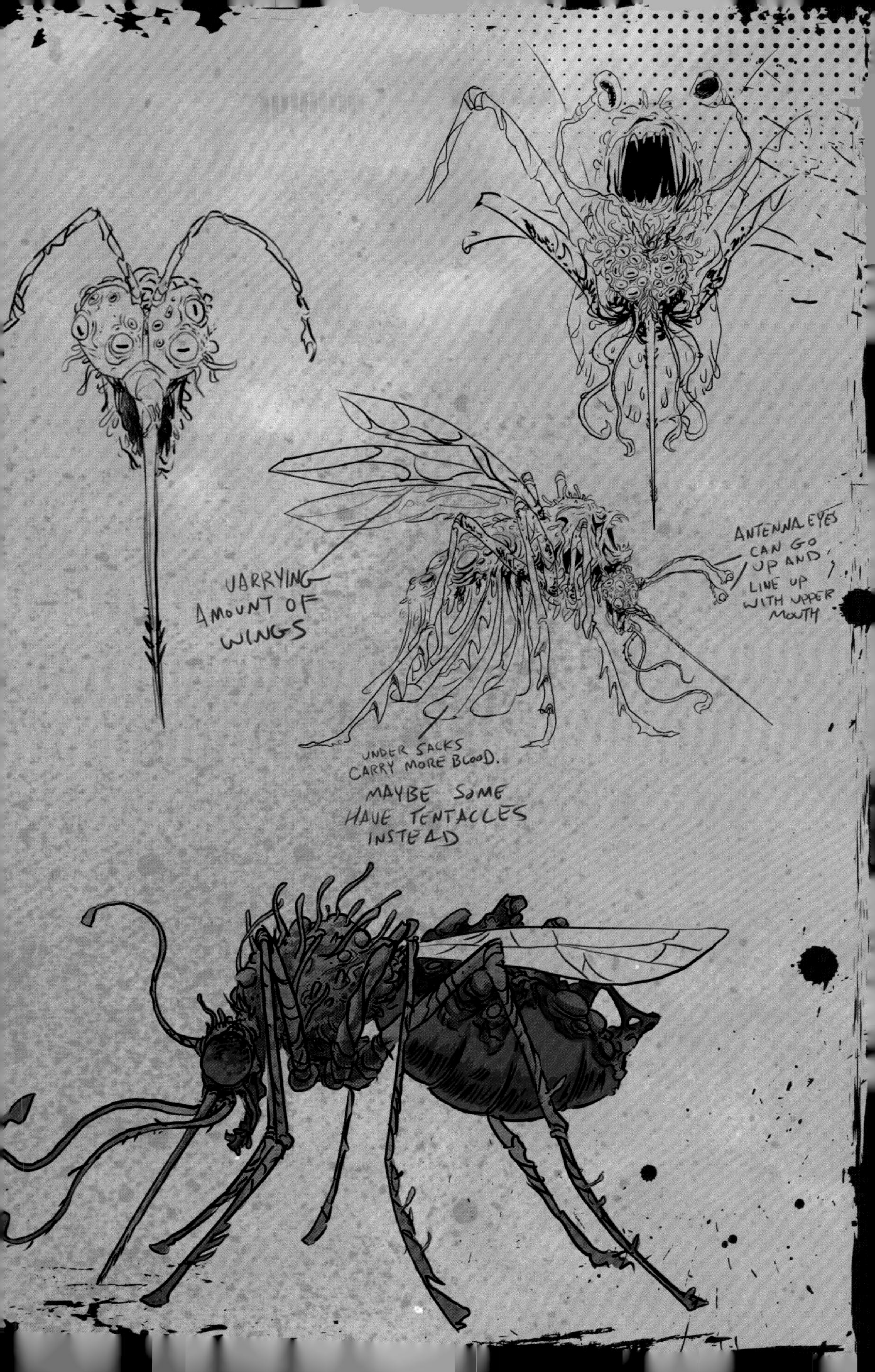

ANTENNA EYES CAN GO UP AND LINE UP WITH UPPER MOUTH
VARRYING AMOUNT OF WINGS
UNDER SACKS CARRY MORE BLOOD.
MAYBE SOME HAVE TENTACLES INSTEAD

Variant Cover B (Lunar exclusive) - Skeeters #1 ✱ Artist: Tervor Henderson

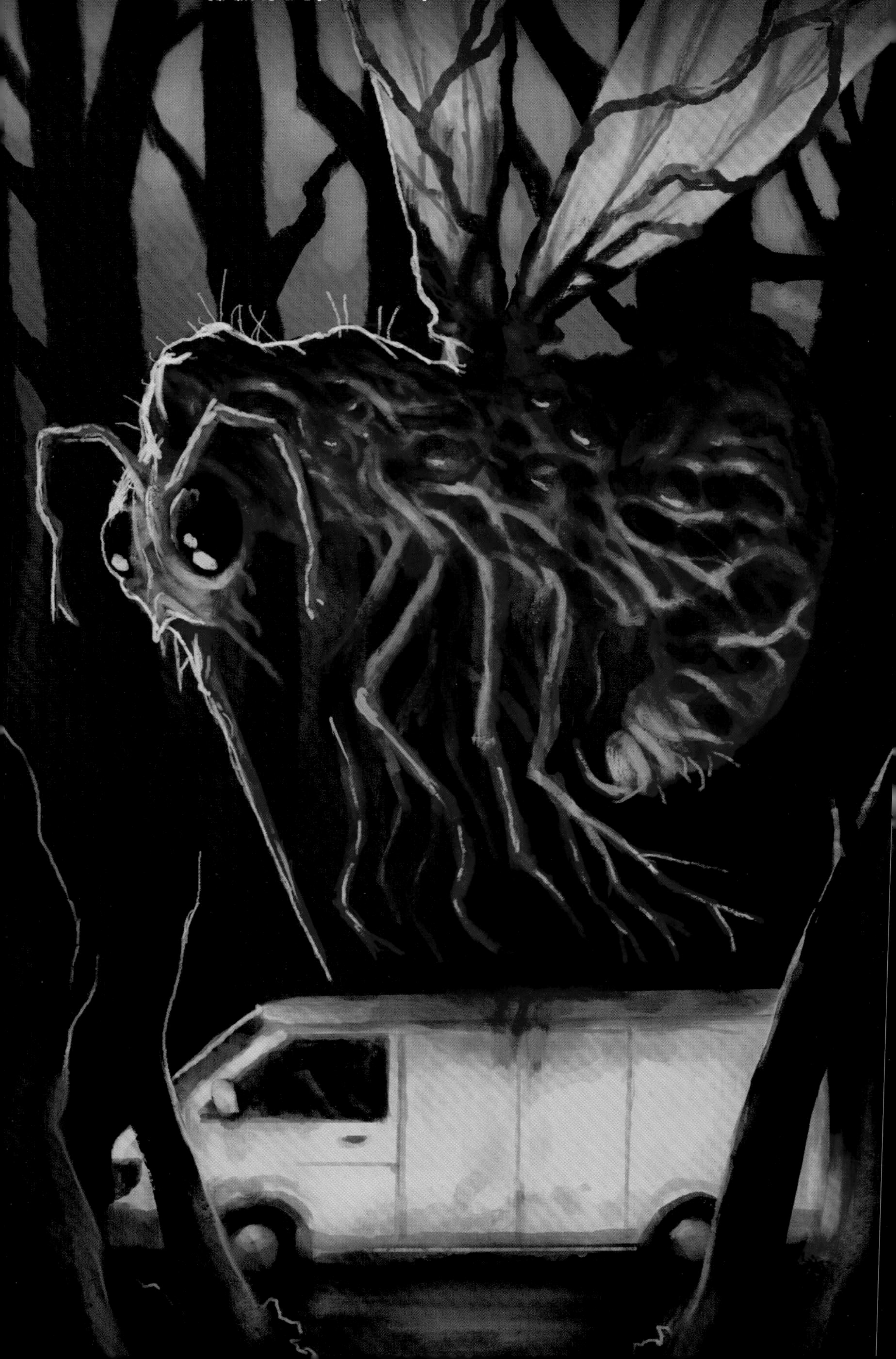

Variant Cover (Four Color Fantasies exclusive) - Skeeters #1 ✺ Artist: Hobbes Holluck

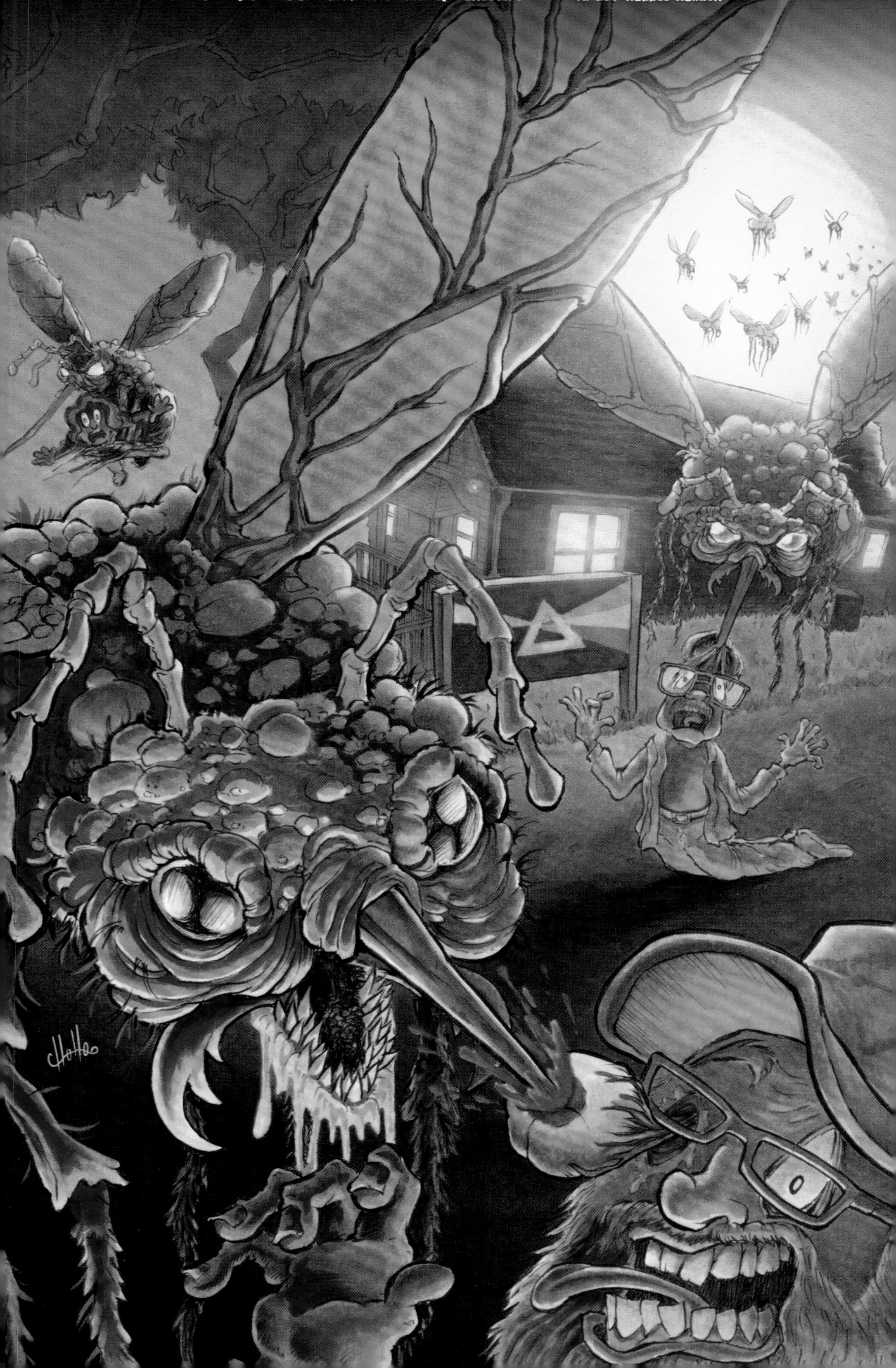

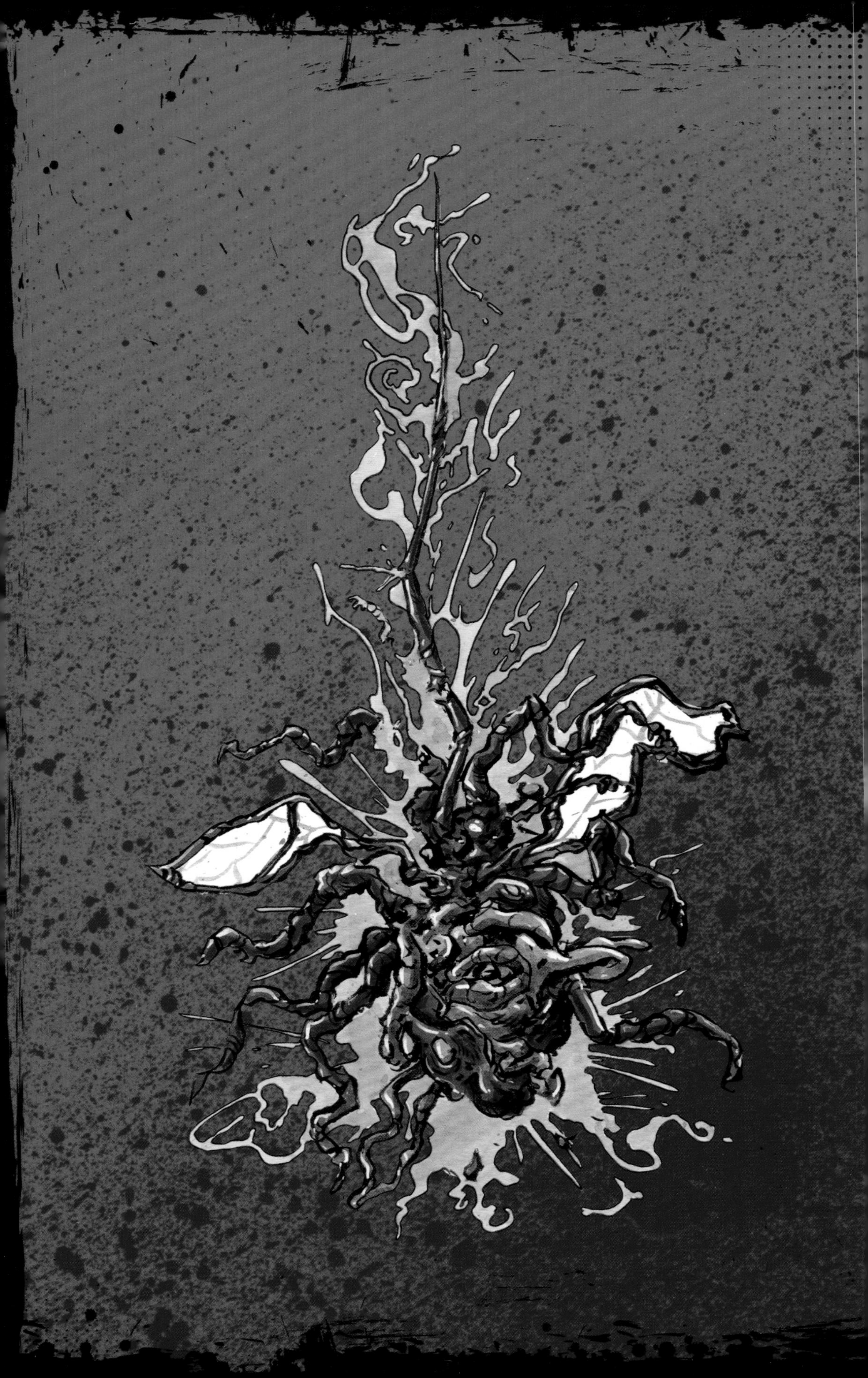